AWARDS AND ACCLAIM

FOR

AFTER THE WIND

Best Nonfiction Books of the Year
Kirkus Reviews

GOLD : Benjamin Franklin Book Award: Best Voice in Nonfiction

WINNER: National Excellence Book Award: Adventure and Memoir

BRONZE: Foreword Reviews' Book of the Year Award: Adventure

WINNER: The Eric Hoffer Book Award: Memoir

BRONZE: Independent Publisher Book Award: Sports

WINNER: Shelf Unbound Best Independently Published Book

WINNER: Pete Delohery Award for Best Sports Book

WINNER: New York Book Festival: Memoir

"A vivid, intimate memoir that with great clarity and attention to detail, tells an unforgettable survival story." — KIRKUS REVIEWS (starred review)

"*After The Wind* is a thoughtful, well-written love story of Kasischke's dedication to his wife and anchor Sandy and his passion for climbing."
— BLUEINK REVIEWS (starred review)

"A through analysis of the 1996 Everest disaster... and the best preparation for my Everest assent."
— JEAN PAVILLARD, IFMGA Swiss Mountain Guide

"Kasischke's account provides an eye-opening look at the perils and extreme conditions on Everest. Evocative illustrations by Jane Cardinal further enhance the text, and includes maps and time lines."
— PUBLISHERS WEEKLY

"Kasischke chronicles the events not only to recover some truth from the sensationalism surrounding that fateful day, but also to share a deeply personal story of the enduring power of love. ... Kasischke attributes his survival to the promises he made to 'live a story he can tell,' and 'come back home' .... *After The Wind* is decidedly genuine in its construction ... and Kasischke presents his story humbly as one man's experience of a horrific day"   — NEW ORLEANS REVIEW

"This riveting book examines what went wrong before and during the expedition ... including a series of ill-advised decisions just below the summit .... Kasischke also examines what holds true when all else fails, when survival is no longer likely. He offers a fascinatingly personal look at what he believes saved him. Ultimately, this is a survival story about love —of mountaineering, of God, and of the deep and abiding bond between a husband and wife."   — THE US REVIEW OF BOOKS

"Kasischke offers a unique perspective ... the voice of experience. Kasischke's perspective and analysis of what happened ... may shock those who have relied on *Into Thin Air,* by Jon Krakauer, as the most accurate account of what happened .... Readers will be drawn into this thrilling book, which combines the author's obvious expertise with a page-turning style and a knack for vivid descriptions. You'll feel like you are there with him in a tent that's barely holding together in a raging storm at 26,000 feet, and you'll perhaps get a glimpse of what courage and fortitude means in a life or death situation ... Readers will truly understand the hard choices that were faced on Everest."   — NEW YORK BOOK FESTIVAL

"Kasischke's book follows his real-life dance with death .... It is a thrilling tale of danger, courage, and love. With beautiful illustrations and thoughtful descriptions, the book is a loving ode to his wife Sandy and to his passion for climbing.   — BLUEINK REVIEWS

NEW TO THIS EDITION
A Reader's Guide: Discussion Questions and Conversation with Author

AFTER
THE
WIND

TRAGEDY ON EVEREST
ONE SURVIVOR'S STORY

LOU KASISCHKE

AFTER THE WIND

Tragedy on Everest — One Survivor's Story

Illustrations by Jane Cardinal

Design by Cynthia Shaw

Library of Congress Control Number: 2015947895

ISBN 978-1-940877-03-7

Printed in United States of America.

The author thanks all those who helped and encouraged him in preparing these pages. A special thanks goes to Laura Kasischke, Jean Pavillard, and James Greayer for their friendship, good judgement, and professional skills and advice.

For more information go to www.afterthewind.com

To Sandy

A Story I Can Tell

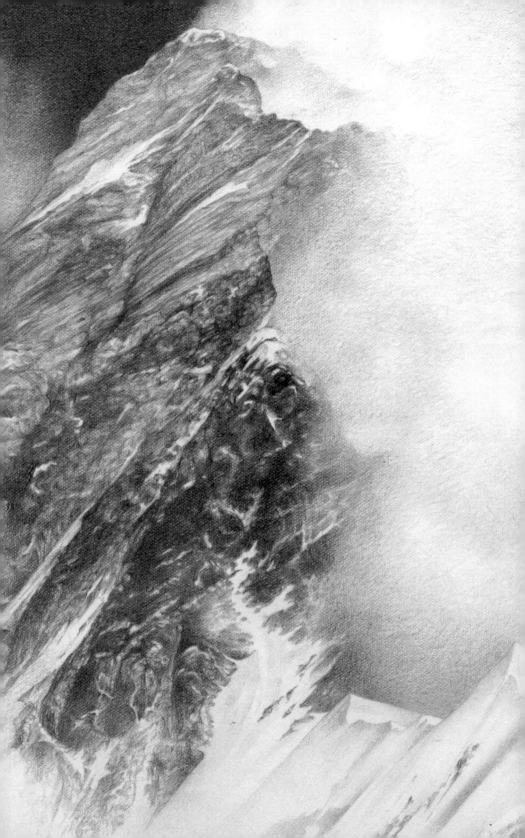

Then a great and powerful wind
 tore the mountain apart...

After the wind came an earthquake...

After the earthquake came a fire...

After the fire came

A still small voice.

1 Kings 19: 11-12
Holy Bible

CONTENTS

AFTER THE WIND

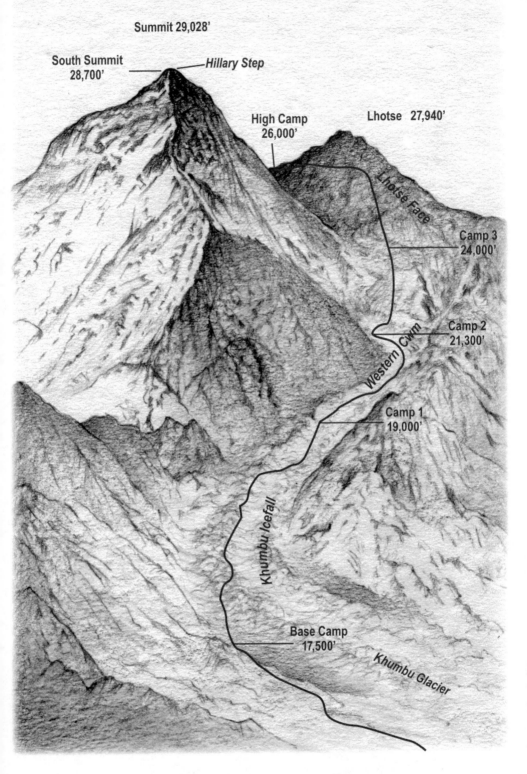

Summit 29,028'

South Summit 28,700' — Hillary Step

High Camp 26,000'

Lhotse 27,940'

Lhotse Face

Camp 3 24,000'

Western Cwm

Camp 2 21,300'

Camp 1 19,000'

Khumbu Icefall

Base Camp 17,500'

Khumbu Glacier

Six Week Route to High Camp

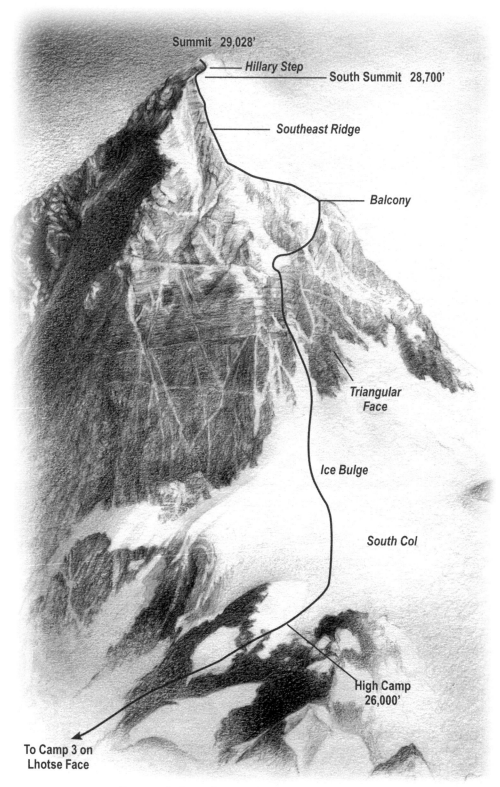

Summit 29,028'

Hillary Step

South Summit 28,700'

Southeast Ridge

Balcony

Triangular Face

Ice Bulge

South Col

High Camp 26,000'

To Camp 3 on Lhotse Face

Summit Day Route from High Camp

NOTE TO READER

NEAR THE TOP of Mount Everest at noon, on 10 May 1996, things went wrong. Some climbers lived. Some climbers died. It was the worst tragedy in Mount Everest history.

I was there. I was a climbing member of the New Zealand-based expedition led by Rob Hall. This is the story I lived.

What went wrong first focuses on the cause of the loss of time at the South Summit in the late morning hours leading up to noon on that fateful day. This loss of time and resulting implications presented a dilemma about what to do. Before noon, there was no life or death Everest story. But then, what happened at noon is the story.

I wrote most of these pages in 1997 and 1998. I wrote my account at that time for two reasons. One was because the events were factually complex and, for me, mixed with many emotions. I wanted to write things down to solidify my understanding, my thoughts, and my reflections. I understood what went wrong. I was there. But for people not there, the aftermath reporting of the events was like fog rolling in to obscure and distort a fair understanding about what actually happened.

My perspective and analysis were also different from much of what was written and reported at that time, particularly the relative importance of things. Too much was written about things that were colorful for storytelling, but did not matter.

What is the truth in this story? It depends on whom you ask. No one has all of it. And some of the truth may never be told.

My personal Everest story, within the bigger historic story, is about my experience of being there — living the horror of it. But my story goes beyond and deeper than about what went wrong. It's also about what went right — how I survived, and perhaps why.

After I finished writing, I decided not to publish my account. Instead, I packed the pages away in a file cabinet.

WHEN I TRAVELED to Nepal in 1996 to climb Everest, I expected a two month climb, to be followed by a return to my everyday life. Just like every other climb. The photos would eventually collect dust. The memories would gradually fade away. The story of climbing Everest would have an end. But instead, what happened to me did not fade away and continues to influence my everyday life, even now 17 years later. The story I lived never ended.

In 1996, I almost selfishly and recklessly died on Everest. In 2011, my wife, Sandy, became seriously ill. We have loved each other for 47 years. We have been married 46 years. Thinking back to the critical moments at noon on 10 May 1996, it was Sandy's love that came with me to Everest that saved my life. She was a source of inner strength when I needed it. That's part of the personal story I tell in these pages.

As life makes its twists and turns, Sandy now needs me. I regret how close I came to not being here for her today. I also like to think today that my love for Sandy is a force within her to help in her health struggles.

I'M PUBLISHING this story now as an expression of my love and thanks to Sandy. As I have shared my Everest experience over the years, many people were interested to know Sandy's part in what happened. My biggest hope and challenge in letting go of these pages is that I write well enough for the reader to understand and value Sandy's part in the story.

As I dusted off and reviewed the pages I wrote so many years ago, I took out things I no longer want to say. Things that are not mine to say. But I added a personally meaningful recent part about my personal story.

I have two stories to tell. One is a story about being there—facing that critical situation at noon, and then living a nightmare in the wind, cold, and thin air, with things going terribly wrong and people dying around me.

The other is a story about what I heard near the top as I listened in sheer silence—after the wind. A story about the voice of the heart. A love story. The story of how I survived.

Lou Kasischke

CHAPTER 1

DILEMMA AT NOON

ON MAY 10, close to noon near the summit of Mount Everest, I gasped for breath.

Four or five breaths for every step. Over and over. And over.

Four or five breaths. Shift my weight. Then step. Over and over. The frigid dry air burned inside me like cold fire. Four or five ragged breaths. Shift my weight and step. My fingers were white and stiff. Frostbite.

I wanted water. More than anything, water. But my water bottles were frozen blocks of ice. Frostbite. No water. Temperature at 30 below zero. High winds. Dehydration. Malnutrition. Little air to breathe.

But none of that mattered. Sheer will kept me going. Breathe, breathe, breathe, gasp, shift my weight. Then step. It was getting steeper.

I was far above the clouds. Almost six miles high. On a narrow ridge just 400 vertical feet from the top of the highest mountain in the world. Snow spindrift whipped around me. The wind sounded like low-flying jets. An ugly storm slowly boiled up from below.

After several weeks of enduring the savage cold and thin air, of climbing rock, snow, and ice, I knew I was close to the top. Thirteen hours of physically and mentally grueling climbing this day was behind me, just to get to this point. The top was minutes away. Four or five

1

breaths. Shift my weight. Then step. I was 400 vertical feet from achieving my goal. The top of Mount Everest. Four or five breaths. Then step. Sheer will.

Nothing could stop me.

Step by step by step. With each step, as a weaker force, I was overcoming a greater one — Everest. I didn't care about anything except reaching the summit. And I was almost there.

I sensed that the climbers above me had slowed down. But at first I did not equate that with a problem. I checked my watch. It was close to noon.

Noon? How could it be that late? Rob Hall, our expedition leader, had hoped to be on the way down from the top at noon. Trouble?

I tried to be calm, but my mind raced to grasp the implications of the time. I felt alone. Isolated. I couldn't talk with anyone. All I could hear was the wind and my own breathing. I looked up at the top. I looked at the climbers above me. I realized things had gone wrong. Very wrong. Climbers were still climbing up, but it was late.

I decided I didn't care. Being late didn't matter much at that moment. This was Everest. Climbing past the safety turnaround time I promised to follow didn't matter at all at that moment. Knowing I would be climbing down in the dark didn't matter. What mattered was the top. And I was almost there. Others were still going. Me too. If they could, I could. Nothing could stop me.

The already high risk of being there just rocketed far beyond recklessness. This, too, I knew. But I was close. I could get to the top. I wanted to keep going. I had to keep going. But it was too late. We were out of time.

The frostbitten fingers? I didn't care about those, either. Go. Keep going. Others are still going. Me too. I can do this. In climbing, there is only one thing worse than not reaching the summit. And that is when others do, and you don't.

I chipped away ice that had caked over my face so I could breathe what little oxygen there is six miles above sea level. With my head down and gasping for air, I continued to climb. Four or five breaths. Then step. Step by step. That first and only voice I heard within me said — *I can do this.*

Then it happened.

A veiled force overpowered me. I jammed my ice axe into the snow directly in front of me. I held tight, as my knees buckled. My heart pounded in my ears. Everything else went quiet. Stone silent.

I didn't know what I would hear — after the wind — when I listened to the sound of sheer silence. But I was about to find out.

MERE moments later, physical toughness and sheer will to climb a mountain of rock, snow, and ice meant nothing. What meant everything was what it would take to overcome a mountain of ambition and pressure to succeed, and to make a hard choice. Was I prepared for that challenge?

Hours later, I would be fighting for my life. Hours later, others would be dying on the mountain.

Years later, I would be fighting to understand. Years later, I wanted to forget. Years later, I could never forget.

Today, I give thanks.

CHAPTER 2

THE RITUAL

MY WIFE, Sandy, claims she was always the last to know what mountain I would climb next. That was not true. My mother was always last. But for sure, Dee, my assistant at work, was the first. Dee typed the letters, overheard the phone calls with my climbing friends, and faxed messages to strange places around the world, helping to make logistical arrangements. I purposefully did all my climbing planning at work. This was so Sandy didn't know my plans until the right moment. After all, climbing plans quickly changed or were cancelled because of a partner's schedule conflicts or logistical problems. I saw no point in starting the ritual about a climb with Sandy before plans advanced to the stage where most elements were in place. After decades of climbing, I had learned the importance of this strategy.

By 1995, I had been a climber for many years. I'd climbed many of the classic mountains around the world, including the highest on six continents. I was always thinking about or planning my next challenge. One June afternoon, I asked Dee to fax a message to Rob Hall, a professional mountain climber and Mount Everest expedition leader from New Zealand. When Dee read the message, she didn't say a word. But I got a look and a slight nod of the head that spoke louder than words. Dee knew it would be a big deal at home.

My message was simply an inquiry. If Rob was organizing a climbing team and getting a permit from Nepal to climb Everest in 1996, I wanted to be considered as a team member. It was just an inquiry, I said silently as I returned Dee's look and nod with my own shoulder shrug and grin.

Rob was regarded in the mountaineering community as the best in leading professional Everest expeditions. I had known him for a few years. We had climbed in Antarctica at the same time. We had mutual climbing partners, and I closely followed his Everest expeditions in 1993 and 1994.

But my fax message was just an inquiry. Who knew, Rob might not be going back again. As for me, thoughts about climbing Everest would probably fade away. That would have been okay. There were many other mountains I wanted to climb. Climbing Everest was not a passion I needed to fulfill. It seemed like a special thing to do if it worked out with Rob, but no big deal if it didn't.

Over the next few months of letters and calls, Rob confirmed he was organizing a team and securing a permit. We talked at length about leadership aspects of the climb and the specific leadership team. This was critical to my thinking and any commitment by me.

Rob Hall

On recent expeditions, Ed Viesturs of the United States and Guy Cotter of New Zealand assisted Rob. These were two people with exceptionally strong credentials and reputations as veteran Himalayan climbers and expedition leaders. In combination with Rob in prior years, they had the best record for safety on Everest. These were climbers for whom safety, not risk taking, was paramount. They were my kind of leaders. In the end, a specific condition of my participation (which became part of a written agreement) was the leadership team consisting of Hall, Viesturs, and Cotter.

After all the calls and correspondence, Dee knew that matters were serious. Several times she gave me the look that said, "I can't wait to see what happens at home when this one comes out." But until that time not a word was said to anyone, especially Sandy. No point in engaging Sandy too quickly. That required strategy. Timing was critical. I told Rob I had some work to do on the home front—the ritual.

MOST OF my friends understand the athletic challenge of being a climber. They know I love mountains and all mountain sports—skiing, ski mountaineering, and climbing. They know my history as an endurance athlete. They recognize the physical and mental challenges involved. They can see the beauty and imagine what a thrill it must be to stand on top and look around, as clouds go floating by underneath you. But they also know the dangers, the cold, the harsh environment, the hardships, the suffering—and they frequently ask "why." They point out that mountain climbing is irrational and conflicts with the innate sense of survival. To that point, I agree. And I agree that, perhaps, from just a rational perspective, climbing is only for people of unsound mind. But from an emotional perspective, climbing makes perfect sense and is an obvious choice. I also point out to them that climbing is about the richness of living a story. A whole story. Standing on top of the mountain is only part of the story. And frequently not even the most important part. The climbing story I live is not one single moment. In the story of getting to the top, many moments are more meaningful and more worthy of memory.

The main actors in the climbing stories are sometimes the place, the mountain, the history, the rigors of the climb, the obstacles overcome, the beauty, the wonder, and the feeling of deep satisfaction from the accomplishment. Sometimes the main actors are the people: what happened to each of us, and why we did what we did. Sometimes it's the mistakes we made, how we responded, and what we learned. Sometimes it's the Third World places and cultures. Always it's about the accumulation of very specific special moments for remembrance, such as crossing a raging river without a bridge, traveling by public bus across the plains of Africa or the highlands of Peru with people sitting on top and hanging over the sides and chickens, pigs and goats as fellow passengers. And, of course, sometimes it's about bad experiences I want to forget. The ones I don't tell Sandy.

Still, I admit that my journal later goes into a file cabinet, the summit is forgotten, and the photos collect dust on the wall or table, or never make it out of the file cabinet. It is a great story I lived. But the earth did not stop turning, no one else really cared, and it was just a big rock covered with snow. Still, the story I live is my keepsake. It lives within me. And the quest to live whatever the next story will be is a major motivating force for the next climb.

ON MY end and Rob's, Everest was a go. But one more thing was needed. Just as Rob needed to secure a permit from Nepal, and just as Everest can only be climbed with expedition team support, I needed the support of Sandy. I love Sandy very much. She needed to be thinking the right way on this. After all, we were talking about Everest—not just another climb.

I couldn't climb Everest or any mountain without Sandy. And I wouldn't want to. I could never draw the rewards from climbing I sought if it came at the price of an erosion of our marriage. I knew of too many cases where climbers wrecked their marriages over climbing. That would not happen to me. And it was not a matter of just getting Sandy's approval. That would not be enough. I needed more. Sandy might have been the next to last to learn about my next climb, but her support was at the top of the list of what I needed to climb any mountain, or accomplish any of my goals in life.

Sandy was a first grade school teacher when we met. It was on a blind date at a party, with music and dancing. For me, it was love at first sight. I was on my best behavior. But Sandy barely noticed, even my best dance moves. It took awhile for her to fall in love with me. We were married in 1967 by my father, a Lutheran minister. We had

Sandy Kasischke

two sons, Doug and Gregg, in short order. We worked hard and did the things typical families did. In almost all respects, we are very much alike. In one big respect, however, we are very different. I tend to be self centered (I didn't always understand this about myself), but Sandy gives everything of herself to others, especially to me.

After we were married, Sandy continued to work as a first grade teacher for many years. She worked and took care of our children pretty much single handed, while I worked full-time and went to night school. She never complained. She always gave of herself and supported my goals, whatever they were. One exception developed over time: my climbing. Gathering her support for my climbing goals took a special process — the ritual.

For decades, a step-by-step ritual evolved between us. I would mention a new climb. Then came the questions. I knew them all. And Sandy knew how to deliver them. "How can you leave the boys and me for weeks and months at a time? How can you take the time away from work?" More questions always followed, separated by a few days. "How would you like it if I were gone for weeks with no communication? Are you being fair to me?" She wanted answers. She would stand in front of me, stare into my eyes, and wait for an answer. One of Sandy's favorites was this: "Tell me again how you can train so long, leave the comforts of our home and the love of your sons and me, enter such a cold and hostile environment, try so hard and suffer so much, to accomplish something absolutely useless?" I never admitted to Sandy that while climbing, with all the suffering and discomfort, there were frequently times I said to myself, "I will never ever do this again," and all I wanted to do was go home. And then, when I got back home, after about a week or so, I wanted to go climbing again.

The ritual usually dragged on for four to six weeks. All the while, Sandy saw how the tempo of my training activities increased. But the questions kept coming. Sometimes I would get one question. Sometimes a few of the questions at once. Sometimes questions would be written in a note left on my desk. "What are we supposed to do if you don't come back?"

Sandy said it was easier for her to block out the possibility of my dying than deal with the loneliness from my absence. Absence and loneliness, during the endless training and the climb itself, were the hardest parts, she said.

EVEREST! The ritual. This was my biggest challenge with Sandy yet. Dee knew that too, as I could tell from the looks I got during the planning stage with Rob. How could I ever get Sandy to go for this one? Sandy had never heard of or knew little about most of the other mountains. But Everest was different. She knew about the Everest Death Zone. My strategy was to go slow, be patient, and look for the right moment to start the ritual.

One morning in the kitchen at breakfast I was reading the newspaper. The mood seemed right. The sun was shining in the windows. One of our favorite morning talk shows was on the radio. So I made my move. "Hey, remember me telling you about Rob Hall when I was in Antarctica? I read about him climbing Mount Everest. He was leading an expedition and turned around close to the top for safety reasons. What a strong leader." Clumsy. Obvious.

Sandy said, "That's nice." That's all. But Sandy doesn't miss a thing. She knew Everest was on deck. The ritual evolved. Day to day. Week after week. "What responsibility do you have to those who depend on you in the decisions you make about what you do? You have a mother with Alzheimer's, a brother with special needs, a wife, and two sons. And you go off risking your life to climb some stupid mountain."

The ritual never involved strong negative tension. We both knew that if Sandy said no, that was it. I can't think of anything I have ever done that Sandy didn't support. She knows in her heart that I love her more than anything and always have. And I know the same about her. Neither one of us would risk losing the other over climbing, if it ever came to that.

Finally one day Sandy said something like, "You know I don't like the idea, but I don't want to be left out of this or any part of your life. I love you and want to back your goals. If you are going to do this, we are going to be in this together. I will support you, but on one condition." She then asked for a promise: that 1996 would be my one and only attempt on Everest. She knew that it takes most climbers two or three, or sometimes even more, attempts to summit Everest. Rob summited on his third attempt. Sandy said she didn't want to live through this more than once.

I thought that was a fair request. I promised. The odds of me summiting in one attempt were long. I knew that. But reaching the summit wasn't the main reason for going. It struck me at the time that this was the first time I could remember Sandy asking for anything.

AS USUAL, once the ritual was completed, Sandy's attitude changed dramatically. Knowing how important it was for me to train and prepare for a climb, she supported and helped my training practices and activities. I could never have done the hard training, mentally or physically, without Sandy's help.

Sandy drew some lines, however, when it came to helping me train. The winter nights in northern Michigan are very cold (well below zero) and windy. We live on a high bluff overlooking Lake Michigan. High winds frequently hammer the shoreline. Wind and blowing snow roll up over the bluff face. On the coldest and windiest nights, I thought it was good training to set up a camp on the bluff edge. Harsh weather skills are some of the most important, especially in the darkness. Setting up a tent in a strong wind is always a good thing to practice. Cooking, melting snow for water, and functioning in the dark with only a headlamp (sometimes turned off to enhance the training experience) helped to keep me fine tuned with my gear. And I enjoyed it. Sandy agreed this was good for training. But for her to join me was foolish.

Sandy likes to tell about an early morning after one of my all night training sessions climbing up and down the hills at the Boyne Highlands ski area. The plan was for her to pick me up at the north end of the ski area. She was parked in her car waiting when a man from the Boyne security patrol pulled up to her car. He knew me, and what I was doing for training. He asked Sandy how long she had been waiting, and said he hoped not for too long because a large mother bear and two cubs were seen in the ski hills. He also suggested that she warn me about the possible danger. Sandy told him, "I'm sticking right here, but don't worry. Lou is a big believer in self reliance as a climber, and he trains to be able to respond to things that are not expected. Let's see how he handles the bears."

Actually, the bears ran away when they saw or smelled me coming. They didn't seem too concerned. I wasn't either. Maybe they were afraid of me. But, as it turned out, Mount Everest was not.

CHAPTER 3

A STORY I CAN TELL

SANDY'S support made me a more responsible and safer climber. This was not just from her watchful eye and assistance while training, but from a promise. A promise that became an organic part of our relationship with climbing.

The promise stemmed from an event many years ago in the middle of my climbing career, when I was climbing a mountain in South America. My partners and I were stuck for a week at our highest camp in bad weather. Most of the other climbing teams had aborted and gone down out of concern about unstable conditions. Finally, with no margin left for error in terms of remaining food and fuel, and a dubious break in weather, our team and another made a summit attempt. Near the top, when conditions were highly dangerous (especially high winds and avalanche risk), climbers from the other team turned around. We kept going to the top. Matters became even worse on the way down, when we were slowed down in deep snow and high winds. We were lucky to get down, very lucky. Two climbers on our team had great difficulty and suffered major frostbite. We did not celebrate our summit after getting back to camp. Everyone was quiet.

A week later at a place in a nearby town where climbers hung out, my climbing team ran into some of the climbers who had turned around on summit day. The discussion became uncomfortable, and forever meaningful. They said we were reckless. But, not wanting to admit that, we responded defensively by saying they were not aggressive enough.

I knew they were right. And we were wrong. We made a bad judgment call about safety. Our actions were not because we thought we were better climbers than the other team. We never climbed and measured what we did against others in some sort of competitive sense. We were, however, arrogant. And reckless. On that occasion, we didn't think very much about decision making, one way or the other. Each of us waited for someone else to make the hard call. We crossed the line. Fortunately, the two climbers with frostbite did not have serious long-term consequences. But it was very close. And one of them decided to never climb again. So, you could say we got away with it, but at a cost. I never felt good about that climb, knowing that luck played the decisive part in our return to safety.

I didn't tell Sandy what happened on the climb. I knew I couldn't tell her that story. For a long time, I had a bad feeling about my friend's very close call of losing all his fingers to frostbite. Actually, I never told anyone the real story. Not being able to tell anyone what really happened made me want to just forget about that climb. No personal satisfaction or joy ever came from summiting that mountain.

About two years after that climb in South America, during dinner with friends in a crowded and popular restaurant, I finally told the story, including the part about the encounter with the other climbers. I can't imagine what I was thinking. Perhaps a glass or two of wine had something to do with it. Sandy was present. As she absorbed what I was saying, she got up out of her chair and walked out. Sandy didn't say a word. She didn't have to. I knew exactly what had happened. I felt terrible. Sandy was upset and hurt. I immediately followed her out of the restaurant, and we took a long walk and talked.

I remember those moments so well because it turned into a rare and serious clash in our lives. But it also became one of life's great blessings for me. It was pivotal in our lives together. And, as it turned out, pivotal to my survival on Everest. Sandy's words went like this:

Why didn't you tell me? I already know why. You didn't because you couldn't tell me about your irresponsibility and recklessness. You couldn't tell me about your mistakes in judgment. But, somehow it was okay to tell our friends about it. How do you make sense of that? Where does that put me in your life? Am I part of this or not? I have said many times I would support your climbing because I want to be part of everything that's important to you. I want to be part of all your life. We are in this together—even the climbing part, and even the bad parts of climbing. So let's be clear. We have two problems here. One is that you didn't tell me. The other, and more important, is the reason you didn't tell me. This was not about a bad experience, but about your reckless behavior.

I want to know everything important that happens on a climb. I want you to tell me—the good things and the bad things. No secrets. I want no secrets about what happens, in any aspect of our life together. But what's more important, I expect more from you. Being reckless and irresponsible, in any part of your life, but especially climbing because of the high price you pay for mistakes, is not who I want you to be.

By your own account, the other climbing teams had turned around. All of them. Did you have no respect for those other climbers? Did you discuss with the other team their decision to turn back?

I had it coming. At the time, I didn't know where that would leave my future as a climber. I don't remember what I said during those moments with Sandy. I probably said little. I knew by then in our marriage to shut up when I'm wrong and Sandy is on a roll.

There was no immediate resolution of the matter. We moved on in everyday life. But Sandy didn't forget. When the next climb rolled around, and the ritual was reaching its conclusion, Sandy made her position clear.

> Please don't leave me alone in life, especially with a broken heart. For me to continue to support your climbing—for me to continue and be part of this—I need a promise from you.

> I have often heard you tell other people you climb "to live a story," which to me is nothing more than your way of putting a nice face on mountain climbing. But if that's the way you see it, before each climb, I need for you to look me in the eyes and promise to live a story *you can tell*.

"To live a story" then changed in its meaning. Before, it was about the experience of what happened to me and around me. But after, to live a story "I can tell" made it more about the rightness of what I did—my actions and behavior—and how that determined who I would come to be in life.

Of course, what Sandy asked for was not something you should have to promise. But it makes a difference when you look someone in the eyes and say "I promise."

Words have power. And words that embody love have great power as a source of strength in how they influence behavior. That promise I made to Sandy so many years before Everest, and kept over the years, probably saved my life.

CHAPTER 4

THE LAST SUPPER

WHEN THE time came close to leaving for Everest, I knew Sandy was getting nervous, and she expressed this in a unique way. She wanted to have a gathering of our friends. Here is the invitation she sent out:

You are cordially invited to join me

for (what may be)

a "Last Supper"

with Lou on Saturday, March 23, 1996, at 7:30 PM

After dinner, please feel free to toast, roast,

and offer Lou some words of profound wisdom.

Sandy Kasischke

I thought the religious reference to The Last Supper in the text of the invitation was indelicate. It was also suggestive of her lack of enthusiasm for my venture. It was also her way of reminding me of her view of the risks and consequences.

Sixty-four of my family and friends, some of the most important people in my life, gathered to party. Sandy's parents, Ed and Jennie Colosimo, sat at a table with my two sons, Doug and Gregg. We were a close family. My in-laws have been a blessing, as they helped raise our sons while Sandy and I worked full time. Everyone took the invitation terms literally. Some toasted me with heartwarming well-wishes. Some of the finest wits and wordsmiths subjected me to comedic insults with stories that I denied were true. One even suggested, "Lou, you should next set your sight on a big descent—the lowest point in the world."

From the comments that evening, two things stood out. One is that at least I was climbing a mountain my friends had heard of. The second was that many of my friends thought I had already climbed Everest. And that the climb was just a great excuse to have the party. In their minds, climbing Mount Everest was not much different from several others I had climbed. I was not going to let anybody down by not reaching the summit. No one would think differently about me if I reached the summit or not. For that, I was fortunate—because I see today how much influence peer pressure played in the critical decisions made on Everest.

It was also clear the gathering was part of Sandy's plan for my safe return. She knew the power of relationships. She wanted me to have fresh memories of the people, their words, and their caring for the strength it would give me, when and if needed. The evening ended with most remarks focused on wisdom and safety. One friend read the poem *If*, by Rudyard Kipling. A Kasischke cousin read a thoughtful poem he had written for the occasion. I think all of it was by Sandy's design. My family and friends talked about keeping safety as my highest priority and to always "be smart" about my climbing. People said they would keep my safety in their prayers, and I said, "I will keep all of your good wishes and prayers in my pocket with me and take them out when I need them."

Sandy was also asked to give our friends periodic updates of what happened on the mountain. No one could have guessed about the ultimate significance of those updates.

A SPECIAL moment occurred after the Last Supper party. A moment that would become important to the life and death outcome six weeks later.

Sandy and I stood in our kitchen. With tears in our eyes, we reminisced about the evening and the value of our friends and family. At that moment, I lost all enthusiasm to leave and climb a mountain. No other place was more important to me than right there. Sandy put her arms around me, looked at me, and said, "I want you to go live your story on Everest, but I want you to say out loud, 'I promise to come back home'." Without pause, I did as Sandy requested. I said the words: "I promise to come back home."

This may not seem like much. In fact, it seems an odd subject of a promise. After all, coming back is always part of going away. Every mountain climbing trip starts and ends back home. But between

Sandy and me, the words "come back home" have much special importance below the surface. They have a private history that goes back longer than I can remember. This goes to our very private way of communicating our feelings and touching each other.

For as long as I can remember, I would call Sandy as I left work and say, "I'm coming home." When I walked through the door of the house, before I saw Sandy, I would say, "I'm home." This sounds common and ordinary. But between us, "coming home" or "being home" didn't just mean traveling to or arriving at a destination or address.

Sometimes a few words can capture the essence of something much bigger. For us, "coming home" and "being home" express our loving relationship in its essence — being together, being with each other, togetherness. "Coming home," and "being home" are expressions of love. The words are a verbal embrace.

At that moment, standing in the kitchen holding each other, the words "come back home" were used by Sandy to give voice to her heart of the human pain of our parting and her yearning for us to be together again. When she asked me to say the same words, she wanted my heart to hear that voice with the power of a promise. The words had nothing to do with logic or rational thinking — of starting and ending back home. They related to love. A matter of the heart. Wherever my actions took me on Everest, I believe Sandy wanted them to be influenced by that voice of the heart.

The streets were choked in chaos.

CHAPTER 5

KATMANDU AND 1995

KATMANDU lies 4,500 feet above sea level, in a fertile valley of the east Himalaya Mountains of Asia. China is to the north, and India to the south. Katmandu is the capital of Nepal and the center of everything that happens there.

The name Katmandu always fascinated me. Many years ago when first hearing this name, I wondered if it was a real place or just a term used to symbolize something far and exotic, rising from the clouds like Shangri-La, or an imagined place astride an ancient trade or pilgrim route from India to Tibet, China, and Mongolia. In the same way, I wondered about Timbuktu. Was that really a place, or just an expression, like, "from here to Timbuktu"?

Somewhere along the line I figured out that both were real cities: Katmandu in Nepal, and Timbuktu in Mali. But they still symbolized mystery. What I discovered on arrival was that the reality was not too far removed from the mystery.

I ARRIVED at Katmandu International Airport via Detroit to Tokyo, Tokyo to Bangkok, and Bangkok to Katmandu. Before leaving the Bangkok airport, I saw Beck Weathers, one of our expedition members, ahead of me in the check-in line for the flight to Katmandu. I watched as Beck was told at the airline counter that he didn't have a reservation. Of course he did, but this is a common occurrence in

21

some countries. Beck made the usual verbal protest, but he knew exactly what it would take to "process" the reservation: two or maybe three twenty dollar bills. In all my travels around the world, one important aspect to keep moving, especially at border crossings, is the United States twenty dollar bill. I am always prepared with several in my pocket, and it appeared Beck was also. I liked what I saw and looked forward to climbing with him.

Seaborn "Beck" Weathers

Seaborn "Beck" Weathers, a Texan in his late forties, was married with two children. He was extremely witty and knowledgeable. He never stopped talking. His spirit was infectious. Beck had a strong climbing background, with several big climbs around the world, and he was especially serious about matters of training and preparation.

I never could have imagined the horror that lay in store for Beck. Nothing could really explain Beck, or how tough of a guy he was, until six weeks later when he walked out of the void at 26,000 feet. It was then that I knew what boxing legend Jack Dempsey meant when he defined a champion as "someone who gets up when he can't."

Beck and I met in the Katmandu airport among the official frenzy of passports, visa, immigration, customs, currency exchange, and luggage retrieval. I exchanged 200 United States dollars for Nepal rupees.

I collected my bags, all of which safely made it. My climbing gear bags were large and heavy. Airlines are notorious for taking bags off the plane at the last minute for weight control reasons. And heavy bags are high target candidates. For easy identification I packed my gear in large orange bags. Whenever I left on a climbing trip, Sandy always waited around in the boarding area for an hour or so, just in case the plane returned. She said she wanted to be there to take me home. This also gave her the opportunity to watch from the boarding area to make sure my orange bags didn't come off just before take off, when the airline does its final weight check. When you have multiple connections, you never know where the bags will end up. On one occasion, my destination was Switzerland, and my gear landed in India. Not this time. Everything was safely in Nepal.

While Beck and I contemplated our next move and how to get to our hotel meeting place, Andy Harris, one of the expedition's assistant leaders, approached us.

Andy was a professional mountain guide from New Zealand, certified by the International Federation of Mountain Guides Association (IFMGA). This is the highest credential a mountain guide can earn. Andy had much experience in Antarctica and the rugged mountain ranges of the New Zealand Alps. He was 32 years old and engaged to be married. He was physically imposing, but talked with a polite New Zealand accent.

Andy Harris

Jon Krakauer from the United States, another member of our expedition, was also on the same flight from Bangkok. Jon made his living as a writer. The four of us piled our gear on top of the roof of a tiny, Japanese-made cab, squeezed inside, and we were off to the narrow streets of the Thamel district of Katmandu. We were headed to the Hotel Garuda. The streets were choked in chaos, with barking dogs, cows, rickshaws, small cars, trucks, people, and bicycles. Black clouds of diesel exhaust were everywhere. The buildings were ancient.

FROM THE beginning of Everest climbing history, expeditions have had a business aspect to them. Leaders and some climbers have always used publicity as a platform to raise money to pay for their next expedition. This year was no different from most earlier expeditions, in which some climbers and most leaders sought attention and recognition from the Everest challenge.

The first attempts to climb Everest were paid for by English newspapers. After that came radio, then television, book rights, and bargaining for exclusive rights to photos and video and dispatches from the mountain. Expedition leaders and some climbers have been very creative over the years in concocting the next science project, experiment, or "environmental clean up" as an excuse to raise donations from others to foot the bill for their next climb. Just as in auto racing and other sports, you see the patches on the clothing.

Rob Hall made his living as a leader of professional climbing expeditions. As such, each of us in the expedition knew that Rob's business interests influenced his decision making. For Rob to seek publicity was not unexpected. But it was another matter — in the extreme — for Rob to form an alliance with a national outdoor magazine to actually embed a writer in the climbing team. That's exactly what happened, however. Jon Krakauer was embedded in our team specifically as part of a financial alliance between Rob and *Outside* magazine. I had never heard of that happening on a professional expedition. Never. From the first moment in Katmandu that I learned of the alliance, I knew, without any doubt, that Jon's presence and purpose for being there would create major performance pressures and much added risk. This could have serious adverse consequences. This was, without any doubt, against the safety interests of the climbing members. Everest is already a very dangerous place, without deliberately jacking up the risks.

I was quiet about it. But I had a bad feeling. It wasn't just about the conflict of interest with Rob. Jon's reason for being on the expedition

Jon Krakauer

was different than ours. I felt uneasy about climbing with someone who was doing so as part of his job and to advance his career. Jon's purposes would involve decision making and risk taking influences different from the rest of the team. Jon was also there to find and tell a story readers would find exciting. And that just might end up being about me, and that conflicted with what I thought was my private quest.

Rob was casual about the issue and said, "Jon is only going to climb Everest and write a story about his experience." That sounded simple enough, but it didn't fool anybody. We all knew Rob viewed Jon as paid hired help to crank up publicity for Rob and his expedition business. In the alliance with *Outside* magazine, Rob fronted most of the cash in exchange for Jon's story and discounted future ad space.

Climbing Everest is very dangerous. Many decisions would be made by the leadership and by individual climbers. Would any of these decisions made on the mountain, especially relating to safety and risk taking, be influenced by an embedded writer with a powerful pen?

There is no question that media presence influences what happens on the mountain and off. Just look at what happens to judges, lawyers, and jurors when the media spotlight is introduced into the courtroom. Behavior changes. Everything changes. And everyone knows it.

WE ARRIVED at the Garuda Hotel, with its big iron gates across half of the building front that were pulled shut at 10 PM for protection. The Garuda was a climber's hotel. You find hotels like it in popular climbing areas around the world. These are usually "budget" hotels, and popular because of the history of the climbers staying there. Everything about the place, such as the photographs and posters on the wall, sent the message that this was where Himalayan climbers stayed. This included even the world's best, such as Reinhold Messner, Peter Habeler, and, of course, Rob.

I checked in at the desk and started the three trip process of carrying my gear up four flights to Room 406. On my last trip up the desk clerk handed me a fax. It was from Sandy:

> ... As usual, I waited until your plane finally took off. No orange bags came off so that part worked ok. But I kept hoping you would change your mind and get off the plane. I waited a couple more hours just in case the plane came back. I wanted to be there to take you back home. ...

Without reading the whole thing, I put the fax in my pocket and doubled my speed up the four flights. I wanted to be alone in my room when I read the rest. Predictably, it included many questions, about when and how we would be communicating. Sandy wrote, "I love you" three times and repeated the usual "climb smart" and "come back home." And then: finally, there was one more example of her support for me:

> ... On reading the two books you left about Everest, I see in the appendixes that those who reach the summit record their ages in years plus days. Now, this is important: when *you* summit, you will be 53 years, *287* days, plus all the days in May until the day you summit. You can't just say "almost 54," and I didn't want you to forget that this is a leap year. 29 days in Feb.

I shook my head with a big smile. This is Sandy. I was lonesome for her and home, but also excited to be in Nepal, sitting on the bed in my room, alone, reading that note. I love quiet moments like this. In my inner speech—by which I mean my thoughts—I actually converse with Sandy.

When climbing exposed terrain, climbers belay each other with a rope for safety. For the deadly events I faced in about six weeks ahead, the safety rope I needed was already in place and connected. It was Sandy back home, her image, and her voice.

After getting organized in our rooms, Beck, Andy, Jon, and I decided to walk around the city. It's amazing to think this fabled and ancient city had no road to the outside world for cars until 1956. Along the dusty streets we saw the hustle of three-wheeled bicycle cabs and ragged children accosting most everyone to sell hashish. We planned to meet later for dinner at an open-air courtyard restaurant. We would be joined by three of our other teammates, Stuart Hutchison, Yasuko Namba, and Doug Hansen.

And by the man himself, Rob.

UNTIL THE early 1990s, most Everest expeditions were not organized well enough to manage the high risks at the level I was willing to accept. Many were organized as government or science sponsored projects using taxpayer dollars. The leadership and climbers were frequently inexperienced at high altitude. Climbers were selected based on who they knew, or their government contracts, rather than climbing expertise. Some expeditions had no organizational sense for working as a team; these were essentially expense sharing arrangements. Some were organized through want ads in the climbing journals and notices posted in alpine climbing huts and on the Internet. This equivalent of computer blind dating was not my idea of selecting partners to climb with.

Everest expeditions reached higher standards when expense funding changed. All Everest expeditions are commercial in the sense that someone has to pay the expenses. Once expeditions became self funded, rather than government funded with taxpayer dollars, expeditions advanced to a higher level.

Beginning in the early 1990s, some Everest expeditions were professionally organized by internationally certified mountain guides. These were highly respected professionals with strong track records for safety. Professional mountain guiding is a 175 year old respected profession, especially in Europe.

Professionally organized climbing significantly improved the sport. Professional alpinists led the way to developing higher standards, better skills, and more responsible climbers and climbing values. This advancement, in turn, attracted a higher caliber of climber, who brought to climbing a broad array of experiences, especially in high stakes decision making.

Safety is the professional climbing leader's primary responsibility. In mountain climbing, risk cannot be eliminated. But evaluating risk and managing it to an acceptable level is the major concern of the professional leader. These leaders are not paid to take risks. They are paid for their judgment about which risks are worth taking. Statistics show that fatality rates materially dropped with the higher standards and the higher skills that came from professional expeditions. In 1995, professional expeditions were the best opportunity to climb Everest as safely as possible.

But in 1995, I still had doubts about my future on an Everest expedition. The climbing risks were extremely high and unique at the high altitudes of Everest. Professional leadership, with proven experience above 26,000 feet, was in short supply. The most essential leadership quality I looked for was a track record of good judgment in decision making while in the Everest Death Zone. Everyone can make the easy decision. But not everyone can make the tough decision. I was looking for a leader who had a record of having the guts to make the hard call.

A TALL, spare figure of a man strode into the courtyard at the restaurant. Rob was 35 years old. But he looked much older behind his thick black beard. This was his eighth Everest expedition. In the climbing community, Rob was regarded as a world class professional climber and expedition leader. He had the best record of success on the mountain, if you measured success in terms of the number of climbers reaching the top. He also had a flair for showcasing himself and his accomplishments, with the record to back it up. Rob held the world record (for a non-Sherpa) for having summited Everest four times. I didn't think about it at the time, but this was the first I had ever encountered an expedition leader who kept track of the number of his team climbers reaching the top. Rob's tally was 39, with climbers from 10 nationalities.

These impressive statistics about getting to the top were not, however, what brought me to Everest with Rob. Instead, it was quite the opposite. On 10 May 1995, after six weeks of climbing, and with the biggest prize in mountaineering only minutes away, Rob turned the expedition he was leading around at Everest's South Summit. This was only 85 vertical meters below the main summit. Rob and his assistant Everest veteran professional leaders, Guy Cotter and Ed Viesturs, made the decision to turn around at 12:30 PM. They recognized that to continue climbing would make it too late for a safe descent to the high camp 3,000 feet below, located in the area known as the South Col at 26,000 feet. Rob had a predetermined turnaround time, and he stuck to it.

His decision was about time, and safety. Rob's judgment was that it was too late. They were out of time. Rob had the right stuff to make the hard call. I was impressed.

The number of climbers reaching the top under Rob's leadership in the prior year was not my decision point. Rob's turning back while at extreme high altitude, and under the pressure of being so close to the top with no second chance for another attempt, changed my mind about climbing Everest and led me here to live my Everest story.

There was also a feeling that Rob did something I may not have had the strength to do. Did I have the courage and strength to turn around so close to the summit after six weeks of extreme physical and mental effort?

THE EVENING in the courtyard restaurant listening to Rob tell Everest climbing stories got everyone excited about the weeks to come. I enjoyed getting to know my teammates. I usually climbed with people I knew well and with whom I had climbed many times. But this felt new and exciting, and everyone seemed to have impressive climbing experience. I felt comfortable, even though I knew I faced the biggest challenge of my life in the weeks ahead. Still, at least I would do that with interesting and good people. The journey to live my Everest story was having a strong start in Katmandu. But from years of climbing adventures like this, I also knew many of the memories I went home with would be much different than at first expected.

Years later, I can still picture that evening in the courtyard restaurant in Katmandu. I still picture us together in warm companionship and all with great expectations. What's hard to picture is some of these companions freezing to death six weeks later at the top of the world.

AFTER I returned to the Garuda, I felt relaxed for my first night's sleep in Katmandu—despite the pounding noise from the Redrock Bar just across the street from my room. I thought about Sandy and decided to write a short note to be faxed from the hotel.

HOTEL GARUDA (P) Ltd

GPO Box 1771, Thamel, Katmandu, Nepal. Fax #++(9771) 413614 or 472390 Tel 416776

ATTENTION SANDY KASISCHKE, USA, FROM: LOU
KASISCHKE, Room #406 DATE: 30 MAR 96, Page(s) 1

Dear Sandy, Doug + Gregg

All is well. Katmandu is very old and exciting place. Expedition
is all ready. Much more snow in mountains than usual. Will be
more difficult getting gear into Base Camp. But more snow could
be helpful to get through the Khumbu Icefall, the first major challenge. I miss you and love you very much.

                                                    Lou

For faxes and phone calls with Sandy, there was a ten-hour and fifteen minute time difference between Nepal and Michigan. I never
did figure out how the fifteen minutes got included. But it meant that
a Monday 6 PM call or fax from me would be an 8 AM fax or call to
Sandy. I wasn't concerned about the fifteen minutes.

Sandy and I exchanged faxes over the weeks ahead, mostly about
routine matters of daily life. But they were special to me because as I
read them I heard Sandy's voice. We dropped paragraph indentation
and other formalities to get as much on each page as possible. Our
son Gregg was preparing for final exams in college. Our other son
Doug had returned to his life in Los Angeles. Sandy was going out to
dinner with lots of friends, who tried to ease her loneliness. There was
Michigan's cold spring weather to deal with, and golf and travel plans
to make for when I got back. Of course, lots of love was sent back and
forth. It was all pretty ordinary.

Six weeks later, however, Sandy's voice in those pages would be far
from ordinary. That voice would become an important part of what
I needed to survive the worst experience of my life.

31

Silent Witness

CHAPTER 6

INTO THE KHUMBU

JOHN TASKE arrived in Katmandu on the second day. Taske was in his mid-fifties and from Brisbane, Australia. He was a veteran climber, with climbs in the Himalaya and European Alps. He was also a good storyteller, especially Vietnam stories. Taske was a colonel in the military and served two tours in Vietnam with Australia's SAS Commando Forces (the equivalent of our Navy Seals). His tough skin and ruddy complexion was that of someone you expected to have gone through war. Like the others, he was lean and strong.

Taske wore a New York Yankees baseball hat and carried himself with confidence, even in his climbing style. He would prove himself an expert alpinist and a genuine warrior. We later shared an experience near the summit that forged an everlasting, special bond between us.

THE NEXT morning we went back to the Katmandu airport, and boarded a huge and much used Russian Mi-17 helicopter, a leftover from the Soviet-Afghan war. The plan was to fly to Lukla in that Russian beast. From Lukla at 9,200 feet, over the next eight days we would trek to Base Camp at 17,500 feet. We sat along the inside edges of the helicopter, with our knees to our chest and our duffels and other gear loaded in the middle in front of us. The weigh-in of our gear, to make sure we were under the safety weight limit, was interesting.

John Taske

Rather than use the large red platform scales located at check-in, a Nepalese bag handler moved his head back and forth, doing a visual determination at the helicopter door. He would study the bags, scratch his head, and heft one or two duffels to decide which to throw off.

We stuffed cotton in our ears. Thump, thump, thump, as the blades revved faster and faster to find purchase and create lift. Finally, when every bolt in the helicopter and every bone vibrated violently, we lifted off. Everyone had a look of terror, since we all knew this was probably the most dangerous thing we would do until we hit Base Camp (I changed my mind when I learned that eating the food along the way was much more dangerous). We knew the history of crashes because of poor maintenance, poor operation, and low aviation piloting standards in that part of the world. But at that moment, all our concern focused narrowly on the jolting in desperation to take off.

We flew over rice paddies for about 100 miles to the village of Lukla in the Dudh Kosi (milk river) valley. We were up front and personal with the Himalaya. This was the beginning of our trek in the Khumbu. We were at 9,200 feet and on our way. It felt good to land, slip on a backpack, and start what I had trained for, and dreamt about, for so long.

We planned for an eight day trek in the Khumbu. It was fascinating to see the wheat and potato fields, Sherpa teahouses, porters with heavily calloused feet carrying loads I could not have lifted (much less carried), and shaky suspension bridges straddling both sides of the Dudh Kosi river. The milky river carried the glacial silt at a fast pace. The stones on the trail were rubbed smooth from centuries of foot traffic.

There were no roads from Lukla to Base Camp. Trails connected one village to another. Base Camp was only 60 miles away on the trail, but we planned to take eight days to get there. The idea was to go slowly so our bodies would adapt to the thin air, a process known as acclimatization. It's a physiological process during which the body's oxygen delivery system adjusts to the lower quantity of oxygen in the air.

To illustrate the need to follow this process, if you went suddenly from sea level to Base Camp at 17,500 feet, where the available oxygen is about one-half of that at sea level, you would have half an hour to write your last will and testament before you collapsed and died. Furthermore, if you went suddenly to the summit of Everest, where the available oxygen is about one-third of that at sea level, you would become unconscious almost immediately. Death would come in minutes.

AS WE moved along the trail, I frequently saw stacks or piles of mani stones with carved Buddhist mantras, the most common mantra being "Om Mani Padne Hum," translated as "Hail to the jewel in the Lotus." When these mani stones divided the trail, which can be stacked several feet high, it's local custom to show respect by keeping them to your right as you pass.

Our first stop was the village of Phakding, at 9,186 feet. We stayed overnight in a lodge, with dorm style wooden platforms on which to place our sleeping bags, for an evening meal of potatoes, fatty yak meat, noodles, and a few vegetables.

The next morning we moved on to Namche Bazaar, at 11,300 feet. Namche is the Khumbu's largest village, with the modern conve-

niences of a bank, a telephone, and a market. This was the last outpost with any sense of modernity in the high Himalaya.

Along the trail, we encountered many trekkers. They were usually serious people, with well-worn backpacks and hiking boots. Many different languages were spoken. Their goal was just to experience the Khumbu Valley, and perhaps go as far as Everest Base Camp. They felt exuberant with their surroundings, a grand sense of wonder. The trekkers knew they were following the footsteps of legends, and enjoyed seeing the vast glaciers and razor-sharp ridgelines surrounding them, while taking pictures of everything. They spoke with feelings of deep satisfaction, for just being there.

I was in the same place, at the same time, seeing the same things. But sadly, I didn't feel the same as they felt. My climbing goal with all the attendant challenges spoiled it for me. My anxiety about what was to come. My anticipation of the unknown. My expectation of adversity, suffering, and hardship. I couldn't let go of any of that, for just those spectacular moments in the Khumbu, and adopt the trekkers more present appreciative perspective. I remember thinking that someday I would return to enjoy the experience just to see, and not to climb. But I never have and never will go back.

ONE DAY I took a break along the trail and came across Frank Fischbeck. He was polishing his trekking boots. This was not on my list of priorities, but that was Frank.

Frank, a resident of Hong Kong, was also a member of our expedition. He was of British heritage, but was actually a citizen of South Africa. He carried himself with British politeness and decorum, but he climbed with quiet and enduring power. Frank had more Everest experience than the rest of us. He was back for his fourth attempt on the summit. Weather, snow conditions, and other events outside

Mike Groom

his control had blocked his earlier attempts. We were all anxious to talk to Frank to learn as much as we could.

In Namche, the final member of our climbing team arrived. Mike Groom had been co-guiding a trek in one of the area's valleys. I didn't know much about him until Namche. At age 33, his climbing resume was impressive and included heavy drama. Mike had lost all of his toes about ten years earlier while climbing in the Himalayas. He froze his feet after being trapped overnight in the open on nearby Kanchenjunga, the third highest mountain in the world. Mike summited, but paid a heavy price for what climbers call, "getting caught out."

Mike never let the loss of his toes limit his future climbing ambitions. Since that time he climbed K2, Lhotse, and in 1993, Everest. Mike was from Brisbane, Australia, as was Taske. Mike was very quiet and reserved. What you saw was what you got. I was surprised that Mike didn't say much, because he was one of our assistant leaders. I later learned he only occasionally served as a mountain guide and never on Everest.

WHILE in Namche on April 2, I had my first encounter with a problem: keeping food inside me. It was a minor issue until Pheriche two days later. It was not pretty—back and forth from the top bunk in the dorm room to the outhouse that was so small my knees didn't even let the door shut.

Getting stomach or digestion sickness in the harsh environment of Asia's backcountry is considered normal and initially isn't alarming. While moving on the trail, I ate the food I had brought with me and drank bottled water. The meals served in teahouses in the evenings along the way were the usual potatoes, vegetables, soups, and various teas. Sherpa tea, made from milk, tea, sugar and rancid yak butter, takes some getting used to. I usually avoided the yak meat because I would exhaust myself trying to chew it. Rice and noodles were the better way to go. After peeking in the kitchen of one of the teahouses and seeing the cook at work while holding an infant child without a diaper, I started eating fried foods — thinking that frying would kill anything that could make me sick. But as I later discovered, some gastrointestinal bug insisted on staying alive in me.

A SHORT distance below the village of Lobuche we ran out of dry land. This is where the Khumbu glacier begins its twelve-mile rise to Base Camp. In this area, a place called Chukpö Laré, there was an imposing row of more than 30 stone chö-lung shrines. Memorials for the dead. These were erected by Sherpa, more as a place for ceremony and ritual than as a monument. If a Sherpa died on the mountain and his body was recovered, it was brought there for cremation, and the ashes were placed inside one of the stone shrines.

I saw other memorial monuments to dead climbers lining the trail to Base Camp. It's hard now to comprehend that one year later, not far from Chukpö Laré, stone monuments would stand in memoriam of climbers from our expedition. And my heart aches to know how close I came to having one of those bear my name.

Base Camp

CHAPTER 7

BASE CAMP — 17,500 FEET

ONE CRITICAL function in a climbing expedition on Everest is logistics. Tons of food, equipment, and supplies have to be moved halfway around the world, across borders, and then 60 miles up the Khumbu Valley to Base Camp. There are no roads or vehicles from Lukla to Base Camp.

From Lukla, the original plan was for yaks to carry the food, gear, and supplies to Base Camp. But the snow got deeper as we moved past the row of memorials. The Sherpa yak herders found it difficult to lead the yaks through the deep snow because their feet sank too deeply. The Sherpa herders yelled and waved their arms and pushed the yaks. But there is a line the Sherpa herder will not cross when it comes to the safety of his animals.

The deep snow prevented the yaks from going beyond Lobuche at 16,200 feet, and porters (hired locally for the assignment) took over the carrying for the remaining seven miles to Base Camp.

Lobuche looks like a worn-out western town. I smelled it before I saw it. A few teahouses and huts were built on the slope above the trail. Its several stone toilets were like open sewers. The joke was that the toilet doors were padlocked shut. You needed a key, as though it was an executive washroom. Climbers and Sherpa alike avoided them.

While at Lobuche, a Sherpa from Base Camp came to tell Rob about a bad accident. Ngawang Tenzing, a Sherpa from our expedition doing advance work, had fallen through a snow bridge and into a crevasse at 20,000 feet and was injured with a broken femur. This was serious. Rob's facial expression showed it. The plan for going to Base Camp changed.

We stayed behind in Lobuche another day, while Rob and Mike went ahead to coordinate a complicated rescue down to Base Camp. The rest of us stayed in Lobuche until things at Base Camp stabilized. The rescue took a whole day and involved about 35 people, who evacuated Ngawang through the highly dangerous Khumbu Icefall.

I was still sick. But I looked forward to Base Camp, which I hoped would afford a bit of privacy in dealing with the runs.

TO GET to Base Camp from Lobuche, we hiked up the Khumbu glacier, which slides downhill from the base of Everest. This river of ice is said to be a thousand or more feet thick in some places. A partial trail was already established through the ice and rubble. The first climbers periodically marked the route with stones stacked one on top of another. If the yaks had been able to get through, they, too, would have left behind their own trail markers.

Base Camp was at 17,500 feet. The bottom of Everest is far higher than any point in the contiguous United States. With less available oxygen, my lungs had to work much harder to function there and above. At this stage of our climb, it was a struggle just being there. And it was only the beginning.

Our camp was located on a combination of rubble and ice high on the glacier, close to the foot of the notorious Khumbu Icefall. This was the traditional area used by expeditions for 50 years. The Sherpa used picks and shovels to level the ice and rubble to locate a cook tent, mess tent, and an equipment and communications tent.

Each of the big tents had blue tarps as roofs, and was surrounded by smaller tents for the climbers and Sherpa. We shared the area with other climbing expeditions from around the world. It was a colorful sight to see all the tents and the prayer flags strung about by the Sherpa.

Colorful prayer flags lit up the icy sky. The flags contained Buddhist prayers that the Sherpa believe the wind reads and sends aloft, petitioning the gods for permission to climb and for safe passage on the journey.

I WAS happy to move into my tent and get organized. I had one duffel bag on each side of the tent, with my sleeping bag in the middle. Everything I needed at a moment's notice had a place: water bottle, short wave radio, pee bottle, food bag, two books, pen and paper, and tape cassette player.

All my mountaineering gear was marked "Louk," which most people read and pronounce as "Luke." I liked that because Luke is a biblical name, and the biblical author, Luke, told a great story. Most climbers also call me Louk. You understand why after one look at my last name.

I wrote my daily journal entries on a stenographer's pad. I brought two books, a mystery novel, and the Bible. I like reading the Bible when I have large blocks of quiet time and can read slowly, with time to think deeply about what I'm reading. Being the son of a Lutheran minister influenced my faith and religious beliefs. My faith helps and comforts me when facing life's challenges. My parents were the first to teach me about the power of prayer and about prayer as a place to go for help. To this day, I still say the prayers my mother taught me as a youngster.

How about praying to climb Everest? Would divine intervention make me stronger or make the mountain softer and easier to climb? I'm kidding, of course. I know prayer doesn't work that way. I tried it in college to pass my exams.

My most important possession was a favorite picture of Sandy and me. It was taken a year before at Christmas time. I used it as my bookmark. I looked at it several times a day when I was at camp. I really missed being home. I missed being with Sandy. I liked being at home. I liked my work, my family, my friends, and my home at sea level in Michigan. For me, climbing mountains was never about an escape from the routines of everyday life. I liked my everyday life. One of the hardest parts about being away climbing was being away.

I lived mostly in the same clothes. For some things I had a few extra, such as socks and shorts. After I couldn't stand the stink any more, the dirty socks or shorts were stuffed under the duffel in my tent. My fleece jacket was my pillow. I knew how to roll it up just right for sleeping. It has become a close friend over the years.

After getting organized in the tent, I set up a communication plan with Sandy. Usually, I had little contact with Sandy while I was in the backcountry. While on a climbing trip, if I were in a city while moving between places, like Quito, Ecuador or Zermatt, Switzerland, I called Sandy. But in the mountains or backcountry, we had no contact.

Actually, limited contact always seemed to work best, given Sandy's feelings about climbing and the risks. Several years ago I had called Sandy from the summit of Crestone Needle in Colorado. This is one of the more interesting mountains in Colorado to climb, with some rock climbing challenge. Sandy wasn't excited, or even interested when I called her from the summit on a cell phone. I got a chilled response: "That's nice. I'm glad you're happy." These words look friendly enough on paper, but the way they were said conveyed more than the words. Every now and then I forgot that Sandy didn't experience the joy I felt from mountain climbing, but that chilly response reminded me.

Communication from Everest, however, was more frequent and different. We had a briefcase-sized satellite phone powered by batteries charged by a solar energy collector at Base Camp. When it wasn't too cold and the stored solar energy gave us power, I would call or fax a message to Sandy, and vice versa.

I preferred to receive faxes. That way, I literally held the words. I carried them around in my shirt pocket and brought them into my sleeping bag at night. Sandy's exact words meant much to me. They were a sustaining force. In a phone call, her words were quickly gone. But with a fax, I saw her thoughts and the images formed from the words. I heard the sounds. The rhythm. I could even see Sandy thinking the words while writing them. I read slowly, word by word, knowing ahead almost exactly the next word to follow. But most importantly, I heard Sandy's voice as I looked at the words on paper. I could *hear* her voice. And I could look at the words again the next day and any day after, just to silently hear her voice again.

ON MY first day at Base Camp, except for my stomach problem, I was feeling pretty good. Base Camp was comfortable, although short on oxygen to breathe. Technically, at the Base Camp altitude, you have about one-half of the oxygen available at sea level. This usually meant a headache, light-headedness, shortness of breath, loss of appetite, fatigue, weakness, and irritability. Like a big hangover.

Dinner time was always interesting. A bell rang when the cook was ready. The standard dress code included down parka, hat, gloves, and big warm boots. My headlamp was a necessity in order to navigate in the dark across the ice back to my tent.

On the trek into Base Camp, the climbing team members made life fascinating, especially at dinner time. Stuart Hutchison, a Canadian in his early thirties, was exceptionally intelligent and quick witted. Stu loved to tell jokes and stories at dinner. He and Beck were the best storytellers. Taske was close behind. It seemed like the stories and jokes never ran out. Both Stu and Beck could also quickly move to serious subjects and deliver on the spot a well organized, articulate lecture on science or political subjects. It was a good thing I was more of a listener than a talker, because I couldn't match up.

Rob said he wanted Stu as part of the expedition because of his 15 years climbing experience in the Himalaya and the Alaskan Range. He had been on three Himalaya expeditions, to the north face of Everest, K2 (the world's second highest mountain), and Broad Peak, as well as many difficult climbs in the Alaskan Range and summiting Mt. McKinley (Denali) two times (and once on the more challenging West Rib route). This was Stu's second attempt on Everest. He aborted his first attempt in 1994 to help rescue another climber.

While in Katmandu, Stu had Buddha eyes sewn on the back of his fleece jacket at one of the many sewing shops along the Thamel marketplace. Those Buddha eyes came to symbolize something about him: compassionate, ever watchful. Stu became one of my best friends on the expedition.

In the mess tent at dinner, Yasuko Namba, a climbing member from Japan, always sat in the same place. From the very beginning, two things stood out about Yasuko. First, though her English was strong, she didn't like to talk too much. She only spoke when spoken to. She was a naturally shy, quiet person. But underneath that quiet exterior was a committed, determined, goal-oriented mindset. Second, she was about one-half my size. Yasuko was about 5 feet tall and weighed about 95 pounds. I am 6 feet 3 inches and weigh 190. That being said, I never figured out how she could eat more than I did. She usually ate her own special Japanese meals and then as much Western food as the rest of us. I joked with her about that. She always gave me a big smile, but said little in response.

Yasuko Namba

Yasuko was one of the leading female climbers in Japan, and had climbed on earlier expeditions around the world with Rob. She was a national figure in Japan and all of Asia, where climbers are held in high esteem. She was 47 years old, but looked more like 30. She would be the oldest woman to climb Everest, and the second Japanese woman. The Asian media were following her climb and the world record she was attempting to set.

I frequently sat at dinner with Doug Hansen, a team member in his mid 40s from Seattle. I identified with him in several ways. We were tall, lean, and born and raised in modest financial backgrounds. And we both found our athletic strength in endurance sports. Like me, he ran marathons, although he ran many more than I had. Both of us also like to run stadium steps to train. And we were both passionate about climbing.

Doug had a long resume in the European Alps and Asia and had climbed before with Rob. Significantly, he was a member of Rob's 1995 Everest expedition that turned around at the South Summit, 85 meters from the top.

Every day since the 1995 turn around, Doug said he thought about Everest. That seemed like exaggeration. But as time passed, I believed him. Indeed, one year later, Doug was back for another attempt, fully committed to dissolving his profound disappointment and finishing off that final 85 meters.

Doug Hansen

Doug was very popular back home. I think he received more messages than anyone else. At dinnertime, Doug was happy to share his news with the rest of us. He was divorced, with two children. Doug's daughter seemed to be his chief cheerleader. Doug and I got along well. I liked him very much. We both shared a deep interest in the history of Himalaya climbing. While in the village of Namche, Doug came across an antique ice axe for sale. He wasn't sure he had enough cash to buy it as a souvenir. I had extra cash with me and lent Doug enough to buy it. He said he had just the right place to display the axe at home.

ON THAT first evening at Base Camp, while in the mess tent, Doug remarked, "Did you hear that 11 expedition permits were issued this year?" Eleven struck me as a very high number. In the previous decade the Nepal government limited the number of annual permits to three or four. (1993 was an exception because it was the fortieth anniversary of the first ascent.) In 1994, four permits were issued, and in 1995, three permits. My expectation was that two or three other teams would also be there.

Nepal's issuance of a higher number of permits was a response to the advent of professional expeditions. These have been good for Nepal. Professional expeditions treated the environment more respectfully and responsibly. The trash left behind on Everest was the product of the unethical and selfish practices of earlier climbers. Professional expeditions now routinely clean up the mess left behind by those climbers. Professional expeditions have also looked out for the local Sherpa interests and fueled a strong economy and higher standard of living in the Khumbu.

What effect would 11 permits have? Should I be alarmed or even concerned? Would it make climbing more dangerous or have any effect at all? I was in no position to know what impact more climbers would have. Everest is a big mountain, so perhaps 11 teams was no big deal. "Should be room for everyone. Let's wait and hear what Rob has to say," Taske said.

Rob said he wasn't concerned and I accepted that, especially after I learned the other expeditions had climbing teams of small numbers, much smaller than ours. All teams had Sherpa support, but compared to ours, much smaller numbers. It was hard for me to see a problem, based on the number of permits issued. But in life, and mountain climbing as well, trouble doesn't always signal it's on its way.

AFTER dinner the first night, Base Camp Manager Helen Wilton handed me a fax from Sandy. Helen was 39 years old, and a veteran Everest Base Camp manager from New Zealand. Over the next several weeks, whenever I was in Base Camp, to see Helen walking in my direction holding sheets of paper was a joyous moment. I knew it was news from home. Sandy's faxes were about everyday life in Michigan, but I reread them over and over. They connected me to her.

To: Lou Kasischke   From: Sandy Kasischke (one page) 4-10-96

Dear Lou, Received 2 pages of your fax in good condition at 5 AM. I sent off the information to everyone on your "list." I selected what I felt was important. A good portion of it was quoted directly from your fax. I was very happy + relieved to receive your call + the fax. I was getting worried—especially since Doris called + said there was an avalanche on Everest + people were killed. I'm sorry you are so sick. This is a new experience for you to add to your collection. I hope you are eating + drinking so that you will *really* be ready to move on up the mountain. Be sure you are well before you go any further. I know you can do this if you are healthy + if the weather cooperates. But once again, I want you to come back home. ...

Everything is O.K. here. I miss you so much. I'm not doing the decorating until you get home. I don't want to do it without you. I get very depressed—especially at night + on the weekends. I know that no matter how bad I think I have it, you have it even worse. At least I am safe, healthy, warm, etc. I love you and want you with me.

How cold is it? Are your hands + feet warm? Does the Kodak camera work OK? No pictures from Kodak yet. Is there a lot of snow at base camp? Tell me what you do each day. Tell me about the ceremony with the Sherpa. Has the doctor arrived at Base Camp? Please fax + call as much as you can. It helps me. This is the worse I have felt about you being gone + worrying about you. I can't believe how much I miss you. Please remember how much I love you and how much I want you here with me. Stay safe + healthy. I'm praying for you. I love you with all my heart. ...

Love Sandy

CHAPTER 8

THE LEADERSHIP TEAM

OUR EXPEDITION leadership team started out with a serious question mark. From the beginning in 1995, the planned leadership team was Rob Hall, Ed Viesturs, and Guy Cotter. Ed and Guy were Everest veterans. They were important to my decision to climb with Rob's expedition because of their strong supportive actions, especially in 1995, on Rob's previous expeditions. I conditioned my participation on that leadership team. But I received a phone call from Rob a couple of weeks before I left for Everest telling me the planned team wasn't going to work out. Ed and Guy had other commitments. Instead, Mike and Andy would be Rob's assistant leaders.

I knew nothing about Mike or Andy at that time.

One concern about Andy developed soon after we met. Andy spoke of himself as a novice at high altitude climbing and the highest peak he'd climbed was less than 22,000 feet. Almost everyone on our team had more high altitude experience than Andy, yet he was to be one of our leaders. I avoided thinking about Andy's lack of high altitude experience and focused on his strong climbing ability and his selfless good nature and positive attitude.

Mike was hired by Rob only five weeks earlier. Mike was not a certi- fied professional mountain guide and was reluctant to serve in a leadership capacity. His presence was more about helping out his friend Rob, whose team was caught short-handed.

So, our expedition leadership team started out with some basic and important organizational weaknesses. Andy had no climbing experience on Everest. Andy had no high altitude leadership or decision making experience. Mike only occasionally served in a climbing leadership role, and had no Everest leadership experience. Rob had only known Mike for two years. Rob, Andy, and Mike had never worked together. Andy and Mike had never met until Everest.

Could they work effectively together? How would this new — inexperienced and untested — leadership team play out in the dangerous area of Everest.

This was not the place for a practice round.

CHAPTER 9

THE BIG PICTURE

MY EVEREST objective was simple and clear—to climb it. People sometimes asked me why. In 1995, my answer was simple, logical, and sensible. Everest is special. Everest is different than any other mountain in the world. It's the highest. It's an icon. It's famous. It's the essence of the high Himalaya. It's the symbol of the highest achievement in any endeavor. No other mountain comes even close. In terms of raw logic, climbing the highest one is more logical than climbing any other. Even more logical, it was the only mountain my mother-in-law Jennie was familiar with.

British climber George Mallory, one of the first to attempt to climb Everest, famously answered the "why climb Everest?" question by saying, "Because it's there." What a great answer. I love the simplicity.

And I have no idea what it means.

Still, it leaves me with the idea that it means something—something deep and something secret. I love it. Maybe someday I'll figure it out, as soon as I figure out what "it" is. Is _it_ the mountain or is _it_ something else?

Everest is also such a huge physical and mental challenge that I knew there would be an interesting story from the climb, even if interesting only to me. What would that story be? That as much as anything

Summit 29,028'

South Summit
28,700'

Hillary Step

High Camp
26,000'

Lhotse 27,940'

Lhotse Face

Camp 3
24,000'

Western Cwm

Camp 2
21,300'

Camp 1
19,000'

Khumbu Icefall

Base Camp
17,500'

Khumbu Glacier

Six Week Route to High Camp

intrigued me. Would I feel or find something more important than the summit I sought? I wanted to live that story.

The story of the experience, whatever that would be, was what mattered. It was special to me to see and experience famous places in mountaineering history — the Khumbu Valley, Khumbu Icefall, Lhotse Face, South Col, Triangular Face, Southeast Ridge, South Summit, Hillary Step, and, of course, the top. After all, there is only one highest mountain in the world.

Still, climbing Everest does not measure your greatness as a climber. To climb it is mostly about the willingness to take the high risks and the human struggle to physically endure the extreme altitude that almost reaches outer space. Some of the world's best climbers have not and cannot climb Everest. But that's not because they lack climbing talent and expertise. It's because, for one reason or another, their bodies are unable to acclimatize to the thin air in the extreme high altitude. Swiss climber Andre Roch on the 1952 Swiss expedition said it well, "The trouble with Everest is not that it's a hard mountain. It's just a little bit too high."

The popular belief in the non-climbing community is that climbing Everest validates you as a climber. Some believe you are not a "real" climber unless you have climbed it. But within the climbing community, this is not true. If you climb Everest, it's great you had that experience. But it doesn't make you a big deal. By the time I arrived, 66 Americans had already climbed Everest. I was not going to make the six o'clock news.

I also know what did not motivate me. The idea of finding my limits or testing myself against Everest didn't appeal to me. I've never been enamored with the idea of going to the edge of my limits and looking at the other side. Besides, if you go past your limits on Everest, you die. It's not like running in a marathon, where if you exceed your limits and keel over, someone helps you to an aid station, and then calls you a cab for a ride.

THE PLAN was to climb the mountain in the classic way. This meant that during April and May we established five camps, with each about a day's climb apart. Base Camp at 17,500 feet, and four additional camps at 19,000 feet (Camp 1), 21,300 feet (Camp 2), 24,000 feet (Camp 3), and 26,000 feet (Camp 4 or High Camp). We climbed to and occupied each camp on a schedule of climbing and resting that allowed the body time and opportunity to make the many physiological changes needed to function with less oxygen at the increasing altitudes. Push higher and recover. Push higher yet and recover. The gradual process was the main focus of our climbing activities for the six weeks before summit day. This was for acclimatization. This is how climbers are able to climb at the extreme altitude of Everest. Reaching the top largely depends on how well a climber becomes acclimatized.

I discovered long ago I have a genetic chemistry well suited for high altitude mountain climbing. I picked the right parents, I guess, to have high altitude tolerance genes. I had climbed the highest mountains in the world outside the Himalaya. My body adapted well to oxygen deprivation. This gave me confidence that I could make a serious attempt to reach the summit.

The general strategy was to be healthy, ready, and in position to go to the top during a brief period in May. This is the window of time when historically the weather patterns shift and the jet stream wind currents that normally blast the upper face (making Everest impossible to climb) moved north. From his experience, Rob projected the window to be from May 5 to May 15. But we had no official weather forecast. During that window of time, the strategy was to be ready and in position, and hopefully still healthy and motivated, to go to the summit from High Camp. Mike Groom frequently said that the key to giving the climb a fair shot was to still be motivated. Until summit day, from the suffering it took to get that high, Everest was going to work hard to beat out of you every ounce of motivation. The mountain would work to make you want never to hear the word Everest again.

FOR FOUR weeks, I was at one of five camps or climbing in between. From my tent at each campsite, as I looked around, I saw different features of one of the most famous places on earth: Mount Everest. It's a different experience from each camp.

From Base Camp, I looked up at the Khumbu Icefall. At Camp 1, I stared into the wall of Nuptse, the Valley of Silence, the Lhotse Face, and the west ridge of Everest. From the rocky moraine of the Camp 2 site, I saw much of the same as Camp 1, but Camp 3 was different. At Camp 3, on the ice shelf with our tents perched on the Lhotse Face, the only view was down the Lhotse Face and across the Valley of Silence at the pyramid shape of Mount Pumori. These are famous sites and it was a privilege just to see them. The experience was a big part of the answer to the "why climb" Everest question. Just being there.

In addition to what I saw, I experienced the sounds coming from above and below. On the mountain walls next to Base Camp and above, avalanches of snow, ice, and rock crashed down in a roar that echoed around the valleys. Then came the wind, and the unrelenting flapping noise of the tent and of the prayer flags strung on the long strings around the camp. Early each morning before the Sherpa left camp for climbing, I heard the crackling noise of juniper branches burning in the lhap-so's stone altar. One constant noise at each camp was people coughing because of the dry air. This is the infamous Khumbu Cough. I also heard the sounds of footsteps crunching and squeaking in the snow, of crampons attached to climbing boots biting in with each step forward, and of people talking and greeting each other in different languages. Beneath my tent at Base Camp were the sounds of the Khumbu glacier moaning and cracking, as the glacial ice and rock slowly made its way down the valley. I was always re-minded that my tent and sleeping bag were sprawled across moving blocks of ice. Every now and then I had to adjust things in the tent to account for the moving action.

But from High Camp, I saw nothing. There was either no visibility or it was dark. High Camp was a place I wish I'd never heard of. High Camp was a nightmare.

ESPECIALLY in my quiet time in my sleeping bag, the most impor-tant sounds were those of words. Not words heard by my ears, but heard within me—"I love you." "Come back home." The sounds of Sandy's voice. The words and sounds of her loneliness and affection.

It was also beyond my imagination that words spoken in a tent or news about any action taken at a remote mountain campsite three miles high could almost instantly make their way around the world and be known by millions of people. And almost instantly again re-turn to another tent 20 feet away—via the Internet. Today I take this for granted. But not in 1996.

Sandy knew more about what was happening on the mountain and in Base Camp than I did. I would call Sandy and say "Hey, what's hap-pening on Everest?" That was amusing, until I saw how the Internet and the media could combine their unchecked power to influence what actually happened on the mountain.

My concern about Jon Krakauer's unhealthy influence as an em-bedded writer was confirmed early when we discovered that a Jon Krakauer "Inside Edition" performance scorecard was showing up on the Internet. In a satellite phone call, Sandy told me that someone named Jon Krakauer (Sandy didn't know he was part of our expedi-tion) was doing a play-by-play for the Outside Online Internet site about his personal performance assessment of the people climbing. She said, "It's all over the Internet. I'm getting many calls about it."

I had no idea what she was talking about. But since Jon worked for *Outside* magazine and Sandy was referring to Outside Online, the magazine's Internet site, I was concerned. This was troubling. My intuitive fears and concerns were proven right.

It was a problem—a very bad feeling—when you were doing the hardest and most dangerous thing that you have ever done, and potentially struggling for your life, to learn that a writer for a major magazine had been hired to scribble notes about your every move for a juicy story. But much, much worse than reporting facts, he was giving his own subjective judgment performance scorecard that heavily influences public perception.

None of us had consented to this. Everest was a private challenge. I felt betrayed by Rob, for converting our private quest into something the whole world could read about, just so he could prime the publicity pump. Rob's breach of trust felt very real.

In fairness to Jon, when asked about it, he said he didn't realize the interviews he gave to the Outside Online reporter would show up on the Internet.

Jon's performance scorecard ended open candor among the climbers and convinced us that Jon's embedded presence was dangerous for us. Everyone also then knew that Jon's performance pressures would not just relate to a North American readership. Jon had a world-wide audience for his views. Only time would tell how the performance pressures from his presence would affect the outcome.

AFTER FOUR weeks of climbing, my feelings were mixed. I felt humility, anxiety, excitement, and self doubt. You name it: I experienced the full gambit. This was Everest. This was big. This was serious. This was not some casual weekend climb in the mountains.

I always had some self doubt whenever I faced big challenges, but it has never stopped me. I have also grown to expect and even accept that self doubt can help lead me to achievement. What I didn't expect on Everest was that my natural self doubt could reach into a sense of inadequacy. But Everest can do that to you, as veterans of the mountain repeatedly warned me. Reality was setting in, and from the shorter climbs between camps I understood how really hard it was to climb Everest.

When climbing, fatigue came quickly and with great force in the extreme thin air. After all, it's the thin air that made Everest—Everest. I needed my head to keep my body moving. Climbers know that if they have trained and have the necessary physical strength and endurance, fatigue and suffering are managed from the head.

On any big climb or endurance challenge, I knew I had to overcome not just the actual physical fatigue and suffering, but also my natural resistance to them. This was that natural internal struggle, where part of you wants to quit, even though another part of you wants to keep going. You must be a good sufferer. What I planned for from my experience and training was to gain confidence in my stamina. You train the mind to keep pushing when the body says, "I don't want to do this any more." The longer you could suffer meant the longer you could go toward your true physical limit before giving in. It's rare that an endurance athlete will ever reach his true physical limit. You almost always "give in" before then.

It's the mind not the body that must win the struggle. The body will follow (however reluctantly) if the inner voice says, "I can do this." I know that the minute my inner voice says, "I can't do this," the climb is over.

On Everest, it was a constant struggle, as I went higher and higher and it kept getting harder and harder. Especially after I felt sick and cold most of the time and the thrill of being on Everest and in the high Himalaya had worn off. Especially when every part of my body was begging to stop. Especially when I looked up and felt like the top appeared 10,000 miles away.

MY CHALLENGE to be a good sufferer was compounded by getting sick with an intestinal problem I couldn't control. I never would have expected that my biggest worry in climbing Mount Everest would be about digestion. Avalanche, high wind, climbing conditions, accident, high altitude sickness, or any one of many obstacles were more likely to be the source of concern, I thought. But not food digestion. Nevertheless, this was just as serious. Food is fuel to climb. It's the source for the needed energy. And without the energy, I couldn't climb Everest. This directly affected my physical capacity, and just as forcefully, my confidence in my mental toughness.

Beginning in the village of Namche and continuing for the next few weeks, I couldn't keep food inside of me. I'd picked up some kind of bug along the line, probably (but not necessarily) from the food or water.

I had never been sick on a climb before, aside from headaches and minor ailments. I'd always taken strange comfort in what I thought was a cast iron digestive system, even in my travels in the Third World. Because of the effects of high altitude on natural body functions, including healing, people say, "If you get sick on Everest, you stay sick." It's frequently said that the climbers who do the best are those who manage over six weeks to stay the healthiest.

The physical low turned into an emotional low. I started struggling with anxiety. This was something I was not accustomed to. I started to lose mental focus and motivation. If I didn't reach the summit, I'd figured I would have lived a good story about why I didn't, such as being stopped by a violent storm, high avalanche risk, or another event of high drama. I couldn't think of anything worse than to be knocked out because of diarrhea.

As a rule, I do not take any medication while climbing, especially high altitude climbing. The exception is a low dose of Tylenol for headaches or Ibuprofen as an anti-inflammatory for muscle strains. My concern was that medication might hinder or distort my natural bodily responses in the acclimatization process. But I needed a remedy. I was concerned about losing any more weight and depleting my fat storage for fuel. I decided to take medication. Dr. Carolyn Mackenzie, our expedition physician, gave me the drug Cipro, a long established antibiotic.

On a long high altitude climb, some believe it's best to gain 10 or 15 pounds before you go, to have sufficient fat storage to burn as fuel. The thinking is that you may need it if you get sick or for another reason you can't keep the calorie intake rate up with the calorie consumption rate. The downside is that you have to carry the extra weight, which in turn requires more fuel and energy. I made a conscious, calculated decision not to gain weight ahead of the climb. My thinking was I never get sick and I didn't want the extra burden to carry.

I finally decided the best thing was not to worry about it too much. Jon and Taske both recovered from being sick. Andy was sick off and on, and he had recovered. I had to be patient.

AFTER FOUR weeks of climbing together, I thought Rob had fulfilled his obligation as expedition leader to assemble a team out of a group of individual climbers. Each had the required skills, experience, self reliance, and ability to make the individual decisions needed to work together. Most climbers are ordinary people, and usually high achievers in other parts of life. Only a relatively few devote themselves primarily to climbing. I admired those like Rob and Andy who were committed full time to climbing and became professionals. It was a great choice for a career. The rest of us were serious, part-time climbers, proud of being amateurs. The origin of the word amateur is the Latin root — to love. By definition, we climbed for just the love of the sport.

Mountaineering self reliance is the main measure of the experience one should have to make a serious attempt to climb Everest. Mountaineering self reliance obviously includes the physical endurance and strength and climbing skills needed to get up and down, especially extreme harsh weather skills. But more importantly, it requires that you can understand the climbing situation you are in, the risks and your own abilities, and have the qualities of humility and character to be able to exercise good judgment in decision making. This includes being able to make decisions for yourself and to take care of yourself, especially in trouble situations.

Mileage recorded in time logged in the mountains or vertical feet climbed is not what's important. A climber can have many years of climbing and many big summits but be consistently thoughtless, reckless, and irresponsible.

Getting away with past hairball mountaineering stunts doesn't count for anything. Unfortunately, in the climbing world it is not uncommon for a climber to have performed some hairball stunt on a difficult peak, survived only through sheer luck, and thereby instantly garnered a lifelong reputation in the climbing community as a great and experienced climber. In mountaineering, you can get a reputation for being bold and courageous by doing something stupid and reckless — an accident that didn't quite happen.

I took much comfort in the decision making experience of several Hall expedition members. My comfort included, such as with Frank and Stu, experience on Everest itself. Several others had extensive non-climbing life and career experiences (such as in medicine and the military) that regularly required high risk tough decision making. People like Taske, Beck, and Stu had the proven skill and presence of mind to act in ambiguous, uncertain situations with incomplete data and in the stress of limited time and sometimes life and death consequences. Most everyone can make easy decisions. But not everyone can make the hard calls. Decision making is frequently what makes the life and death difference in mountain climbing. Each of us expected much from the other in that regard.

Still, climbing Everest is not just about technical skills and decision making. It is a team effort. It's about the people. We each had to climb the mountain individually, but for any of us to succeed, others must also. And for that to happen, we needed to work together.

Rob was a Mount Everest expert engaged to provide his leadership expertise and judgment, especially on matters of logistics and decision making to manage risk. He was not the hired help or nurse to tend to our basic needs. Some, actually several, in our expedition were better technical climbers than Rob. But that was not relevant. No one on our team came close to having Rob's specialized Everest knowledge.

Our individual responsibility was to be supportive of Rob, but not passive. If we were passive, we were weak. We would and should have as much influence on Rob as he had on us. The premium on this would come on summit day. We would all be strung out physically. But it would be everyone's responsibility to help in the management of the summit day climbing plan, and especially regarding time. Rob said, "Time is what counts. We must be, where we need to be, on time."

I felt confident about my teammates. As I looked at the members one by one, I saw that most were leaders of other people in their work career. They knew that every decision has consequences. And Rob would only be able to lead them to within the limits they could accept in terms of their own judgment, values, and tolerance for risk.

Serious climbers also know the possibility of a leader needing help or even needing to be rescued by the others. In fact, many times it's the more likely situation. For example, either Rob, Mike, or Andy would be up front, and if anyone fell into a crevasse, it would probably be that leader. The rest of us must have the skills and be ready to rescue the leader. For these reasons, practicing crevasse rescue techniques was always a high priority in my preparation for any glacial climb.

Good climbing members also never wait for the leader to ask for help. Rob needed strong teammates who spoke up and stepped up. He said, "I want no sheep on this team, especially on summit day." All indications at the lower elevations were that our climbing members were good teammates. But it was easy to be a good teammate when things were easy or going as planned. It would be when things were hard or going wrong that we would see if we were a team.

CHAPTER 10

KHUMBU ICEFALL

THE MOST difficult challenge, and the most feared area to climb on Everest from the Nepal side, is the Khumbu Icefall. While at Base Camp, I was constantly reminded of its presence. As I looked out my tent door, the Icefall was right in my face — 2,000 vertical feet of falling ice blocks the size of apartment buildings.

As snow accumulates on a mountain face over a period of years, it turns to ice. That means it glaciates. The weight of the ice mass is what causes a glacier to move down the mountain side. Some describe a glacier as a flowing river of ice. For about two miles, the Khumbu glacier flows down the side of Everest. But at about 19,500 feet, it abruptly falls over a steep section of bedrock to 17,500 feet, the elevation of Base Camp.

Picture a 2,000 foot high and 400 foot thick waterfall. But instead of water, picture huge blocks of ice weighing 40 tons each. That's what we were climbing, a mass of ice, falling 2,000 feet over a cliff.

Over the weeks before summit day, we climbed the Icefall several times, up to Camps 1, 2, and 3 and back down to Base Camp in preparation for the final push to the summit. It was the most technically demanding part of climbing Everest. The Icefall is one of the historic and legendary places in mountaineering. It is a place like none other on Everest.

The risks were always extreme because the Icefall was moving. The amount it actually moves each day varies with its weight, the sun, and the air temperature. Some days it doesn't move at all. Some days it moves a centimeter or two. Most days it moves much more. On average, it moves two to three feet each day—slowly moving unstable blocks of ice. The moving action causes deep cracks to open and close, and high towers of ice called seracs, to collapse without warning and send thousands of tons of ice crashing down.

Even the sounds in the Icefall were scary. One minute, a cracking noise. The next a creak, and then another creak. And sometimes a roar as a section of ice towers collapsed and toppled over. But the worst sound and sight was a rushing noise caused from the force of a wall of air that was pushed ahead by an avalanche and accompanied by what looked like smoke rising above the surface, which was actually loose powder snow swirling from the forces.

When I first saw the Icefall from a distance, it seemed impossible to climb. As I climbed through it, in some places the only possible route was under overhanging shaky blocks of ice.

TO PROP up my motivation while climbing, my inner voice frequently said, "I can do this." But in the Icefall, that voice spoke with less conviction. The Icefall is so feared because climbing it is in many ways a game of Russian roulette. As a climber, you have no control over the ice blocks. But you know that each and every one you pass beneath or over will one day collapse, sending thousands of tons of ice crashing down and crushing everything in its path with a thunderous roar. Of all the perils a climber faces on Everest, no single place has more objective dangers. Over the years, more climbers have died there than in any other area. The first American to die climbing Everest was crushed in the Icefall by falling blocks of ice. He was part of the first American expedition to summit Everest in 1963.

The skills and strengths needed to climb Everest are varied. Sometimes it was the strength and stamina of an endurance athlete. And sometimes, as in the Icefall, you needed the concentration and anxiety control skills of an expert sharpshooter who pulls the trigger between heartbeats.

ON THE morning before our first climb in the Icefall, our Sherpa conducted a special ceremony: the puja. The puja is a ritual for purification and a request to the mountain spirits for permission to climb and for protection along the way. The Sherpa worship site is called a lhap-so.

An essential part of the ceremony takes place at a stone altar built by the Sherpa. In the center and at the top of the altar the Sherpa erected a tharshing, a tall flagpole from which the prayer flags flew. Members of the expedition brought offerings of food and drink to the stone altar, while a lama from the Tengboche Monastery in the Khumbu Valley read prayers out loud.

Both climbers and their equipment were purified as part of the ceremony. Our ropes, ice axes, crampons, and other gear were passed through smoke from smoldering juniper branches while the lama read prayers. The Sherpa gave each of us a red nylon string, called a sangdi, as part of the blessing. The Sherpa believe that the sangdi provides protection from harm. We tied it around our necks, where it stayed during the expedition.

While those beliefs are not part of my personal Christian faith and belief system, I felt it important to participate and show my respect to the Sherpa and their beliefs. They were an essential part of the climbing team and they gave us their blessing. And Everest was, after all, in their country.

WE STARTED climbing in the Icefall just before first light. This was before the heat of the sun would loosen the ice blocks. To climb Everest from Nepal on the Southeast Ridge route, we first had to get through the Icefall. We had no choice.

One unique thing about climbing the Khumbu Icefall is the use of ladders in some places. The practice started when the British first climbed Everest in 1953. They climbed the same Southeast Ridge route. This was how it was done then, and every expedition climbing Everest's Southeast Ridge route in the last 50 some years has followed this practice. The use of ladders in some locations is not only the traditional way to climb the Icefall, it is the only way to bridge the enormous gaps between the giant ice blocks. At some points it is necessary to lash together two or even three ladders.

The overall mental effect of climbing on these ladders was quiet alarm. We had to walk over those precarious bridges in our crampons, which are two-inch long metal spikes on the bottom of our boots.

My neighbors in northern Michigan laughed and told stories about seeing me practice in my back yard walking across a fully extended aluminum ladder. My friend next door was a commercial painter and, it being wintertime, he had little use for his extra long aluminum ladder. I set the ladder on cement blocks at each end, and practiced walking across with crampons, wearing a full pack. The ladder sagged as I approached the middle. Sometimes I practiced on the ladder after a hard workout. The idea was to practice concentration and effectiveness when totally exhausted.

The only difference during practice was that I was only a few feet off the snow in my backyard. On Everest in the Khumbu Icefall, below the two ends of the ladder was a hole 10 stories deep. To get a feel for the difference, think about a piece of wood 2x4 laid on the floor. Almost anyone can concentrate on the board and easily walk along it. But suppose you put that board 10 stories high? Now it becomes much harder. It's difficult to concentrate on the board because you are also concerned about what happens if you fall off. The consequence of making a mistake is a major influence on your ability to perform. Practicing was one thing. In the real action, it was entirely different.

The recommended technique is the same as if walking on eggshells. Don't look down. Don't stop. Move as fast as possible. Breathe. Make no mistakes. My crampons rang out on the aluminum rungs. The ladders creaked and sagged under my weight as I tried to float like a butterfly over the void. Breathe. Don't look down. Don't stop. Make no mistakes. I grasped the lines strung across the gap. They wobbled from side to side. Each time I prayed (I wasn't taking any chances) to get across as quickly as possible. If I made a mistake, it would be a big problem. A very big problem. Climbing in the Icefall did not allow for time to deal with problems. Focus, focus on my next move, and keep moving. Fast. I needed to be mentally calm and quiet to be efficient and fast. I needed those sharpshooter concentration skills.

On one occasion I was behind Taske. Two long ladders were lashed together. He was in the middle. The ladders sagged and lifted as he

moved across, shifting his weight from one foot to another. I waited and watched. I wanted Taske to cross so I could get across. He moved steadily and the ladders moved up and down in his rhythm. All of a sudden, the ladders shook from the rhythm being broken. Crampons have 12 two-inch spikes. The rear two spikes on his back foot were pinched between rungs on the ladder. Taske couldn't move his back foot forward. He tried to stay in balance like a high wire act in the circus. I choked with anxiety. There was nothing I could do. The ladders would not support both our weight, and for me to touch them could throw Taske off balance.

What he did next, I never could have done. Staying in balance, he did a deep squat, paused to be secure with his balance, shifted all his weight to his front foot, wiggled the back foot to free the pinched spikes, and stood back up. He then proceeded across. As he reached the other side, he looked back and said, "Hey, mate, what did you think of that one? When I looked down, I thought I could see all the way to America."

Breathe. Don't look down.

SHERPA assistance, the use of fixed rope for safety in exposed areas, fixed camps, and a leadership structure are the generally accepted practices of the classical and ethical style of climbing Everest. Let's face it, as with ladders in the Icefall, if any one of these practices were removed, almost nobody would stand on top of Everest.

The Everest climbing challenge takes an organized, leadership-driven team effort, and this was true from the beginning. In 1953, even though the impression left by the media is that Edmund Hillary, along with Tenzing Norgay, were the "conquerors of Everest," like most things in life, there was much more to that story.

In fact, it was the Swiss expedition in 1952, one year before the first ascent that established the Southeast Ridge route to the top. Supported by Sherpa, the Swiss were the first to climb through the Khumbu Icefall, up the Western Cwm, up the Lhotse Face, over the Geneva Spur, and to establish high camp on the South Col. From there, and pursuant to a disciplined Swiss-like leadership structure, Raymond Lambert and, of all people, Tenzing Norgay, using supplemental oxygen equipment, climbed up the Southeast Ridge and established another camp at 27,230 feet. From there, they climbed to 28,200 feet, almost to the South Summit. They were very close to the top.

Two things were important about that effort for the British expedition the next year. The first was that the Swiss expedition climbers established the route to within 800 vertical feet of the top and proved that it was climbable. Until then, a big barrier was psychological and physiological—it wasn't known if a human being could go that high and live. Lambert and Norgay established they could. They did not turn back before the top because of psychology or physiology, but because of the wind and difficult snow conditions.

The second and even more important thing for the follow-up British expedition was that Tenzing Norgay was one of those climbers. Norgay knew the route. He was there, near the top. He could guide

Hillary. (The British, along with Edmund Hillary, in 1951, the year before the Swiss, had not even gotten through the Khumbu Icefall.)

The British expedition that followed the Swiss expedition was also highly organized, heavily supported by Sherpa, and subject to a disciplined leadership-followership structure led by Himalayan veteran John Hunt. He had a detailed plan and a highly organized team.

Fourteen Sherpa carried loads of gear and supplies to the camps along the route. Hunt's plan was for climbers Tom Bourdillon, a British physicist working on rocket science, and Charles Evans, a British brain surgeon, to push the route past the Swiss high camp to the South Summit. Hillary and Norgay would then follow them to the top.

The plan worked. Bourdillon and Evans reached the South Summit. They were the first to reach the highest summit ever climbed and stood at the foot of the final short stretch to the top. They examined and analyzed the final 279 vertical feet to the top, cached oxygen supplies for use by Hillary and Norgay, and climbed back down to the South Col camp.

Bourdillon and Evans discussed whether to continue to the top themselves. Ambition told them to keep going. Fame and glory told them to go to the top. But personal responsibility to the team told them to go back down to High Camp, as planned. Even though it meant giving up the glory of being famous, they concluded the risks were too high. Specifically, the risk was that there might not be enough daylight left to safely continue to the top and get back down before dark.

At 1 PM they were at the South Summit. In their judgment it was too late to safely continue. If they were caught out in darkness, any attempted rescue would be disastrous. Although it was tempting, in the team spirit they felt it was best to stick to Hunt's plan of preparing the route for Hillary and Norgay and report back with their analysis of the final short stretch.

Two days later, Hillary and Norgay set out from the South Col camp with three others carrying gear and supplies in their support. They passed the Swiss campsite and carried to 27,900 feet, where the five stopped and dropped the gear and supplies. The three support climbers went down to the South Col camp. Hillary and Norgay camped at 27,900 feet for the night, a little more than 1,000 feet below the summit.

The next morning, after five hours of climbing, Hillary and Norgay passed the South Summit, the Bourdillon and Evans high point, and reached the top. Along the way, Norgay was able to guide Hillary up terrain he had climbed one year earlier with the Swiss. Hillary and Norgay became the first to climb that final 279 vertical feet and reach the top.

THOSE DETAILS of the first ascent show the critical components and the traditional ways that most Everest climbs are still done today: fixed safety ropes in exposed areas, ladders in the Icefall, use of supplemental oxygen for safety on summit day, a professional leadership-followership organizational structure, Sherpa support for the management of supplies and logistics, and a careful eye on the clock and remaining daylight.

Sherpa support plays a critical role on Everest to this day. Virtually no ascent of Everest has occurred without Sherpa assistance. Most Sherpa live in the Khumbu, which encompasses the valleys leading to the base of Everest.

By participating in a climbing expedition, Sherpa attain status among other Sherpa. But they are primarily motivated by the money, not the sport. In 1996, Nepal's per capita income was about $175 per year. Climbing Sherpa can earn $1,500 to $2,500 in a single climbing season. This income has been an important part of the Himalayan economy for many decades. Sherpa income has materially increased the standard of living for individual Sherpa families and many villages in Nepal. Today they have schools and health clinics, thanks to income earned on climbing expeditions.

If I had to carry all my gear, plus my share of expedition food, fuel, supplies, rope, and tents, I could not climb Mount Everest. Neither could 99.8 percent of Everest climbers. That includes Edmund Hillary and Tenzing Norgay. Some uninformed people scoff at climbers who rely on Sherpa support. Indeed it is possible to climb Everest solo and unsupported by Sherpa. As far as I know, it's been done once, and maybe even twice.

CHAPTER 11

THE "SAME DAY" DECISION

AFTER CLIMBING up and down to higher camps over the past four weeks, we were back at Base Camp from May 2 to May 5 to rest before the push to the summit. Summit day was soon. The main event. Rob completed the climbing plan for summit day. The plan included two last minute major decisions. One was highly unlikely. Both were unexpected.

If our expedition were the only team climbing, it would be easy to approach the specific date for a summit attempt with patience and flexibility, and to wait for clarity that the weather window was open. But it would be more challenging to have that patience and to be flexible if a large number of climbers from other expeditions were planning to go to the summit at the first opportunity. That was a possibility in our situation because of the big increase in the number of permits issued by Nepal.

The large number of climbers was, by itself, not the concern. Everest is a big place. But depending on the time of day, a large number of climbers could be a major safety problem, from overcrowding and resulting delays on the final part of the Southeast Ridge route at the area called the Hillary Step. The Hillary Step is a natural terrain chokepoint. For safety, only one person at a time should climb that 40 foot section. We were all aware of the history of the delay danger at the Hillary Step.

Over the previous weeks, few expressed any concern about large numbers. Each expedition did its own thing for readiness, on its own and usually different timetable. The delay danger would probably only present itself if the weather window didn't open until much later than expected. By then, every expedition would be ready and waiting with time running out.

The major expedition leaders had a meeting. Looking at the apparent readiness of most expeditions, Rob and the others were concerned about the potential for dangerous gridlock. They decided to manage the risk of overcrowding at the Hillary Step by having the major climbing teams go for the summit on different days. In other words, spread out. Such a plan had never before been made on Everest. That's why it was an unexpected decision. If the major teams spread out by going to the summit on separate days, no delays would occur at the Hillary Step chokepoint. Other than at the Step, as Rob said, "Everest is a big place."

Rob said May 10 would be the date for our attempt. He had summited Everest in two other years on May 10, and thought it was his lucky day. Other major expeditions would precede us. The Imax expedition's date was May 9. The Yugoslav expedition, the Swedish expedition, and the Spanish had already planned on going even earlier. Other expeditions were following us on May 11, and so on.

Of course, we didn't know—even approximately—what the weather would be on May 10. We didn't know if the acceptable weather window, which had not yet opened, would be open for a safe summit attempt on May 10. We had no evidence that the weather, primarily wind, had begun to stabilize in the upper regions. The plan for the teams to spread out on separate days seemed good, but it was premature to select dates. But Rob said we couldn't wait at Base Camp until weather stabilized. We had to be working our way up, based on reasonable historic expectations, to be in position to seize the opportunity when it came. That made sense. The movement of the world-wide jet stream doesn't necessarily respond to a climber's idea about when it was convenient to climb to the summit. Nature has its own schedule.

When Rob announced the plan, we all knew the date was arbitrary and tentative. It was obvious that the final decision to climb to the summit on May 10 would be determined on the actual facts and circumstances when the time came. May 10 was not carved in stone. At least that was my attitude — and assumption — and the clear perception given to us by Rob.

I didn't think much about this decision at the time. On balance, it seemed that some plan to manage the risk from large numbers on the same day was better than no plan at all. But it left unanswered what would happen if the weather window had not opened when the date came. How would the climbing schedule work then? Would everything back up, or would those with earlier dates move to the back of the schedule, or what else? Designating a fixed date carried some risk that a leader might be influenced to resolve doubts about the weather in favor of sticking to the assigned date. When asked about the unanswered questions, Rob was his usual positive and optimistic self. With a twinkle in his Kiwi eye and a flick of his fingers to the lid of his cap, he said "Don't worry. May 10 is my lucky day."

NOT LONG after we learned about the plan for teams to spread out on *separate days,* Rob announced that he and Scott Fischer, the leader of an American expedition, decided to go to the summit on the *same day* — May 10. The Fischer team was comparable in size to ours. It included some well known and highly respected climbers. Scott and Rob were competitors in the business of professional Everest expeditions.

Like the May 10 decision, this was also unexpected. But this decision — to climb on the same day — was unexpected, unlikely, illogical, and irrational. Bells rang. Alarm bells. When I first heard Rob say it, I tilted my head to see if I'd heard correctly. I looked around at the others. I wasn't alone. We all tried to process the announcement. From what I could tell, we were all puzzled.

The whole point of the major expedition leaders plan to spread out on separate days was to avoid the danger of delay from a large number of climbers going to the summit on the same day. So, why would Rob plan for the two largest expeditions to go to the summit on the same day? The membership of the Hall and Fischer teams was more than all the other teams combined. Rob's "same day" plan was clearly in conflict with the rationale of the "spread out" plan. It made no sense. None. What did it mean to "go on the same day"? Team up? Join together? Work together? And why would competitors even want to go to the summit on the same day?

Rob made that decision without prior consultation with any of our expedition members. We'd never even talked about it as a possibility. Who would think of such a thing? This was a major strategic departure from our expectations and climbing plan. On Rob's prior Everest expeditions, he never planned to go to the summit on the same day with another expedition—large or small in number. This was not the time and place to do a practice round. We were already doing something of a practice round with Rob's untested leadership team.

Many on the team had serious concerns. Adding numbers meant adding problems. What happened to the plan to spread the teams out on separate days? What was the point of that plan, if we had another plan to do the opposite? It was nothing personal about the Fischer team climbers. I understood from others they were good strong climbers, and I had no reason to think otherwise.

If the two teams ended up by chance going on the same day, so be it. We'd all had that experience. That would be outside our control. But to choose to go on the same day—on purpose, as part of a plan—made no sense. The Hall climbers knew that; and we wanted to know why. What was going on?

Questions about Rob's decision were raised. The most basic and the most important fundamental question was why. We had a lengthy discussion. No one except Rob thought that two teams going to the summit on the same day, as a matter of choice, was a good idea.

Someone, I think it was Taske, explained that before summit day and while on the glacier, we can move around and easily pass each other. You can even say there is a theoretical strength in numbers on a glacial climb. But on summit day on Everest, it's a ridgeline climb. We are climbing the Southeast Ridge. There is no strength in numbers. In fact, it's just the opposite. It's weakness. If you end up in the same place on the ridge mixed together, you are forced to work together in large numbers. That can easily cause confusion and create problems for climbers who have never worked together before. And that itself can lead to delays at the worst possible location.

Rob dismissed our questions and played down our concerns with empty, aggressive rhetoric. He said, "Look, you are reading too much into it." When someone said, "We don't even know these people," Rob replied flat out, and in a hard line manner, that none of that mattered. We were not combining teams. Each team would simply be somewhere on the same 3,000 foot route, and probably never in the same place at the same time. We would not be climbing mixed together. Rob specifically said, "We will function separately."

Slam. Just like that. The discussion ended. We would function separately. Not mixed together. Probably never in the same place. Rob concluded by again saying, "Everest is a big place, you know."

Combining team Sherpa for any reason, such as to break trail or fix safety ropes higher on the route, was never mentioned and would have been irrelevant anyway. Our expectation was that one of the other expeditions that preceded us would have fixed whatever rope was needed. And if not fixed by another team, what little rope work was expected (likely only at the Hillary Step) wouldn't be difficult or time consuming. We wouldn't need help to do it.

The "Same Day" Decision

Rob's words reassured me. I felt the downside risk was small. I had higher priorities to focus on. And besides, things were going well for us as a team. Everything was on track. This wasn't the moment to challenge Rob's decision making. We trusted him.

But we never did get a good reason (or even a weak one) for why both teams were going to the summit on the same day. The dismissive "didn't matter" response from Rob only begged the question even more. If it didn't matter, why do it?

What exactly was the real reason?

We will never know, for certain. But there was no good reason—none—that supported the interests of the individual climbing members. That point was clear and certain from our group discussion. But for some reason, it served Rob's interest.

I would only later come to understand the real reason. And that if there had been no "same day" decision, there would have been no 1996 tragedy.

Scott Fischer and
Rob Hall

CHAPTER 12

SANDY BACK HOME — MAY 4

ONE OF the biggest problems I faced over the past weeks of climbing was the mental torture that my intestinal problem put me through. I tried to reconcile myself to what appeared may be a dark outcome to my Everest challenge. In some ways, it was probably natural and human, in a time of doubt about the outcome of a big challenge, to look for reasons I could be comfortable with for not accomplishing the challenge. But what was happening to me was not acceptable. Two broken legs would be okay as a reason. But not the runs. I could take no comfort in that reason. It was humiliating.

Sandy knew about my situation. This was one of the disadvantages of regular communication. It made the whole Everest experience harder for Sandy because she knew the problems. Sandy is a natural worrier, especially about family and health matters. Over our long life together, to be a better husband, I tried to spare Sandy specific things to worry about. This had the downside effect of forcing me to keep my problems and worries to myself. Sandy always said I was lucky because I never worried about anything.

Three weeks earlier, while I sat in the mess tent with others, Helen Wilton handed me a fax from Sandy. I put it in my pocket to read later when I was alone in my tent. Such a simple thing. A pen, a piece of paper, and some words. But words of great power. With love and care and concern behind them, words that would creep into my being and be a contributing influence in what I did on May 10. Words that would save my life.

Sandy and I had made an irrevocable agreement that 1996 would be my "one and only attempt" on Everest. But this commitment, which Sandy knew I would keep, started to concern her.

Sandy knew my philosophy about dreams and goals, and about how turning around on a mountain fit into that philosophy. A dream is just a goal with a deadline; and if things don't work out at first, you reset the deadline and try again. On a mountain, every time you turn around you can go back. The dream doesn't die. Sandy understood this was my way of thinking, as I had turned around on other mountains when it was not safe to continue. But because of our "one and only attempt" agreement there would be no reset on Everest. Sandy's concern was that I might then push too hard in my weakened physical state.

Saturday, April 13, 1996 (noon)

TO: Lou Kasischke

FROM: Sandy

Dear Lou: I am very concerned about your health. If you keep pushing yourself, how do you expect to regain your health and strength? *You* are more important than the summit of some stupid mountain. Please, please think not just about one day, think about the next many, many days — the rest of your life. You must climb day after day in a weakened state. Then you still must have enough left in you to get back down, then back home, then the rest of your life. *I promise I'll let you try another year if you are too sick to continue this year.* Don't be your usual stubborn self. Think. Think... before you act. I want you to fulfill your dream, but not at the cost you are paying... with your health. Take whatever medications you should be taking. Drink, drink, drink. Rest. Eat. Then think again.

Remember, even though you have the force of all those 64 sets of thumbs pushing you up the mountain, *you* still must do the work. Everyone is wishing you well and hoping for your success. Most of all, everyone wants you back. I will keep your latest illness confidential from most people. If you become even sicker, I think you should come home. If you need me, I'll fly to Katmandu to bring you home. You want to live to be 100 … remember? You don't want to be some sick old man, but a healthy person. You must make the choices now that may affect your life. I'm so sorry this happened to you. I'm sure it is very depressing. I wish I were there to help you and take care of you. Watch what you are eating. Maybe there is a particular food you just can't tolerate. I don't know why the faxes I send to you are not clear. I am using black ink. It is a grey, rainy, depressing day today. I hope you are staying as warm as can be. I guess there is no way I can send you anything but my love and best wishes. I think about and worry about you every minute I am awake. I have not been able to sleep much — even with sleeping pills, so you are in my thoughts almost 24 hours a day. I love you. I miss you. Come back home.

Sandy

Sandy's decision to release me from my promise made me smile. It didn't surprise me. It was just like her — giving of herself for my safety.

On Everest, I spent much time alone with my thoughts. But I routinely spent time rereading all of Sandy's faxes. I thought much about this one in particular. Sandy's release from my promise warmed my heart every time I thought about it. I could hear her voice.

My recovery from intestinal problems, however, was stubborn in coming. As time went on, either from the medication I was taking or the change in routine (I started managing my own water bottles, filling them myself with water I saw for certain was boiling), I started getting better. I thought the problem was completely behind me. I could hold my food and my digestion was as normal as it could be at this extreme altitude. I felt stronger (in part because I was sleeping better from having less anxiety) and I was lighter from the loss of maybe 15 pounds in body fat. I didn't know the exact amount of weight loss, but it was significant enough I could tell from my clothes and comments from others.

But the difficulties of communicating with the other side of the world made matters even more difficult for Sandy.

Sunday, April 14, 1996 (8:30 AM)

TO: Lou Kasischke

FROM: Sandy Kasischke

Dear Lou: I tried for hours, starting at 12 AM today, to send you the letter I wrote yesterday. I could not get through. ... I assume that since I have not heard from you, that you are sick — or — sick again. I'm very very concerned + worried. I'm also very sorry this happened to you. Maybe God wants you to be happy with all of your past accomplishments. You have so much to be thankful for. Maybe this mountain is not meant for you this year. As I said, you can try again another year, if you want to. Don't do something stupid just because you're there + feel like you have to climb even though you're sick.

TO: Sandy Kasischke

15 April

I received your faxes. Sorry I worried you because of my G/I problems. But I'm better now. The Cipro worked. I feel strong again and my appetite is back. So, don't worry I'm fine. It's expected that some people will fall ill and the expedition has the flexibility to deal with different problems. ... Everest is a very serious undertaking and without question is the hardest thing I've ever done. I was sick but that's now history. Time for me to move on and get back to work on this — one day at a time. Everyone is great to be with. No problems. So, get behind me and push, as I know you will. No matter what happens, this will be a good story I lived, even with the runs. At this moment, I'm more worried about you + your health and about Gregg and his exam. I want him to do well as much as I want to climb Mt. Everest. The experience (even before I left for Asia) has also brought me closer to you and shown me your true value to me. So, we have much to be thankful for. So, be positive and tell everyone I'm back in action and fighting my way up. ...

But by April 22, my intestinal problem doubled down its assault on my system. I reached the lowest point I experienced on my way up the mountain.

> "Very discouraged and demoralized. Don't report this, but I see this thing getting away from me for this reason. It dehydrates me and weakens me. I eat and one-half hour later it's out. I was extremely weak climbing back down to Base Camp from a higher camp. I'm losing my motivation, which I must fight off. I'm back on Cipro."

That is what I wrote to Sandy after we climbed and occupied Camp 1 and Camp 2. I asked Sandy to help me be positive and take it one day at a time. Her next fax was upbeat. She knew I needed a mental lift. "No problems here whatsoever—except that I miss you very much and would rather have you with me more than anything." Even her handwriting looked happier. She signed with "Love, Sandy, Doug, Gregg + The Baby," including a tiny drawing of "The Baby" (our new cat).

By the end of April, I was better, physically and mentally. My motivation to keep going was there, even though I wanted it over with. From our communications, Sandy could tell that I was finally over my intestinal problems, and she began thinking about my homecoming, although with more than a touch of sarcasm.

> ... My idea for your welcome home — or whatever — party. A slide presentation of your "vacation to Asia." We can invite others to bring slides of their trips, pets, grandkids, etc. (Joke) What do you think? ... Maybe we could do a dessert buffet since you need to gain weight. We could do a great invitation: "You are cordially invited to help Lou gain weight at a Gala Dessert Buffet" etc.

By May, Sandy not only wanted this whole thing over with and me back home, but she pretty much wanted Everest to be my retirement from mountaineering.

> Everyone wants to know if Everest is the end. It better be. Enough is enough. I want to do normal stuff—not sit home alone for weeks and months alone while you go off to weird places by yourself to live some stupid story.

And then on May 4, two days before we began our push for the summit, Sandy wrote:

> Once again, good luck. I hope you make it. And then it's time to come back home. By the way, I changed my mind. You may not go back next year. ... I trust that your intelligence will be in charge of all your decisions.

She reversed her release. Can you believe that? Now that she sensed that my health and self confidence were restored, and she didn't have to worry about my decision making, she wanted the old deal back. It brought a big smile to my face. This is part of why I love her so much. She is so predictable.

ON THE evening of May 5, I organized my backpack and gear to leave the next morning. Careful thought went into what I would carry on my back, especially at these extreme altitudes. Whatever I took must be an absolute necessity. For me, this included the faxes from Sandy. I bundled them up and put them in a small Ziploc bag. If I got stuck in a storm with time on my hands, I didn't want to be without the faxes to read. I wanted to hear Sandy's voice.

Valley of Silence

CHAPTER 13

BEFORE FIRST LIGHT

MY ALARM went off at 3:45 AM on May 6. The first sensations I had were the smell and crackling of burning juniper branches. This meant the Sherpa were getting ready. I was pleased to realize I had slept fairly well, considering what I was about to undertake. I finished packing my backpack. I had everything organized and set to go from the evening before.

I then went to the mess tent to eat and drink as much as possible: tea and more tea, oatmeal, yogurt, eggs, oatmeal, bread with jam, and more oatmeal. Oatmeal is great as fuel, but by then I despised it.

Eating and drinking had been a priority for the past few rest days. Nutrition, hydration, and rest were the essential physical prerequisites before the hardest and most dangerous challenge I had ever faced. My body was beaten up from five weeks of climbing. My mind and spirit as well. Many times I didn't think I could remain standing. But the preparation was over. The big show had come.

You could feel the tension. People in the mess tent were quiet. This was it. The move up for the last time. This time, to the top. I was nervous, but I tried not to show it. I just focused on eating and drinking. Rob moved around with his usual confidence. I had come to expect that flair of his. He had experienced these moments many times before. This was his natural environment, and he was comfortable in it.

Just before first light, we walked out of Base Camp. Juniper branches still smoldered in the stone altar. We were all together in quiet order, just the way Rob liked to do things. We crossed the glacier to the base of the Khumbu Icefall, put our crampons on, and started climbing. We were ready, and we intended to go all the way, if everything worked out as hoped and planned. Four days to the top of the highest point on earth. The target for this first day was Camp 2, which is at 21,300 feet. This meant 3,800 vertical feet of climbing in a one day push.

The plan was to spend May 7 at Camp 2, resting, evaluating conditions, and making final plans, preparations, and decisions. May 7 was the day for big decisions about health, readiness, and weather. If the evidence showed the weather window opened or was opening, and if everything else was still a go, on May 8 we would climb straight up the Lhotse Face to 24,000 feet. There we would spend a wild night perched on a small ice shelf. On the morning of May 9, if everything was still a go, we planned to climb further up the Lhotse Face to about 25,000 feet. Next, we would traverse the Lhotse Face, climb up and over the Geneva Spur, and then up to the South Col (the mountain pass between Everest and its neighbor, Lhotse) and High Camp at 26,000 feet. We would rest a few hours and then, assuming everything was still a go, continue to climb late that night. We planned to reach the summit by about 11 AM the next day, May 10, and be back to High Camp well before dark. The long march.

That was the plan—weather permitting. But, first we had to climb the Khumbu Icefall for the last time.

By now I knew what to expect in the Icefall. The experience of having climbed there on five different days gave me the self confidence and resulting ability to climb faster. Progress was good and Camp 1 appeared not long after sunrise. It was a great relief to know I only had to journey through that deadly ice one more time—when coming down and almost back home.

Camp 1 was at the top of the Icefall, at 19,500 feet. We stopped for a few moments to rest and pick up the gear stored from earlier climbs. Camp 1 was a small cluster of tents located on the first plateau after exiting the Icefall. It is a breathtakingly beautiful location. From there, I looked up the valley at the Khumbu glacier, which rises another 2,000 feet, to the foot of the imposing Lhotse Face. To the left was the massive Southwest Face of Everest and to the right were the steep walls of Nuptse. From Camp 1, I still could not see the summit of Everest because the West Ridge blocks its view.

From Camp 1, the climbing route is up the valley. It was a snow climb, but with many dangerous crevasses lurking below our feet. For the next two miles of glaciated terrain, the walls and connected ridges of Everest, Lhotse, and Nuptse, the major peaks of the Mount Everest Massif, surround me. These walls of rock and ice rise thousands of feet.

The valley is named the Western Cwm (pronounced "coom," the Welsh word for valley). It's also known by a more descriptive and evocative name—the Valley of Silence. That's because it is a quiet place, sheltered from the sounds of wind. It's a place where you can allow your mind to calm and just consider the journey ahead and behind. The only sounds you hear are your own breathing—until the roar of avalanches of snow and ice crashing down the walls of Nuptse, Lhotse, and Everest shatter that silence. These avalanches feed the Khumbu glacier.

On average, each avalanche carried 100,000 tons of snow and ice and moved at a speed of 200 miles an hour. They are among the most deadly and destructive forces of nature. A high percentage of climbers who die on Everest are killed by avalanche.

Another risk here for climbers are the hidden crevasses, which are deep holes in the glacial ice you can't see when they're covered by snow bridges formed by wind-blown snow. If you fall through a snow bridge and into a crevasse, you will likely be crushed to death by the snow and ice that falls on top of you. If a fallen climber is not crushed to death, he or she will land in a place much colder and with little light. As the body's core temperature goes down, the blood goes to the vital organs (brain, heart, and lungs) and away from the hands and feet. So the hands and feet won't work as needed to climb out of the crevasse, and the climber is completely dependent on rescuers. Without rescue, the climber will die in a few hours from the extreme cold.

WHEN WE first ascended the Valley of Silence, we climbed the early section roped together as a team. This was the only time on Everest we were roped together. If someone fell in a crevasse, the other climbers on the rope could arrest the fall, so the fallen climber didn't go in too far and it would be easier to pull him or her out.

Andy made the decision to rope up because of what happened earlier in the climb when our advance team of Sherpa moved through this area. The Sherpa were not roped together and Ngawang Tenzing fell into a crevasse. Fortunately, Ngawang didn't fall too far because he landed on an ice platform and was rescued quickly enough to avoid freezing to death.

Roping up on higher angle non-crevasse terrain on Everest is a different story. You do not climb that terrain roped together. At the extreme altitude of Everest, a rope team with three or four people rarely has the ability and physical strength to arrest the fall of another. The falling climber would probably take the whole team down. Instead, you either fix safety ropes to the mountain itself with anchors or follow a time-consuming procedure in which the lead climber is attached to a solid anchor and belays the other climbers.

In the 1953 first ascent of Everest, Edmund Hillary and Tenzing Norgay didn't know each other before the climb. But a special bond was formed between them while climbing in the Khumbu Icefall. Hillary fell into a crevasse while crossing a hidden snow bridge. Norgay arrested the fall and was able to rescue Hillary using traditional safety and rescue mountaineering techniques. Hillary later gratefully credited Norgay with saving his life.

ONE OF the unique aspects of climbing in the Cwm is the temperature. It can range from 90 degrees in the sun to 40 below zero in the dark. While climbing in the sun you roast because the sun reflects off the walls of Nuptse and Everest and from the glacier snowfield, creating a solar oven. But as a cloud rolls in to cover the sun, the temperature can plunge 50 degrees in minutes.

In the Cwm, just after passing the west ridge, I got my first sight of the summit, still 8,000 feet above. I stood still for a long time just looking up. I took a few photos. That was it. That was where I was headed and it seemed like the difference between the earth and the moon.

Then, at the end of the Valley of Silence, we came to a steep ice face known as the Lhotse Face. Camp 2 was near the base of the Lhotse Face at 21,300 feet. The camp was located on an area of rocks (called a moraine) piled up on the side of the valley by glacial movement. Camp 2 consisted of a cook tent, mess tent, and smaller sleeping tents.

I arrived at Camp 2 in the mid-afternoon on May 6. The climb from Base Camp to Camp 2 was physically difficult. It had been a long haul from Base Camp. I was exhausted, physically and mentally spent. I wanted to get off my feet and into my tent. I needed 20 minutes to just lie there until I could think about recovery and what still lay ahead of me.

CAMP 2 was usually isolated from the wind and as comfortable as any place could be 21,300 feet above sea level. Our plan at Camp 2 on May 7 was to eat, drink, rest, and get ready. It was all about fuel and readiness, both mental and physical, for the climb to the top.

Some say that a goal isn't worth achieving unless you enjoy the journey to get there. I enjoyed the journey, until I got sick in Namche. After that, I didn't. The prospect of summiting the highest mountain in the world was no longer exciting to me, after being beat up so much for so long. But I was still standing. I'd recovered and was healthy. I was still motivated to climb, but it was more like wanting it over with.

I frequently thought about Sandy during the day. I reread her faxes several times. Mostly, I wanted to go back home. It would not be long now. This was almost over. I wanted to place that phone call to Sandy that I had made thousands of times over 28 years of marriage. The call to say "I'm coming home." I was lonesome for Sandy. I was lonesome for our routine together. We had a good life together. I had a good life back home with my work and family. I wanted a bagel and a good cup of coffee. I never wanted to drink another cup of tea as long as I lived, or eat oatmeal. Never. No, I had to amend that thought. Until this was over, I would eat and drink whatever I could and as much as I could. That was fuel. I needed a full tank of gas. After that, never.

SEVERAL times during the day we discussed the wind. Camp 2 was often protected from the wind, but our precise concern was the wind above on the upper reaches of the Everest summit pyramid. Camp 2 was the only place from which we could look above and see the upper ridge traverse between the South Summit and the Hillary Step. From Camp 2, we could hear what was happening above—where we would be in two days if all went well. In that regard, a major decision soon had to be made from Camp 2.

For the first time, climbers started talking more seriously about timing. The wind was raging in the upper regions, as it had been late in the day most every day for the past month. Everest is not just the highest mountain in the world. It is also the only mountain that sticks up into the jet stream that circles the world. The jet stream makes the mountain almost impossible to climb, except for a brief period during the Asian monsoon season when the jet stream moves north of the Himalaya. This is the so called "weather window."

Was the weather window open or opening for our summit attempt? What was the evidence? How would we know for sure? The open weather window is historically narrow. In the last five to ten years, an average of only three days were summit days. This year it might not open until later in the month. There were no official forecasts. It was a judgment call. Knowledge of how the weather works is highly specialized, and Rob had more experience about this than any other leader on the mountain. Still, what did the evidence show?

Rob said that if the wind the next morning was like that afternoon, it was unlikely we would move up. But even if it were calm in the morning, would that be sufficient evidence to think the weather window was open? After all, it was what happened with the wind late in the day that would be most important — not what happened early in the morning.

Rob was always optimistic. I wasn't too concerned. This was his call. We put our trust in his experience and expertise as our leader. Whatever will be, will be, I thought. I saw no reason to rush anything. We could wait. I thought we would wait.

Patience is one of the most important qualities required in high altitude climbing. Not just required — critical. A delay at Camp 2 because of the wind above would not be so bad. Even though it was at 21,300 feet, it was a good camp site, and my body had functioned reasonably well in terms of eating, digesting, and sleeping. I also knew it was the last place before the summit that I could count on the ingestion and reasonable digestion of solid food. I took full advantage of eating as much as I could push down. To me, if we waited for the wind to calm, with more time to rest, eat, and drink, that would be okay. At no time did I feel we were locked into the May 10 summit day. We had the time and the resources to wait.

WHILE resting in my tent, I reflected on Jon Krakauer's presence in the expedition. It was one thing for Jon to write about events after they occurred, and another to influence the occurring events themselves. One risk from Jon's presence was that it created a chill on candor among team climbers and impeded the feedback Rob needed for effective leadership and decision making. Team climbers might be concerned about how their dissent or views would be reported by Jon.

But the biggest risk was the performance pressure his presence created—pressure on both leaders and climbers. The pressure on Rob was to get to the top with as many climbers as possible. It's well established that people behave and perform differently when under the pressure of the media spotlight. Rob, as leader, as well as the other climbers, were under greater pressure to push their personal boundaries of acceptable risk and physical limits. Jon's article in *Outside* magazine could be a huge financial and promotional boost to Rob. But the individual climbers had nothing to gain and everything to lose from Jon's unwelcomed and unchecked power of portrayal of them for the whole world to read. It was undeniable that Jon's presence would affect everyone's behavior. And on Everest, the stakes were high.

It was flat out wrong for Rob to embed Jon in our expedition. But, from Jon's perspective, he had a job to do. We couldn't blame Jon. He was paid for his wordsmith skill to shape a story that kept the reader's attention. Jon was there to advance his career, and, from Rob's business perspective, to advance his.

I WAS also reflecting on my experience with the leadership team over the past few weeks and my earlier concerns about whether they could work together effectively. As a team, they were new and untested. And we were moving into the extreme conditions, when leadership counted the most.

Both Mike and Andy were exceptionally strong as climbers over the past few weeks. But in terms of the leadership, Rob ran the show. He hadn't delegated much of the planning or any of the decision making to Mike and Andy. At least that was how it appeared. This did not reflect shortcomings in Mike or Andy. It was just Rob's way of running the expedition. At the higher elevations, especially in the Death Zone where leadership and decision making were the toughest, we needed more than a one-man band. Would Rob surrender some of his dominance? Would Mike and Andy be strong enough to overcome Rob's dominance if need be? Would Mike and Andy step up as leaders if Rob was not around?

As a team of leaders and climbers, neither was tested with a tough situation before summit day. We did not know until that day what we were really made of *as a team*. In all of life, it seems that you never really know about yourself or your organization until you are tested by a tough situation. Did Rob have what it takes? Did we? Did I?

THE ONLY person who was discussed as possibly having a health issue was Doug. In recent days, he didn't look well, was uncharacteristically quiet, and had problems talking because of a throat condition. Doug had said on one evening in the mess tent at Base Camp, "My adventure is over." I recall this because, at the same time, he repaid me the cash I had lent to him to buy the antique ice axe back in Namche. But we all had bad days, and some of us expressed our feelings openly. Doug was very open. From rest and recovery, however, Doug's attitude and determination were restored. He was still in the action. But Doug had not acclimatized to the same altitude as the rest of us, which became an issue about the risk to his health as we pushed on to the extreme.

Aside from Doug, when we left Base Camp on May 6, it seemed that the biggest health risk was Ang Dorje's painful tooth. Actually, this was not a minor issue because Ang Dorje was the leader of the Sherpa. Their effectiveness regarding logistics was critical on summit day, when there was little or no margin for error.

CHAPTER 14

THE LHOTSE FACE

IN CAMP 2 on May 8, I sat on the rocky moraine next to my tent to put on my crampons. I then started to climb down to the flat area leading to the snow on the glacier. It was shortly after 7 AM. I was pleased to get going. We had delayed our 6 AM departure while Rob made a final decision about the wind.

At 7 AM Rob made the decision to go. I didn't know if he had consulted with any other expedition planning to move up on May 8. The consensus among the Sherpa of another expedition at Camp 2 was that it was too windy up high, and climbers should wait it out. But we were going. This decision was in Rob's area of expertise. It was his judgment call as our leader. I trusted Rob. We still had flexibility. We weren't locked into anything, if it turned out the time wasn't right.

While waiting for Rob's decision, I put on my crampons at the campsite rather than wait and put them on below in the snow with everyone else. This meant climbing down the rock with crampons, which can be tricky with 12 two-inch long metal spikes attached to the bottom of my boots. But it also meant I wouldn't be the last climber to get moving once on the snow section of the glacier. Being last was usually the case for me because it took me more time than others to attach the crampons. With my size 13 feet, I could not use the modern crampons, known as "step-in." I had the old straps system. They took longer to put on, but I preferred the straps anyway. I felt they were

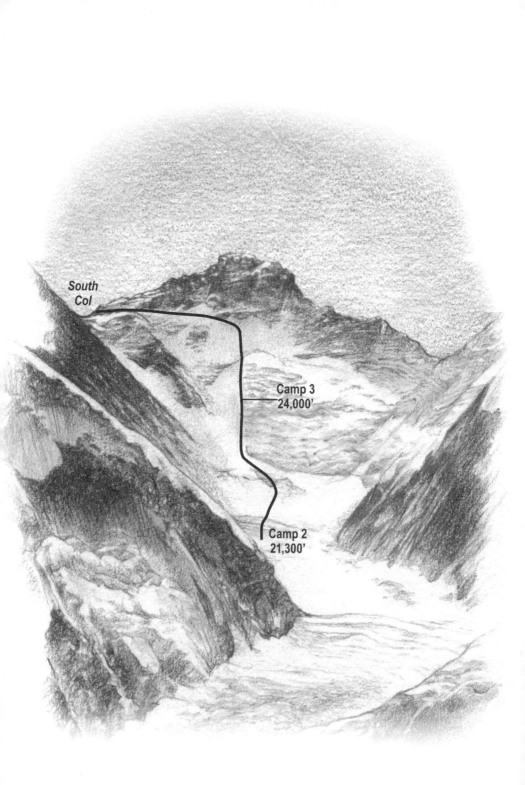

The Lhotse Face

more secure. I have never had a crampon come off, which can be a serious problem at the wrong time or place.

I was excited and anxious. After almost six weeks, we were on the final push for the summit. Once the decision was made to leave Camp 2 it was a single continuous push. Camp 3 and High Camp would only be brief rest stops on the way to the top of the world.

By my calculation and assumptions, we would be on the move for 59 or more hours, with little if any sleep, and little solid food to eat. Sleep deprivation and lack of nutrition, by themselves, magnify the difficulty of all the climbing challenges. Hopefully I could get my body to digest solid food, but I wasn't counting on it. My body would also have to climb 7,800 vertical feet while hypoxic and while my cell structure was dying from oxygen starvation. Also, in very practical terms, others who had climbed the terrain before told me there was no place to sit down and take a rest. If you wanted to rest, it would be while standing and gasping for air.

If everything did not continue as a go for some reason, it was possible to wait above the altitude at Camp 2 for a limited time before going further, or even return to Camp 2 after an aborted attempt and try again later. This commonly occurred and we were prepared for that possibility. We had the time and resources. But we never talked much about that contingency. Rob was always positive. He said, that the idea and priority was to have patience and pull it off the first time and avoid the physical and logistical challenge of a second attempt.

So the early morning of May 8 was a big moment. Despite my initial anxiety, I knew I would feel better once I reached the snow on the glacier and fell into a climbing rhythm. Breathe and move. Breathe and move. Get a flow going. That always worked whenever I climbed, no matter how exhausted I was. For me, the rhythm of moving and breathing led to effectiveness and enjoyment of the experience. Enjoyment? That was not a good word to use to describe my feelings at 22,000 feet, as I moved toward the Everest Death Zone. Actually, I hadn't felt a single moment of true enjoyment since arriving in Nepal in March.

I also knew the next 59 hours would be the big hurt. It would be all misery. Suffer and endure. I thought of this as "the 59 hour long march." Since the time for starting the hour count from Camp 2 until arrival back to Camp 4 from the summit was estimated, I easily could have called it the "60 hour" long march. But somehow, 59 felt much better.

REACHING the base of the Lhotse Face was our first objective. For the last few days, and maybe even a week, I felt pretty good physically and mentally. The climbing conditions were also good, with moderate temperatures and no wind, but that was to be expected in the protected area around Camp 2. Our final goal for the day was Camp 3, at 24,000 feet. It was half way up the Lhotse Face. We had climbed to Camp 3 twice before as part of the process of acclimatizing to the extreme altitude. I knew from two previous experiences that this would be a hard day.

On Everest, the higher you go, the more difficult things become. It keeps getting harder and harder. The Lhotse Face is a 4,000 foot steep wall of blue bulletproof ice, one of the most difficult parts of the climb.

Much would be going on mentally and physically on that part of the climb. I needed to keep my mind and emotions calm. I didn't want to be thinking, analyzing, or worrying about that particular challenge. I wanted to take each move as it came—and to use my energy efficiently. With that in mind, I had done special mental preparation for climbing the steep Lhotse Face.

To build the inner strength that comes from self confidence, I had gone to Peru six months earlier to climb a mountain called Alpamayo.

Alpamayo was a steeper and more difficult ice face climb at high altitude. That climb went well, so I felt prepared for Lhotse. This preparation was important because if I made a mistake on the Lhotse Face, I could fall about a mile.

CLIMBING the Lhotse Face is part of the Southeast Ridge route to climb Everest. Common reference to the Lhotse Face makes it sound as if it's an area of Mount Everest itself. It's not. Lhotse is Everest's next door neighbor and the fourth highest mountain in the world at 27,940 feet. You actually climb most of Lhotse to get to the main pyramid of Everest.

As we approached the Lhotse Face, I could see its slick and shining surface reflect light and glisten. All the snow had either slid off in avalanches or was blasted away by the wind. Camp 3 was half way up the Lhotse Face, at 24,000 feet.

But the first challenge after Camp 2 was to get on the Lhotse Face from the valley floor at the base. The Lhotse Face is covered with glacial ice and at the bottom the glacier breaks away from the face when it hits the base. This breaking off point separating the Lhotse Face from the Western Cwm (the valley floor) is called the bergschrund. We first had to climb over it.

Bergschrunds can be difficult obstacles in any climb. But what makes this 50-vertical-foot "shrund" (as climbers call it) difficult was that I was climbing at more than 22,000 feet, where everything was difficult.

Once over the bergschrund, I clipped a jumar and a carabiner to a fixed rope and started climbing. A jumar is a handheld metal mechanical device attached by a sling from my harness to a fixed rope. The device slides easily upward, but a cam grips the rope under a downward pull. So if a climber falls, the ascender cam locks to the rope and holds the fall. A carabiner (a D-shaped link that snaps open and closed) is also attached from a separate sling to the fixed rope. This is a safety backup system. If you fall and the ascender device (jumar) fails, or is temporarily unclipped while passing a fixed rope anchor, the backup carabiner slides down the rope to a stop at the next anchor point below to arrest the fall.

Safety ropes are commonly fixed in certain high exposure areas. Climbing the Lhotse Face with a fixed rope has been a common practice since the first ascent. A fixed rope is simply a rope anchored to the mountain face and left in place. It keeps climbers moving efficiently and spread out from each other when climbing up and down a difficult or exposed section. A fixed rope eliminates the need for an alternative more time-consuming protection procedure.

Climbers don't literally climb up the fixed rope, or even pull on it. A fixed rope is not an aid in climbing or compensation for lack of skill. Like much equipment used in climbing, fixed ropes are a back-up safety system in case of a fall.

The best practice, and the one I tried to follow, was to climb as if there were no safety rope. By climbing with the mental concentration required as if there were no rope, you climb more efficiently and use less energy. This attitude also avoids a false sense of security that can come from the rope.

The task of fixing safety ropes is usually shared by the climbing expeditions or done by the first expedition team up. In 1996, three expeditions took joint responsibility for fixing rope on the Lhotse Face.

Serious climbers believe that the best climbers are the safest climbers. But it is not uncommon for the elite subculture in the climbing community to speak with condescension about fixed ropes, to imply that seeking safety is somehow a weakness. All climbers have a choice of whether to use fixed ropes for safety. I think it's smart climbing. And, very importantly, I saw all climbers use them in the Khumbu

Icefall, on the Lhotse Face, and other areas on Everest where ropes were fixed.

ON THE Lhotse Face, on the way to Camp 3, we crossed paths with members of the Imax expedition. David Breashears and Ed Viesturs, two highly respected Everest veterans, led this expedition. They were climbing down from Camp 3 to Camp 2. I understood the Imax climbers were scheduled to go to the summit ahead of us, according to the plan adopted among the major expedition leaders. But I saw they were coming down instead.

At the point of crossing paths, the climbing was difficult. All my mental and physical energy was focused on the dangerous moments when climbers pass each other on a fixed rope. I wasn't thinking about why they were descending. I wasn't thinking about whether their reason for turning back could be relevant to us. My only priority was a safe pass on the fixed rope.

A fixed safety rope is tied off to intermediate anchors so that it becomes a series of short, independent sections of rope. This means the ascending climber must remove his jumar from the fixed rope at each anchor, and reattach it above the anchor. This is dangerous, so it's necessary to first move the safety backup carabiner and reattach it above the anchor. Then the jumar can be moved above.

More than one climber can be on a fixed rope, but there should be at least one anchor between each climber. A tricky passing situation can arise, as happened with the Imax climbers, when one climber is coming down a fixed rope while another is climbing up the same rope. This requires each climber to pay close attention to detail, especially on a steep sheet of ice. It's usually safest for the climber moving up to stop at an intermediate anchor and allow the descending climber to make the clipping and unclipping of hardware to make the pass.

This process held my full attention because communications between climbers can be difficult and mistakes are easily made.

Suddenly, a carabiner came sliding down and bouncing off the Lhotse Face. It nearly hit me, and I knew if it hit anyone on the head below me it could kill him instantly. Someone above had dropped it. That was a good reminder to make no mistakes.

David Breashears and Ed Viesturs had closely followed the wind on the upper region of the mountain from their 24,000 foot Camp 3 vantage point. On the evening of May 7, the Imax tents at Camp 3 were battered by gusty winds. Between gusts David and Ed heard the wind up higher roaring like a freight train. Apparently at sunrise May 8, about the time Rob was making his decision from the vantage point of Camp 2, the wind moved from the limited location Rob could see. But David and Ed at Camp 3 had a perfect view of the full Southeast Ridge 3,000 feet above them. They heard the wind pounding the ridge and saw the long plume blowing from the summit. Everest veterans can gauge the wind velocity by the length of this plume.

The Imax leaders decided to abort a summit attempt on their May 9 planned date. In their judgment the safe weather window had not yet opened. It was still too windy up high and not safe. They decided to go down and wait for the weather to stabilize.

This was the same concern that Rob and some Sherpa had in the early morning at the Camp 2 vantage point, where the view of what was happening up high was mostly obstructed. But Rob made the opposite decision.

We knew the wind speeds at Base Camp, Camp 1, and Camp 2 were no indication of what they were at the South Col and above. The lower camps were somewhat sheltered by the surrounding walls of Lhotse and Nuptse. The upper part of Everest is also windier because it is closer to the jet stream, which moves at the 29,000 feet elevation. The jet stream has a direct effect on the upper third, but only an indirect effect lower down. So the good weather we experienced at Camp 2, and as we climbed to Camp 3, was irrelevant to our decision making about what was happening further above.

David and Ed explained their decision and reasons to Rob as they passed. Rob then had new situation information and reasons to re-evaluate his decision.

We kept going to Camp 3.

AS WE got closer to Camp 3, and after nearly six weeks on the mountain, I had my first and only contact with climbers on the Fischer team. Only a few on the Hall team knew who some of the Fischer team were. Previously, I had seen some of them climbing from a distance. I only knew that it was the Fischer team because someone told me. Before May 8, I had never seen up close a single Fischer climber, except for Scott. But on the Lhotse Face, some of us unexpectedly came together on the route, and we talked. I snapped a few photos of them. No one mentioned that we would be going to the summit on the same day. It appeared that they, too, believed it "didn't matter."

Camp 3 Ice Shelf

CHAPTER 15

SUFFERING

ON LHOTSE'S 4,000 foot steep wall of ice, nature provided no place to camp. So we carved a campsite out of the ice, a narrow shelf just wide enough for our tents. The narrow shelf made it hard to get into the tent. I crawled up and slithered in as I moved off the ice face and onto the tent floor. I cautioned myself about the dangers of getting out of the tent and falling down the Lhotse Face. If I were to move between tents, I needed to clip into a safety rope anchored to the ice face, or risk falling 2,000 feet to the Valley of Silence glacier floor below. Precarious in the extreme.

By the time I reached this altitude, the difficulty of the challenges and obstacles I faced (and the needed qualities for high altitude climbing) came sharply into focus. It's all about suffering. Only about suffering. Being a patient sufferer without yielding.

But the mission was still simple: keep going to the top.

Just "keep going" was not so easy without energy. By the time I reached Camp 3, I was on empty. I could not remember ever being so exhausted. For some reason, I was worse off than a week or so earlier when I had climbed to Camp 3. I didn't expect to be out of fuel because I had a good rest day before the climb. I had focused on my nutrition and hydration, and felt rested and restored. It was just one of those inexplicable bad days.

But that was history. For the long march ahead, I needed to physically recover in the short time available at Camp 3. The focus now was on recovery.

Energy and strength comes from hydration, nutrition, and rest. Hydration was the easy part of the equation. I simply needed to drink enough water, and, fortunately, even at high altitude my body was fairly receptive to ingesting water. Seven to eight liters a day, at a minimum, was my program. The stove at Camp 3 worked full time to melt ice for water. I drank every drop available.

Nutrition and rest were another matter. The intake of food had been repulsed by my system for a long time by then. This happens to everyone at extreme altitude, but above about 22,000 feet, the body is not just repulsed by food. The normal digestion of solid food is difficult. I knew from experience on long climbs and as an endurance athlete that nutrition made a huge difference at this point in the climb. Skills, experience, and sheer will to stay motivated and keep pushing through the suffering were all essential ingredients to success. But they were still worthless without adequate nutrition.

I could not force myself to sleep, but I could force myself to eat. And that is what I did at Camp 3. Every moment since arrival I ate, drank, and got ready. I had to recover from the beating I took getting there. Recovery was the key. Soup, cold stew out of a can, crackers, cheese, M&Ms, and cold oatmeal. As much food as I could eat. I looked at it and stared at it. My inner voice said how much I hated it, and I pushed it in. I was not confident my body would digest it, but I had to get it in to have a chance. Soup was the best and easiest to get down.

The final component for performance was sleeping. A good night's sleep was impossible. Any sleep was almost impossible. At Camp 3, I didn't sleep or even doze. I called it "just resting." On hard, long climbs, I used to worry about not sleeping. But many years ago my doctor back home convinced me that lying still and "just resting" could significantly restore my body.

Who would have known on May 8 that I would not sleep or even "just rest" again for four days and nights? If I had known about the nightmare I was facing, I would have happily packed up and bailed out.

Why would anyone ever want to climb Mount Everest?

NO TIME or effort was allocated to anything but eating, drinking, and resting. No socializing or joke telling. People were quiet, even Beck. It was all business at Camp 3, and at that point I just wanted it over with. My morale was so low that the spirit and grandeur of climbing in the high Himalaya was lost on me. Too much suffering. Most everyone told me that Everest first-timers felt that way, but that didn't seem to help.

In those low moments, the basic skills and qualities of a good mountain climber meant little. The challenge was to withstand the insistent wind, the cold, the sleeplessness, the lack of even fair food (I had not eaten a good meal for five or six weeks), and the unrelenting peppering of the tent walls with ice chunks falling down the Lhotse Face. I would have given anything for a few moments of silence, without constant reminders of the hostile environment. And to be able to breathe.

I lay in my sleeping bag thinking how much I hated cold, hated ice and snow, hated cold boots, and hated oatmeal. I hated my ice axe, hated peeing in a bottle and bringing it into my sleeping bag so it wouldn't freeze. I hated my shirt. I hated cracked lips and cracked fingertips. I hated cold oatmeal. I hated wind, hated headaches, and hated not being able to sleep. I hated not being able to breathe. I hated, I hated the wind. I hated all oatmeal. I hated darkness. How many more hours of suffering? I wanted to go home. I hated wind. I hated wind.

Hate.

I don't know how else to describe how I felt.

"SINCE you suffer so much, why do it? Since you want to quit almost every day, why do it? Why put yourself through such misery and hardship, to say nothing of risk, just for that single moment to stand on top of a mountain? There must be some point to it. There has to be a point. I know all of this has a point. Right? Right?"

That was what my inner voice asked and searched for. When other people asked me the same questions, I had a standard (vague) answer: "It's to live a story … about being there, yak, yak, yak."

But I was doing the asking, not someone else. It's one thing to vaguely answer that question for others while sitting on the deck at sea level on a warm summer night having a beer. It was another to answer myself while perched on a small ice shelf at 24,000 feet, waiting for the wind to blow me off, knowing what was ahead, and, even worse, not knowing all of what was ahead. My standard answer was not very convincing, even to me. If it was "to live a story," then I had lived all that story I cared to live.

I knew I did not have to do it. I did not even like doing it any more. It was not as if no one had ever been on top, or that I was going to discover Noah's Ark. The earth would not stop turning if I did this. Doing it did not matter.

How does anyone ever really know why we do what we do?

Is it that doing something that doesn't matter gives one true power of choice — and maybe that matters?

Or, to discover what lies between the vertical feet up and back on summit day?

Or, to discover the part of my destiny that calls for great suffering?

If none of this makes sense it's because that was how my mind worked at 24,000 feet on the evening of May 8. My brain was crippled from fatigue and starvation. I could even feel my brain getting smaller.

The truth is that after I start I can't quit something important without a good reason, such as for safety. My general self assessment that I was a damn fool to keep going would not be a good enough reason. I had underestimated how hard Everest was to climb. If I had known, I never would have come. But once I was there, what was more important than standing on top was knowing I didn't quit just because it was too hard to do. Sandy wanted me to live a story I could tell. Quitting just because it's hard is one story I have never had to tell before and never wanted to tell.

I was at hour 12 of the 59 hour misery countdown on the long march. It would end. In the next 47 hours, I would find out—if I could. And, I would find out (I hoped)—I hadn't quit.

Into the Death Zone

CHAPTER 16

A SLOW DEATH

IN THE early morning of May 9, not far away from our tents on another ice shelf, Chen Yu Nan crawled out of his tent to answer the call of nature. He lost his balance, slipped on the ice, and fell down the Lhotse Face. Chen was a 36-year old Taiwanese steelworker and a climber on the Taiwanese expedition. When he fell, he was neither wearing crampons nor clipped to a safety rope. He was hauled free from the crevasse he fell into, and he seemed to be okay. But he must have suffered some internal injuries in the fall. Chen was later found dangling from the fixed rope on the Lhotse Face. He was dead.

What makes climbing different from most other sports is the heavy punishment for a mistake. And the most common mistake is a momentary loss of concentration. Chen Yu Nan paid the ultimate price.

LATER THAT morning, Rob stuck his head in my tent and said, "It's a go." I didn't think about the weather window. My only thought was "we're going." It was clear and there wasn't much wind at Camp 3 as I crawled out of the tent and prepared to climb.

I was myopic in my preparations. I dressed in my one-piece down suit. Harness on. Hardware ready. Crampons on. I checked and double checked the details. Everything had to be right. Climbers take great pride in their attention to detail. In climbing, details count.

I don't think I slept, but I felt pretty good, so I must have rested. The recovery process worked. I really wanted to get going and start into my climbing rhythm. "Yesterday, I had many enemies beating on my motivation. It was a bad day. Today is a new day. I can do this," said the voice of my ambition and determination as I clipped my jumar on the rope and took my first step.

We climbed straight up the Lhotse Face. The higher you go, the harder the climbing gets. The difficulty is exponential. Climbing at 20,000 feet is twice as hard as climbing at 15,000 feet, and climbing at 25,000 feet is twice as hard as 20,000 feet. I don't know if this is exactly accurate, but it sure feels like it.

At 25,000 feet, we began to traverse the Lhotse face to climb a band of limestone rock known as the Yellow Band. The band is a distinctive feature seen in photographs of Everest and Lhotse. Climbing on the Yellow Band was treacherous because it was a band of rock, and we had crampons on our boots. Each foot had to be placed and tested carefully. Even spraining an ankle at that altitude could be fatal.

I looked forward to the traverse of the Lhotse Face, thinking it would be easier than climbing straight up the steep face. But it was just as difficult. And we did it without taking a break.

Not taking regular breaks was a big difference between some of the other climbers and me. Over my long years as a climber and endurance athlete, I put the highest priority on the regular and disciplined ingestion of calories and fluids while "on the run." For my body, it was not good enough to eat and drink only at camp.

Rob reminded us often that he was there to provide specialized Everest expertise on leadership and logistics issues, but that we had to individually climb the mountain. Each had to make a full range of personal decisions along the way. Refueling is an individual body and mind matter. It's not uncommon for a climber to focus too much on just moving and end up hitting "the wall." The best climbers can feel themselves "running out of gas" and know when to break and ingest food and water.

Each climber also made his own decision, within a general time frame, about pace for moving between camps. Pace is important. Some say speed equals safety. But that's too much of a generalization. Climbing a big mountain is a long-haul endeavor. You must climb at a relatively slow but steady pace that conserves energy and allows you to recover and climb again the next day. And the day after. And the day after that. Climbing is not a series of sprints. You never use energy that doesn't have a pay off. You must be able to pick up the pace when you need to because of changing weather, snow conditions, or any other good reason. But otherwise, make it pay.

I was accustomed to climbing with a much smaller group of people. We usually climbed at about the same pace and stopped to refuel together. But this didn't happen very often on Everest. I knew my body and my needs for performance, so I made refueling stops, but less frequently than I should have. That might have been what went wrong the day before when climbing to Camp 3.

The other challenge above Camp 2 was that frequently there was no good place to sit down or stop for a break. Nowhere. But I found a spot on the Yellow Band to stop and refuel. I drank water and ate a handful of M&Ms and a small piece of cheese.

Everything seemed to be going okay. I had nothing to complain about except, of course, for being beaten half to death with fatigue. My strategy was to get into a rhythm and just go. The mission and target was simple: High Camp at 26,000 feet, our last camp. From there we go to the summit.

The weather was good most of the day. The skies were blue and visibility was good. Even the wind seemed to have subsided. But on the Lhotse Face we were sheltered from the wind that hit the upper regions. From there, it was hard to tell what was happening above.

At midday, the climbers in front, who were in a position to see, said the plume of snow blowing from the Southeast Ridge was a bad sign indicating ferocious wind up high.

In high altitude climbing, the wind is frequently the biggest obstacle. Cold temperatures, snow, and poor visibility don't compare to the high winds that can make it impossible to move, even in clear sunshine. It's the opposing wind that tries to make you crack. Its goal is to defeat your mind, body, and soul. In climbing the wind never seems to be at your back.

I later learned that when I crawled out of my Camp 3 tent we faced yet another decision about whether to keep ascending for our summit bid. Anatoli Boukreev, the experienced Himalayan climber serving as a leader of the Fischer expedition, had a problem with his measure of the wind velocity above 8,000 meters (2,000 feet above Camp 3). He doubted his expedition should have kept ascending and he discussed his reservations with Scott Fischer and Rob Hall. Rob disagreed. Scott said he was going to follow Rob. Scott was an experienced climber, but less experienced in leading Everest expeditions, and it seemed he was deferring to Rob. Once again, Rob's decision was contrary to the judgment of another high altitude veteran, this time Boukreev—the climber with the most Himalayan experience, apart from maybe Rob himself, on either team.

After the Yellow Band, we started to climb over an area of loose rock known as the Geneva Spur, an outcropping of rock that runs vertically down the Lhotse Face from the South Col. This part of the route was marked by old ropes, and it was just before the final stretch to High Camp on the South Col.

That area and above is quite appropriately known as the "Death Zone." It is known as such because, while you are in it, minute by minute your body is dying. Your cell structure dies from the cold and oxygen starvation. This deterioration was once described by Dr. Peter

Hackett, an expert on high altitude physiology, as "slow death by starvation, dehydration, suffocation, and exposure." I agree with everything he said, except one thing: It didn't seem slow to me.

The Sherpa say: "Only the gods live here. This is no place for man." To this, I agree, without exception. In one respect, however, the Sherpa are wrong. Many dead climbers reside here as well. And, as it turned out, some would be my friends and climbing partners. And, there was almost an eternal place for me here too.

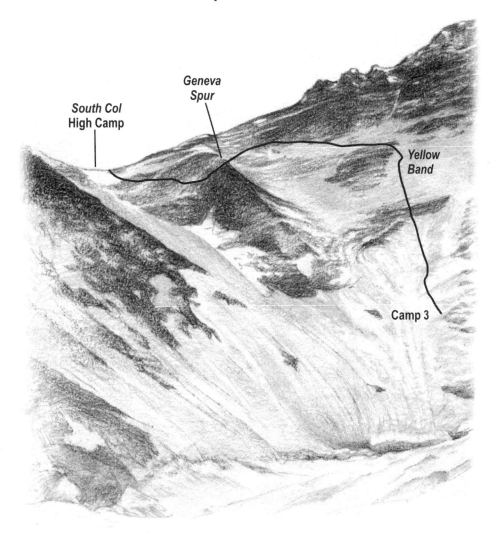

Lhotse Traverse to High Camp

CHAPTER 17

THE SOUTH COL

NOT LONG after we climbed the Geneva Spur, we were near the infamous South Col. I was almost there. This was the area for High Camp, at 26,000 feet—the last stop before the summit. I'd read so much about this place. I'd seen many photographs. I'd imagined myself there countless times.

The South Col is a saddle between Everest and its smaller neighbor, Lhotse. It is a barren plateau of windblown snow, ice, and boulders. It is bordered on the east with a 7,000 foot drop off into China and on the west by a 4,000 foot drop off into Nepal.

The South Col is one of the coldest, most inhospitable places in the world. A place you never want to be on purpose. And the place, which in a little more than 24 hours, I thought I would never leave alive.

When we crossed over the Geneva Spur, the weather had deteriorated. By the time we arrived at the South Col, it was storming with high winds and little visibility. Actually, it had stormed most days that high in the late afternoon, so it was no surprise.

We were getting close to the jet stream. And as a saddle, the South Col is a natural wind tunnel. The winds accelerate in force as they are funneled in between Everest and Lhotse. This was called a camp, but it wasn't a refuge.

Storm or no storm, I was relieved to be there. I didn't care that I couldn't see the famous upper pyramid of Everest. Photographs would have to do. I wanted to get off my feet, rest, and get ready for what happened next. Visibility was almost zero. It was hard to tell where to go.

Several of us arrived at the same time. You couldn't hear anything over the howl of the wind. All of a sudden, there was Rob. He pointed in the direction of the tents. A good thing someone was there to help locate High Camp, as I would soon discover.

I started to crawl into a tent, a North Face "Himalayan Hotel." Doug, Beck, and Andy arrived just ahead. They staked out their space in the tent. We packed four in a tent because it was warmer. At my request, the others agreed to make a small space for me at the end by the door. I first took my crampons off outside and placed them with my ice axe next to the tent door.

CLIMBING in the Death Zone is recognized as one of the most dangerous things in the sport of mountaineering. One of the biggest problems in the Death Zone is that your body barely gets enough oxygen to work with—to metabolize—and generate body heat. The outside 30 to 40 below zero air temperature is not the biggest risk. Freezing to death from the inside out is one of the biggest risks.

To generate body heat, the body must function well. Measured on the body heat score, I was doing well. I was a good, heat-producing engine. My clothing habits and system to manage heat loss had also worked well.

Mobility at this altitude is a must. Immobility can occur for a wide range of reasons, such as injury, sickness, accident, or being late and getting caught out in the open after dark. Immobility is fatal. If you simply stumble from fatigue or trip while wearing your crampons (easy to do), and twist or sprain your ankle, there is a good chance you won't make it back down alive.

High Camp was never intended as a camp, in the sense of spending time there to sleep and eat. It was more of a rest stop on the way to the summit and back. Because the body breaks down so rapidly in the Death Zone, this was not a place you wanted to, or even could, spend much time. At this altitude, even at rest the body deteriorates more than it restores. But it would deteriorate even faster without taking the time to rehydrate and refuel. The idea on arrival was to rest a few hours (you can't sleep at this altitude), and continue again until we reached the top.

I felt okay. Not great, but not terrible. And much better than the day before when I arrived at Camp 3. This surprised me because I understood, correctly or not, that the climb from Camp 3 to High Camp was physically tougher.

SUMMIT day involves choreography of science, art, and nature. The science is in the careful preparations of the body, mind, and spirit, the needed equipment and supplies, the required technical climbing skills, and the summit day plan for execution. The art is the people, what they do or don't do and why, and the constantly changing interplay of people, decisions, and actions. Nature is the final dance partner, to which the people must surrender the lead when nature demands.

The time spent at High Camp before the summit attempt was one of the most important times in the climb—a time for final thoughts and preparation. As I quietly lay in my small space in the tent with my head resting on my backpack, it was a time to bring the big picture together in my head.

I hadn't slept in days. I was hypoxic, malnourished, and dehydrated. I was not very cold, but I couldn't breathe. I didn't have any cracked ribs from coughing. The only things cracked were my lips and fingertips. I had no broken legs or arms. So I guessed I had to keep climbing. But why would anyone do that on purpose? And how many hours before it was over?

Is this what slow death feels like? If so, I had to get up and down pretty quickly. I didn't have much time to work with in the Death Zone. Slow death seemed fast to me.

From the way I saw the weather, nature was in the lead. This was one dance I wanted to sit out.

8 PM. If it were still a go, we had a plan to get to the summit and back. We all knew the plan by heart. The timetable was to leave the South Col for the summit by 11 PM and climb at a pace to reach the Balcony at 27,600 feet by about daybreak. Then to climb the Southeast Ridge to reach the South Summit by 10 AM or before. Then to traverse the ridge over to the Hillary Step, and climb the final stretch to reach the main summit by about 11 AM. After a few minutes on top, we would begin the descent back to High Camp on the South Col.

The rationale for a specific timetable was to get to the top and back down before running out of daylight, supplemental O2, strength, or body heat. We hoped to reach each way-point early, and complete the climb in no more than 18 hours.

We needed to constantly monitor the time, and the geographic way-points that were our guides. Rob had been on Everest seven times before and understood the climbing pace required and the time we needed to safely be back down to High Camp. Climbers had to move at a specific pace to meet Rob's timetable. He said if we climb too fast we risk burning out and not having enough strength to get back down. And if too slowly, we run out of time. He said he would set, manage, and monitor the right pace.

Any loss of time on summit day was our enemy. The Hillary Step is a well known chokepoint vulnerable to delays—both going up and coming down. We knew this, and both Rob and Mike had prior experience there with delays. Rob's plan was for the Step to be fixed with rope to avoid delay. We expected that one of the expeditions preceding us would have fixed that rope. But Rob never assumed anything. He planned to send our two strongest Sherpa one hour ahead of the rest of us to do the work just in case it wasn't done.

Most expeditions in the past did not take the time to fix rope on the ridge traverse from the South Summit to the Hillary Step. It's not essential there. The terrain is exposed, but not difficult. Our team climbers were fully capable of climbing that short traverse without a rope.

IT'S HOUR 37 in the countdown on the 59 hour long march to the summit and back to High Camp. I had 22 more hours to go. For that to actually happen was an intimidating thought. I knew it was not over even then, and that I wasn't safe and on my way home until I was back at Base Camp. But for the 59 hour long march calculation, I was mostly looking at the period of extreme suffering. Once I was back to High Camp from the summit, I wouldn't see the way down as suffering. That would be coming home.

The most important part of any summit day plan is the time agreed upon and set as the turnaround time. This part of the plan focuses on getting back alive. The turnaround time means that, from wherever you are on the mountain, you must be able to reach the top by that set time; and if not, you turn around—right then, from wherever you are. Suppose the set turnaround time was at 1 PM, and you are at the South Summit at 10 AM and you have no reason to think you cannot reach the top by 1 PM. Under the plan, based on time, you would keep going up. Suppose for some reason you were still at the Balcony at 10 AM. In that case, you turn around right then, at 10 AM. You have no chance from the Balcony to reach the summit by 1 PM.

Serious climbers always know where they are and how much time they need. With a 1 PM set turnaround time, if they know there is no chance of reaching the top on time, they would never ignore the time situation and keep climbing until 1 PM, and then turn around. That would be unsafe, irresponsible, and reckless. And pointless.

On Everest, there was no standard turnaround time for all climbing teams, such as absolutely noon or absolutely 1 PM. The turnaround time depends on variables unique to each team. For Rob, the judgment call focused on our planned departure time from High Camp, daylight, budgeted supplies of supplemental O2, the demonstrated strength of team climbers, snow conditions (expected to be good based on reports from others preceding us), and current experience and expectations about late afternoon weather.

Rob set the turnaround time for 1 PM.

Climbing down is the most dangerous and important part of the climb. A basic principle on Everest is that you must be back to High Camp in daylight. Do not get caught out in the dark. Once you lose daylight, everything changes — for the worse. Darkness would occur about 6:30 PM. But late afternoon bad weather could bring on "effective darkness" much earlier, just as it did when we arrived at High Camp.

In the dark, you can't see where you are going. You lose sight of the camp below in the vastness of the mountain. Landmarks disappear. Even if your headlamp is still working, which is not likely in the extreme cold and from using it the night before, it's still easy, especially in poor weather, to take the route in the wrong direction and go over the edge.

It is also much colder after the sun goes down, when the temperature can drop 40 or 50 degrees. On summit day, you are hypoxic, extremely dehydrated, and fatigued after two days of solid climbing with little or no food, water, and sleep. Everything is hard. You are at your limits, mentally and physically. And you may face the typical late afternoon storms, especially high winds. The weather tends to change for the worse as the temperature drops and the winds pick up. Being back to High Camp in daylight is one of the most important reasons that Everest expedition leaders, especially on large expeditions, have a predetermined turnaround time. Save your life if you follow it. Lose your life if you don't.

Rob said, "If you are not back to High Camp in daylight, you will die." He spoke bluntly for good reason. If you look at Everest climbing history, his admonition was usually true in good weather, and almost always true in bad weather. Most of those in history who managed to survive the night in the open did so in good weather, and in most cases ended up losing some fingers and toes to frostbite. In the first American expedition to summit Everest in 1963, two climbers lost their toes to frostbite after being too late in going to the summit and were caught out by darkness coming down. They were forced to biv-ouac overnight at 28,000 feet.

A fair rule of thumb for large expeditions in normal conditions on Everest is that from the South Col it's an 18-hour round trip—if things go on schedule. Twelve hours up and six hours down. Our plan was to start from High Camp at 11 PM on May 9, and reach the sum-mit by about 11 AM on May 10, and then be back to High Camp no later than 5 PM. The time schedule allowed for one and a half hours as a cushion for error in terms of daylight. But that was only if the late afternoon weather was good. With bad weather expected, there was no cushion for error.

Rob's turnaround time calculation was not just about daylight. Just as critical was supplemental O2. Rob had supplies for 18 hours of O2 for each climber on the planned 18 hour climb. For this we had no margin for error. Eighteen hours, and that was it. Running out on the descent by being late would mean big trouble.

Given our scheduled 11 PM departure time, and the expected 12 hours up and 6 hours down, the turnaround time should have been about 11 AM or soon after. The 1 PM time set by Rob was already on the late side when we considered the O2 supply aspect. A 1 PM turnaround time would work only in the most ideal circumstances and was the outside, absolute last chance time to still be climbing up when we figured in the O2 supply aspect of the calculation.

The turnaround time was unconditional. And we needed to stick to it, no matter what. We sat in an oblong circle in the tent. Rob looked each of us in the eyes and we each gave our promise to Rob, to each other, and to ourselves to stick to the turnaround time.

Rob spoke strongly. He said, "I want no dissension up there on this. My word on the turnaround time is absolute law." Rob intentionally created the high drama when he asked, as leader, for our explicit eye-to-eye promise and commitment. The drama was designed to bind us together as a group—a bind in *trust*, for the safety of all. This made it a team decision—not just a Rob Hall decision. This is how we were organized. Not all Everest expeditions chose to organize this way. But this was who we were. To climb up beyond the turnaround time would breach the agreement we had with each other and put everyone in jeopardy.

WHAT IF the turnaround time came, but some kept going? What do you do? Some say there is only one thing worse than not reaching the summit—and that is when others do and you don't. When you prepare to face a challenge, how do you prepare for that one—when some stick to the agreed turnaround time and some don't? Where do you go for strength to resolve the dilemma?

We weren't planning on things going wrong. Facing the turnaround time was something I hoped would never happen. To get to that point meant something went wrong—bad weather, accident, delay, or sickness. And when things go wrong, turning around wouldn't necessarily mean you get down safely. Things could continue to go wrong—and maybe get worse. But if they did, the turnaround time was the safety net.

A safety net—if we followed it.

AFTER WE arrived at High Camp, the wind roared even louder. Maybe it just seemed that way because I was inside the windbreaker of a tent and not outside. It didn't matter, however, because all I wanted to do was lie down and rest. I desperately wanted to just be still and find some quiet. It was difficult to hear each other inside the tent over the sound of the wind. Suddenly, I thought I heard a voice — a voice outside.

"Let me in or I'm going to die out here." I snapped up and unzipped the door flap and a man with a bushy black beard covered with snow fell through the doorway. He shivered uncontrollably. His face and beard were caked with ice. I had never seen him before. He was Bruce Herrod, a British climber and a member of a South African based expedition.

When Bruce arrived at the South Col, he was met with the same fierce winds and snow I had faced. But now the visibility had turned to zero — a virtual whiteout. Bruce was alone. He was lost. He had stumbled around on the Col looking for any tent as a refuge. He eventually found our tent. Bruce was in an extremely deteriorated physical condition. The climb from Camp 3 had ravaged him with overwhelming fatigue, hypoxia, and what appeared to be hypo-thermia. He was incoherent. Bruce was in big trouble. Bruce was a visceral reminder of what happens if you are caught out in the Death Zone. What happens was inches from my face. This is what happens. "So, Lou, don't get caught out," said my inner voice.

Bruce was also right on top of me. I didn't have much room in the tent to begin with. Now I had to figure out how to share it with Bruce. I was not compassionate. I was frustrated and angry that his misfortune had fallen my way. He was not part of our expedition. This was not my problem. I had things to do. I had to get re-hydrated, refueled, rested, and ready to do the most dangerous and hardest thing that I'd ever done. I'm ashamed to write this, but that's how it was. These were my cold, uncaring thoughts. My thoughts focused only on me.

Bruce was also not helpful. I couldn't understand what he was saying through his strong accent and shaking voice. He kept pulling his hat off. I put it on. He pulled it off. I put it on. "Come on, man, try to cooperate in the help I'm trying to give you." I was trying to give him water to drink, but he didn't seem interested.

After awhile Bruce calmed down and became more cooperative. I think it must have been after he warmed up. But I still couldn't do much to help myself get ready to climb with Bruce partially sprawled on top of me. After he became warmer, it was clear he was a very nice guy, but I still wanted to get rid of him and "tend to my own knitting" (one of my mother's favorite expressions).

After three hours, I needed to figure out a way to evict Bruce. No one from his expedition came looking for him, and he was in no shape to go out and find other housing. Around 7:30 PM, I looked outside and the visibility had somewhat improved. Andy crawled out to see if he could locate Bruce's expedition tents. The winds were still high. Andy found the tents and came back to escort Bruce to the South Africans.

Bruce Herrod

Bruce's situation was unfortunate at the time (poor me for having to help) because it had adversely affected my mental state, physical recovery, and readiness. In climbing, situations like this come up. You hope they don't, but they do. You may not want to help someone in need, but as a matter of humanity and decency you always do. Someday it might be me who needed help. I knew and believed this. And I did help. I just wasn't happy doing it.

I can't say that anything Bruce did was irresponsible. He got lost in a whiteout, which could happen to anyone, including me. One ethical question climbers ask frequently is what responsibility do you have as a climber to another climber who is reckless or irresponsible? Does it make a difference if that person is a stranger? These questions are in all of life, not just in climbing. And the answer is clear and simple: you help. That's the right thing to do. If you don't help, you will never feel good about yourself, no matter how hard you try to rationalize or justify it. And you will never have the respect of others, who know you could have helped but didn't.

I NEVER saw Bruce again. I learned he was an experienced and re-spected Himalayan climber and Antarctic explorer who usually had a big smile on his face. Bruce held a doctorate from Cambridge and spent many years as a geophysicist with the British Antarctic Society and as a leader of wilderness adventures in high and wild places around the world. I never had the chance to hear his side of the story of being alone, lost, and nearly frozen, and our time together in that storm. I never got the chance to know this fascinating guy, or to see the big smile others talked about.

Sixteen days later, Bruce was dead. One year later, a climber found his body hanging upside down on a rope on the Hillary Step near the top. Bruce died alone.

What happened is not clear. Bruce reached the summit on May 25 and radioed Base Camp at 5:15 PM with the news. Bruce was on top many hours past any responsible turnaround time. For an unknown reason, he fell behind the others in his expedition when they went for the summit. Bruce was alone, again.

The climber who found Bruce the next year cut his body loose and let it fall down the mountain face to a grave of Everest ice and snow—the most dignified thing that could be done for him. It's not possible at that extreme altitude and highly dangerous location to bring a body back down.

The speculation is that, when Bruce rappelled down the Hillary Step, he slipped or his crampons got caught on one of the old fixed ropes. But whatever happened, it flipped him over and he was unable to regain an upright position. He then hung upside down until he died.

Is this a story I can tell?

CHAPTER 18

DECISIONS AT HIGH CAMP

NO WAY would we leave for the summit in three hours, said my inner voice. The winds hammered against the side of our tent. Winds had been raging up high since midday. Good thing four of us were inside the tent to hold it down.

To me, it was absolutely certain that Rob would not lead our team for the summit that evening, even if the winds calmed. We debated the issue in our tent, although it wasn't much of a debate. Beck, Doug, and I were convinced we should wait. Andy said nothing. Andy was a loyal lieutenant. From his body language, I knew Andy agreed, but he didn't want to say anything that would conflict with Rob. Rob would make the call. Andy knew that. So did I.

I didn't think it was a tough decision to make. We understood the weather window issue. We knew May 10 was arbitrary when selected a week earlier. It was a wait-and-see decision making process. So, what did we see? We saw no precedent of stable weather up high. Late afternoon high winds and storms were still common at the higher elevations. We heard the high winds in the upper region from Camp 2 on May 7. Leaving Camp 2 the following day was doubtful. On the morning of May 8, we deferred our start time because of concern about the wind up high. Winds were stiff at Camp 3 that evening. After leaving Camp 3 it was storming once we were no longer sheltered by the Lhotse Face and came over the Geneva Spur. If we had another storm the next day on May 10 when we were trying to climb down—just as we had that afternoon and were having in the early evening of May 9—it would be big trouble. All the evidence pointed toward bad weather the next day, on May 10. It was more likely to be hostile than not.

To me, it was also an easy decision because it didn't change our quest. It would not be a decision to abort. It was just to wait a day. Not much would be lost, and we had the resources to wait. No climbing expedition that preceded us had reached the top—apparently because of high winds.

My concerns were also caused by another influence. I had just finished caring for Bruce. That was a close look at what happens to a climber caught out in late afternoon bad weather. It was a frightening image. Caught out—one of the things high altitude climbers fear the most. Bruce couldn't find his way. Why? No visibility. After all, we were at 26,000 feet. Clouds rolled in and Bruce couldn't see. The consequences were steep. Bruce would have died without help. So, what if late afternoon tomorrow I couldn't find my way because of weather? Whose tent would I find? Would I find any tent or anyone to help? This immediate and vivid experience showed me what could quickly go wrong. And it also provided real meaning to the underlying rationale for other summit day climbing principles—the turnaround time and getting back in daylight.

Anatoli Boukreev and Bruce Herrod's South African expedition, also camped on the South Col, felt that no attempt should be made under the current weather conditions. This was the second time Anatoli spoke out in opposition. The first was at Camp 3. The Imax expedition also decided not to go to the summit on May 9 because of likely adverse weather.

My bad feelings were not limited to the weather. While tending to Bruce, I'd lost valuable preparation time. I needed more time to hydrate, try to eat something, rest, and get better organized. I needed more time to be prepared. But unless we waited, there wasn't any more time. My vote was to wait.

9 PM. ONE of the Sherpa brought around half a bowl of warm water. It didn't seem like any soup mix was in it. Eating for performance was usually my top priority while in camp. But right then nothing more was available, and I didn't even care that much. Too many other big issues were on my mind, diluting (like my soup) that priority.

9:30 PM. An hour and a half before our planned departure the wind had calmed. But we still had no word from Rob. I didn't know whom Rob was consulting with if anyone. He was in another tent.

10 PM. The winds stayed calm. Word came from Rob: "We're going. Be ready to start climbing at 11."

Rob never consulted with Andy or any of us on the decision. Because the stakes were so high and the weather so questionable, for Rob to make a major strategic decision unilaterally was not a good sign. Our tent was full of experienced and well informed climbers who had serious thoughts about what to do and why. Maybe Rob sensed he would not get a consensus. Maybe this was more of Rob as the one-man band. But, in the next 24 hours above 26,000 feet, decision making would be tougher and more critical, and would likely take more than a one-man band.

AS HE PASSED the word, Rob also knew each of us had our individual go/no go decision to make. Do I follow Rob's lead or not? Moments earlier, I thought Rob faced an easy decision. No way would we go. There was no evidence of stable weather.

But for Rob, the weather risk was acceptable. What about me, and the rest of us? I had a choice. Now I faced a hard call. This was a moment I had hoped not to face—a moment I might not have the courage to face.

I could go, or sit tight if I believed the weather danger was unacceptable. We had no official forecast, but what did that matter at 26,000 feet above sea level? Looking outside and thinking about what has been happening—that was the best forecast. What ever happened to the idea of only going to the summit after the weather window opened? What evidence did we have the window was open?

I looked at the others. No one said anything out loud. But all their eyes said, "I guess we're going." And everyone started to get ready. Except me. I was watching to see if anyone would make a move to dissent. Would I be the only one? Maybe each waited for someone else to say something. My body language, by not getting ready, was sending that message of dissent and of looking for support. But this was met with only silence, and getting ready.

I had a sick feeling in my stomach: Rob had made the wrong decision. After five minutes of doing and saying nothing, I decided to follow. My inner voice said, "It's not perfect, but it's your only opportunity." If I wanted to climb Everest, it was now or never. I would never have another chance—ever. There were no second chances in our expedition. I would never be back on Everest. I'd promised Sandy only one attempt.

I'd also promised Sandy to only live a story I could tell. Was this a story I could tell Sandy? I asked myself that question, but I didn't want to listen for the answer. I needed to think. But asking the question amounted to a second thought about my already shaky decision to go. I was sprawled out with my head resting on my backpack. I still made no move to get ready. I needed to think.

ROB frequently talked about his leadership, teamwork, and self leadership. He made it clear that his leadership and support resources on summit day had serious limits. Rob couldn't do much beyond making decisions for risk management and safety. Everything was at the extreme above 26,000 feet. The raw reality was that if anything went wrong, despite being on a team of climbers, each was on his own. You must be able to take care of yourself. Others always try to help someone in need, but not much can be done to help another. In the Death Zone, the only rescue is self rescue.

At no time did Rob say the Sherpa were there on summit day (or any day) to assist a climber or even to help one in trouble. Neither did any of us have that expectation. As was true of all of us, any Sherpa would aid a climber in trouble to the extent possible, as a matter of basic humanity, if that situation occurred. But the Sherpa's job was only to support logistics. They were not paid and had no incentive to take the highly dangerous risks to serve as fireman in the event of fire. The Sherpa were not a paid or trained rescue squad.

For self leadership, each of us had our own personal limits, on both risk tolerance and physical reserves. Only we knew our limits. Rob couldn't know how much energy I still had in the tank. He couldn't know when I'd reached the limit of risk I was willing to accept. All that was up to me to know, and to act as a self leader.

ROB EXPECTED any one of us to "say no" to any decision he made to keep going in the climb, such as that moment at High Camp, if it conflicted with the limit of our personal risk tolerance or physical reserve, or our personal judgment. To do so would not say that Rob was necessarily making a wrong decision. It would only say that it was not the right decision for me. I knew this in the abstract. I just didn't expect to face such an important individual decision right then.

I could always turn around later if things didn't look right, I thought. I could go and wait and see. I had an option to reverse course. "You're not making a final decision," said my inner voice.

But I also knew that to exercise the option to turn back later would require extraordinary inner strength once I started going for it, as the pressures to keep going would intensify as I got closer. This was the specific warning I was given in advance by Everest experts. I could easily lose self control the closer I got.

I have also had many experiences while climbing where I had doubts, put off the hard call, and things got better. And I was later grateful I didn't say no when I was first concerned. If I'd acted on the impulse to say no to my goal every time it first came in my head, chances are I never would have summited any mountain.

So I finally decided to go and to take the risk—for now. Wait and see.

I started to get ready as quickly as I could. I had to make do with the time I had. I felt cold inside. I wanted to be organized and still have some quiet time before leaving the tent, and it seemed like the others felt the same. No one talked. Even Beck was quiet. I thought about and talked to Sandy inside of me; I didn't mention any of my promises to her. I told her I wanted to come home. I wanted this over with.

I said a prayer. I don't remember any specific petition. I probably asked for help to be stronger or for Everest to be softer and easier. Either way, I'd take what I could get.

Was this a story I could tell? Was I climbing smart? Was this a story I wanted to live?

CHAPTER 19

ABOVE THE SOUTH COL

10:40 PM. Almost time to go. Andy, Beck, Doug, and I were quiet. No chatter. Too much tension. Too much anxiety. We each faced the most difficult and most dangerous thing any of us had ever done. Things were not perfect. But we were going.

"Twenty minutes." The word came from Rob. "Twenty minutes and we move out." That meant eleven o'clock. Right on time.

I was very methodical when it came to readiness. Maybe I was even a bit neurotic. As I lay in my climbing suit resting my head on my backpack, I rehearsed in my mind what I would do in those final 20 minutes, and the sequence in which I would do it. Whatever it was, I wanted to do it once and get it right. I wanted to be efficient so I didn't have to rush. I did not want to be late so others would have to wait. When I have to rush, I make mistakes with my gear.

I organized my pack and double checked everything. Extra eye protection. Heavy duty expedition mittens in case my expedition gloves were insufficient. One chocolate bar. I had two one liter bottles of water that I put in my pack positioned against my back. I hoped the body heat from my back would prevent them from freezing. I also had a smaller thermos to keep inside my climbing suit that I could get to without taking off my backpack. That was it.

10:55 PM. I was first out of the tent because I was on the end by the door. But I wanted out early anyway. I was ready. Everything was ready: crampons, hardware, harness, and knots. That was within my control, and there was no room for mistakes. The stories are unending of climbers who died because they failed in the simplest of gear details, such as not following the basic safety procedure of doubling back the waist strap on the harness. I checked and double checked. I even double checked my crampon straps with my bare hands, just to make sure. I did not want a crampon to come off, especially up that high. Good, I thought. I even felt I was ready inside. I expected to be more anxious. Good. It would be a climb of a little more than 3,000 vertical feet to the top and another 3,000 feet back down. Twelve hours up, six down. As we moved out of High Camp, we first had to navigate around the tents and support lines, being careful not to snag any lines with the crampons.

It was clear with not much wind. But it was extremely cold, 30 to 40 below zero. Every part of my body was cold. But I was moving. I just wanted to get into my rhythm.

As we left camp, I overheard Rob radio Base Camp: "We're going. All are strong. We'll set world records." Yasuko being the oldest woman to summit Everest and Rob summiting for the fifth time were the only records I was aware of. But Rob also had in mind a world record for the largest number of people from one expedition summiting on a single day. He clearly expected all of us to summit. Rob was record oriented. He knew the publicity value of world records for expedition business purposes.

Once we started moving I felt good. My anxiety disappeared as I concentrated on rhythm and technique. I was moving. Up. I also started to generate body heat and warm up. The terrain began with a flat section of rocks on the South Col and then to a steep but short bulge of blue ice. Then it was hard snow, as we entered a system of gullies that quickly steepened. This area was known as the Triangular Face.

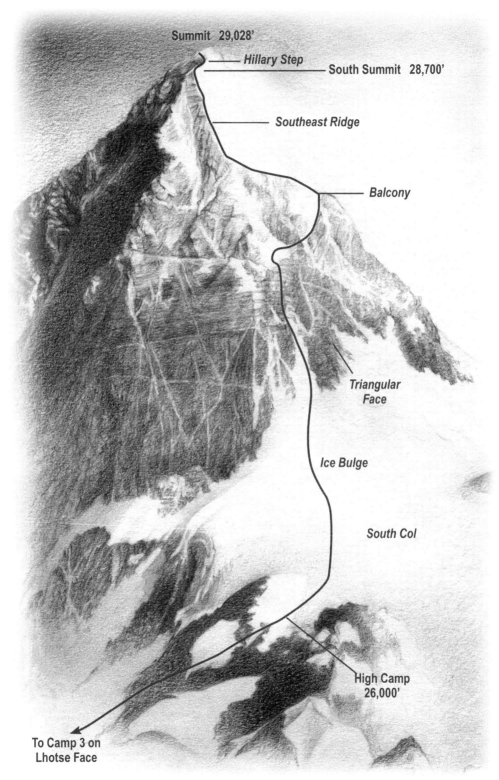

Summit 29,028'

Hillary Step

South Summit 28,700'

Southeast Ridge

Balcony

*Triangular
Face*

Ice Bulge

South Col

High Camp
26,000'

To Camp 3 on
Lhotse Face

Summit Day Route from High Camp

As I zigzagged up the mountain face, I moved my ice axe to my uphill hand. I had duct taped insulating closed-cell foam to the axe head to help prevent my fingers from freezing when gripping the metal. I was going to the top of the world and I felt good, even a little joyful.

As I climbed, I tried to memorize the terrain. This distracted me from negative thoughts. It was also a good climbing practice, for safety. As you climb up, you also think ahead about climbing down. All of us had looked at photographs of the route many times. But this was the real thing. It was somewhat different from the photographs, but not much. I wanted to understand the terrain features of what I was climbing, and impress those in my brain. If there were problems later, such as a storm or a visibility whiteout on the way down, the memory bank would help me find the route.

I looked around and behind, and I thought about what I saw. I was on a section of ice, followed by hard snow, then a short section of fixed rope, a left and then a right turn up terraced rock shelves, a snow gully, and a rock ridge on the right. I pictured those things as a sort of a handrail, in case I needed it later.

It was dark and we used our headlamps. Circles of light danced on the mountain face ahead and behind me. The sky was clear and bright from the moon and stars. I saw well without my headlamp. I turned it off to save battery life. When I did, I was suddenly very alone. Even though I saw the lights of the other climbers, as people they disappeared. It was just the mountain and me. All I heard was my own breathing. There was no other sound. I felt so far away from Sandy. I wondered what she would think if she could see me now. In the next 24 hours I would be planning my trip back home. This was almost over.

Those moments of climbing in the dark reminded me of the many all-night climbs on the ski hills at the Boyne Highlands ski resort as part of my training. I was always alone. I usually climbed without a headlamp. Climbing in the snow in the dark is good training, especially when it's cold and windy. It's important to have exceptional bad weather skills and experience in darkness. You must be at ease with those conditions. You must be well organized to cope and function efficiently, and to make gear changes in the dark and in high winds, such as putting on crampons or making other hardware or clothing adjustments. Being able to set up a tent in the dark and in bad weather is an especially important skill. Even though the Boyne ski hill terrain was easy, everything changed in the dark. The climbing became more difficult. It required careful concentration because mistakes were easier to make. I needed those skills to be fine tuned for Everest.

Another favorite climbing practice focused on efficiency. By concentrating on being efficient, I not only tuned fatigue out of my head, but I also recruited the strongest muscles and created less fatigue in the first place. First, I looked for a rhythm between my breathing and the steps I took. I settled into my metronome like pace, one that I could sustain for long periods. I pictured very precisely in my mind what was happening with my lungs, muscles, and bones. I saw air moving in and out of my lungs. I saw my nose moving over my toes to get my torso into the correct balance position. I saw my muscles flex as they pushed to the next step. In between steps, I saw my muscles relax and rest for an instant as my full body weight was positioned on the bones of my back leg. With intense concentration I studied every step, even the most routine on easy ground. This minimized wasted and exhausting effort, and it minimized mistakes. Most climbing mistakes occur during a momentary lapse in concentration.

To manage fatigue, sometimes I played a mind game with myself by saying, "I can do anything for another 20 minutes." It's a joke with some of my regular climbing partners when someone asks how much longer to the summit. No matter how long it may be, the answer is, "20 more minutes." When 20 minutes is up, the same is true for another 20.

So, 18 more hours in 20 minute segments is 54. So, 20 more minutes, 54 more times and the long march would be over.

WITHIN a few hours of starting out, I saw Frank Fischbeck and Rob in deep conversation. Frank had decided to turn back. I couldn't hear what they were saying, but Rob's body language was that of acknowledgment and understanding. Rob made no effort to persuade or encourage Frank otherwise, and I understood why. I respected Rob for how he handled the moment. That was what I expected from him. Rob always said he depended on each of us to be self leaders and to make our own decisions at critical moments, especially about our individual physical and risk limits on summit day.

Rob and I had several discussions about leadership. He was smart and experienced about the role of the leader as motivator. We discussed the tricky nature of encouraging others to act, even though each climber must accept personal responsibility for his or her decisions. Rob knew there was a time for the leader to be a motivating force to push others harder. But he also knew there was a time not to push. When you push, you walk the fine line between being a positive motivating force and pushing someone too far. In the case of Everest, and especially on summit day in the Death Zone, pushing too far could easily mean dying.

Frank was a strong climber with much experience. He was also an independent thinker. One day you would find him climbing in front, and on another day in the back. This was his fourth attempt on Everest, so he acted on valuable experience. He was unlikely to turn back without careful consideration. On the evening of May 9, Frank was in another tent, so I didn't hear his views on the weather decision. But it turned out he too had been vocal, and thought that going for the summit that evening was a bad idea. Frank now acted on what he thought was right.

I felt no emotion as I watched Frank climb away from me. At that moment I had no good reason to go back. I was going to the top.

NOT LONG after Frank turned back, I saw the headlamp of some-one else turning around and climbing down. That light became Doug. As he passed me, he said he was cold and feeling bad. Doug was sensitive to being cold after his feet were frostbitten on the 1995 attempt. Over the previous weeks he worried about his feet and pos-sible additional frostbite. Doug knew the tissue was more vulnerable the second time.

Doug's turn around didn't surprise me, or add to my own appre-hension about the day. The cold and pressures of the moment kept me focused on just my next step. Again, I had no emotion about Doug's decision.

Doug was in the tent with me at High Camp. He had not been happy with Rob's decision to go for the summit. From his appearance, he didn't seem physically well. Combined with his earlier health prob-lems, all of this must have been too much. Doug made the individual hard call decision that Rob expected from each of us.

Doug also had not been part of the same acclimatization plan as the rest of us. When we made our first climb to Camp 3, we turned around a short distance from Camp 3 and climbed 2,000 feet back down to Camp 2. I remember the incident well because I was ex-hausted and looked forward to reaching Camp 3. I knew it would take more energy to climb back down to Camp 2. But that was what we did. Later that evening, in the Camp 2 mess tent, there were con-flicting thoughts about why we turned around. One was that Doug was sick or severely cold. The other reason was that it was too windy. I didn't think it was too windy. But it didn't matter what the reason was — we went down. Doug looked awful and only made a brief ap-pearance that evening. It appeared poor health would take him out.

The next day we went back up to Camp 3 to spend the night at 24,000 feet for acclimatization purposes. Doug didn't go with us. The next time I saw Doug at Base Camp he didn't look well, and he couldn't talk. Among other problems, he had a serious throat problem. Still, as time passed, Doug's strong will and improvement in health brought him back into the game. Most of us went through the same cycle at one time or another during the climb.

On our later climb to Camp 2 on May 6, someone raised the question with Rob about Doug's ability to go to the summit without being part of the acclimatization process above 21,300 feet. Doug had never slept above 21,300 feet. Rob said he wasn't concerned about Doug's acclimatization because based on the 1995 climb, he was sure Doug could perform all the way to the South Summit.

Rob's answer didn't seem reasonable. From my understanding of acclimatization science, Doug's 1995 climb shouldn't matter. Doug even said he'd had problems at the South Summit altitude in 1995. Besides, 1995 was 1995. That was last year. Doug may even have been fully acclimatized then, and still had problems. But, once again, I accepted that Rob was the expert, and I didn't think much more about it at the time.

Now on summit day, Doug decided, based on his own judgment, that the best thing for him was to turn around. Again, this was the individual decision making Rob expected from each of us. Doug was the best judge about his own readiness.

As Doug moved below me, the rest of us continued to climb. I was surprised I felt as good as I did. I liked the pace. But I had a problem with my supplemental oxygen system (O2 as climbers call it). For one thing, I hated the mask, which made it more difficult to exhale. I couldn't breathe out a hard, fast exhalation, as I was accustomed to doing as part of my breathing rhythm.

I had never used O2 before Everest and I trusted Rob to have a good system for use. The mask was a Russian-made Vietnam War relic, and highly questionable. It had one small hole at the end from which to expel air, and that hole continually froze over with ice. The very small hole on the side to bring in ambient air, which was most of the oxygen I breathed, also froze over. Only a very small amount of what I actually breathed came from the supplemental system.

Rob's ancient system was not designed for mountain climbing—an aggressive hard breathing situation. The modern mask systems used by the other expeditions in 1996 were much more advanced.

My mother had severe bronchial asthma. When I was growing up it was frightening to watch her. She always said her problem was "I can't get air out." On Everest, I finally felt for myself what my mother was talking about.

I could feel no difference with the O2 system on or off. I became convinced that my system was not working properly. Ice could have formed in the line, the valves might not be operating correctly, or the regulator could be malfunctioning. Trying to use it impaired my breathing rhythm and performance. So, I unloosened the mask and let it hang. I felt better without it.

IT WAS established long ago that Everest can be climbed without supplemental O2. Early expeditions didn't use it. In 1924, twenty-nine years before Hillary and Norgay first reached the top (with O2), Edward Norton, a British climber with the Third British Everest Expedition, climbed to within 900 feet of the summit without O2. He turned back because of oncoming snowblindness from not wearing his protective goggles part of the time.

To use O2 or not is a decision that revolves around safety. Almost everyone (approximately 98 to 99 percent) who climbs Everest uses O2 on summit day. At our planned usage rate (2 liters per minute), the amount of supplement is quite minimal compared to the total you breathe. But it adds just enough fuel to your body's metabolism to help produce body heat to prevent hypothermia and frostbite. And since it is a good treatment for altitude sickness (one of the most serious and common risks), it's also a good preventative safety measure. So, most climbers feel that climbing without O2 involves taking unnecessary risks.

One big disadvantage of using O2 is that as you climb higher, your body can become dependent on it. After dependency sets in, you can have a big problem if you run out or the system malfunctions before getting back down to High Camp. The effects from the sudden removal vary with individual physiology (natural body chemistry). Most climbers can just keep moving, but with more difficulty. Some can't move at all from the debilitating effects on the body. At what altitude you run out is also a big factor. To run out at 29,000 feet near the summit is a much bigger problem than running out close to High Camp at 26,000 feet. And you can't predict how anyone will react because the relevant variables (natural body chemistry, nutrition, hydration, acclimatization, exhaustion, and body temperature) are always changing. In most cases, if you run out, you're in a worse position than if you had not used it at all.

A few climbers choose to go to the summit without O2. That's part of the freedom of the hills. But it's hard to make that as a matter of distinction (or "pureness" as some say). These few climbers are almost always with others using O2, climbing on the route prepared by others using O2, using fixed ropes set by others using O2, living in camp sites prepared and stocked by others using O2, and surrounded by others using O2, who are available to rescue them if they become hypothermic or get altitude sickness. Besides, for performance, what counts the most on Everest is an individual's natural body chemistry adjustment to oxygen deprivation. It's not a matter of how tough you are. And the matter of pureness gets muddy. What is pureness? Who decides it? Is O2 not pure?

THE AREA called the Balcony was our first key way-point. It was still a few hours away. We climbed through a long section of fixed rope. After exiting the rope, I wondered why that section was fixed with rope. From what I could see, the mountain face was wide open and the exposure seemed minimal. It was not a delay chokepoint. But I also knew it would be good for route finding on the way down. So I put it in my memory bank. I couldn't tell if this rope was fixed by our Sherpa team climbing ahead of us, or if it was done by one of the other teams that preceded us. In the past several days, at least three teams had made unsuccessful attempts on the summit. All reached very high points before being turned back by high winds. The Yugoslavs, who preceded us by one day, climbed all the way to the Hillary Step before turning back. Based on route information feedback, it appeared the only place the Sherpa needed to fix rope was the Hillary Step.

When we left High Camp for the summit, it was dark and unbelievably cold. Everyone was bundled in big down suits with almost their entire faces covered. I couldn't tell one person from another. I was focused on myself, how cold it was, and my next step. Nothing else mattered. I assumed two of our Sherpa had left one hour ahead to fix rope to avoid delay, as Rob said they would. I didn't think about that any more. But as it turned out, no Sherpa left early.

We then climbed a section that looked like terraced shelves of broken shale. It was strange terrain and, on one occasion, I sat down on one of the shelves to rest. It was during this moment that I looked back and saw Rob coming up, and he did something that struck me. He made his move to the next rock shelf by putting one knee up and then the other, and then standing. That was a move you would not expect from someone of Rob's skill level. I also noticed he was shaking and looked cold. I thought Rob might be having a problem. Actually, seeing Rob suffering boosted my self confidence in a perverse way. I wasn't the only one suffering.

I got to my feet and pressed on, searching to get my rhythm back, moving to the rhythm of my breathing, and shutting out thoughts of fatigue. One foot in front of another, we climbed up a steep gully of dry, sugar-like deep snow. It was like climbing up a sand dune because the snow would give out under foot as you started to move up. It was very fatiguing. Off to the right was a rock ridge of more broken shale. It was not inviting, but climbers up ahead moved to the ridge to save energy.

The sun came up over the horizon in the east and cast its golden light on the ridge just above. Beck Weathers was in front of me. As climbers ahead of Beck moved out of the gully to the rock ridge, Beck kept moving up the gully. I came up behind him to get his attention and said, "Beck, move right to the ridge." He turned around and looked straight past me. He appeared to be having trouble focusing his eyes. He finally said he couldn't see.

I saw some climbers sitting down for a rest break at the top of the gully. I knew we would be taking a break there, too. Beck started to take off his pack. I said, "Beck, no, keep going. We'll be breaking in a few minutes." He squinted in the direction I pointed, and said, "If you don't mind, Lou, I'll just sashay on your heels a little." I moved ahead and we climbed in close tandem. I was so focused on the climbing challenges to get to the Balcony that in the moment it didn't seem to matter that Beck "couldn't see."

CHAPTER 20

THE BALCONY

"WE'RE ON TIME," I overheard Rob say. His first time way-point was to be on the Balcony on the Southeast Ridge at about daybreak. Pace management brought us there on schedule. The sun had just come up. Being on the Southeast Ridge meant we were off the Triangular Face. Now we start the final part of the climb—the ridge to the summit.

Oddly enough, I was feeling much better than I'd expected. Climbing to the top was happening. Climbing at a steady pace through the night, in a good rhythm, was good for my mind and body. And now for the morning reward. I got to sit down. The Balcony was a small, flat surface of snow a few meters wide, and one of the only places on summit day where you could actually sit down to rest.

When Everest was first climbed in 1953, the Balcony was the site of the last camp. At that time, no one believed climbers had the physical capacity to reach the summit and return all the way down to the South Col in a single push.

Two particular jobs needed attention. Since the sun had come up, eye protection was critical. At that high altitude, the intensity of the ultra-violet rays was very dangerous. The biggest danger was sunburn of the cornea—snowblindness. I always carried two pieces of eye protection. One piece was dark-lens glacier glasses with side shields designed for climbers. The side shields are leather patches so the sun's rays cannot hit the eyes from the side. My alternative piece for protection was ski goggles. I preferred the glacier glasses because there is less tendency for the lens to fog.

The final chore at the Balcony was changing the O2 canister. The O2 plan was that the first of three canisters would be about gone by then. We each carried two, and a Sherpa carried a third to leave at the South Summit for use on the way down. I told Rob again, as I had mentioned to him earlier when we were on the move, that my system was not working. That I actually felt better without it. Rob was aware I had taken the mask off for most of the time in getting to the Balcony. He was an expert with this equipment. He fussed with the regulator and banged on the mask a couple of times and said it should be better and to try again.

"According to the gauge, my first canister is still over half full," I said.

"Good, that's great, leave it in the bank, mate, and change it later."

I had no explanation for why so much was left in the canister. I looked at the other climbers, for signs that we were about to go. And to see how everyone else was doing.

Doug. There he was, at the Balcony. I was surprised. But I was too busy focusing on my own readiness to talk to him or to think much about how he'd gotten back in the climb to the top. Doug had obviously changed his mind about going down to High Camp. I just gave him a smile and a thumbs up, and he returned the gestures.

Beck. Beck had impaired vision. He needed to get down to safety. And he needed help to do so. I was standing close to Rob and Beck at the Balcony.

"You wait here. We'll pick you up on the way down," I overheard Rob say. Beck nodded his head. Beck's impaired vision was caused by oxygen starvation and Lasik eye surgery he had undergone a few years earlier.

Beck was out of the climb. I looked at him but felt nothing. The climb was so physically and mentally difficult, and so intense at that moment, that focus on myself dominated everything. I was incapable of feeling anything for anyone else. At that extreme altitude, when you are suffering from fatigue, malnutrition, dehydration, hypoxia, and sleep deprivation, you don't have much emotional capacity—let alone empathy.

But Beck needed help. Resources were available to help him. Rob faced a leadership dilemma. To leave Beck waiting at the Balcony until we returned, Rob preserved full leadership and Sherpa support resources for the summit attempt. But that delayed getting Beck the help he needed and put him at risk. Waiting is something you never do at high altitude, except in an emergency. Waiting meant Beck would use valuable energy just trying to stay warm. Getting cold could mean dying.

To send Mike or Andy down with Beck on a short rope would help Beck without delay, but would dilute leadership resources for the summit attempt. It would result in Mike or Andy foregoing the summit. Andy had never summited Everest, and it would be a major disappointment for him to go down then, with only a few hours left. If Mike assisted Beck down, that would leave Rob with only Andy to assist him. But Andy was an unknown quantity because he had no experience at that altitude. Rob could send one of the Sherpa down with Beck, but perhaps none of the Sherpa had the skills to assist him on a short rope. Also, the Sherpa's only paying job was logistics.

Rob decided to handle Beck's problem later. Rob didn't foresee problems or delays up ahead. We'd soon be back for Beck? Was that the assumption?

Most of the climbers probably didn't know of Rob's decision. Those who did were absorbed with their own problems and situation. Rob needed decision making help at that moment. He needed someone to question his decision. No one spoke up.

It was a poor decision for any leader to leave a sick or injured climber alone. It is one of the unwritten rules of mountaineering. Too many things can go wrong when a climber is alone, especially at 27,600 feet. And Beck would be alone and waiting for a long time. Also, at the planned flow rate, he would be out of O2 before someone saw him again. Without generating body heat by moving, it would be very difficult for Beck to stay warm. And what if we were delayed getting back? What if the weather turned bad?

Assisting Beck to safety was a team priority that Rob subordinated to the goal of the summit.

Rob made the wrong decision.

IT WAS time to go. I took a moment to look around and snap a few photos. I suddenly enjoyed the unbelievable setting. From there, I could look over the infamous Kangshung Face into the plains of China/Tibet. The Kangshung glacier was 10,000 feet below. I could see Kanchenjunga, the world's third highest peak and Makalu, the fifth highest. Each were bathing in the rising sun. All are famous sights for students of mountaineering. It was absolutely breathtaking. I will never forget that moment of beauty and calm among all the suffering. Just being there was part of the answer to the "why climb Everest" question. I reminded myself that few people have ever seen those sights.

But that feeling was fleeting. My thoughts quickly returned to suffering. I felt better when Rob said, "Everything is fine, just keep pace." Keep pace—that was my focus, my mantra. Actually my mantra, which is a Sanskrit word meaning "instrument of the mind," was a familiar carryover from other climbs—"keep pace and climb smart." Over and over, "keep pace and climb smart." "I can do this." Another mantra. A voice I heard over and over. "I can do this."

Beck was left alone.

Enjoying the scenery was over. It was time to go. In fact, there would never be another single moment on Everest—ever—that I would experience as enjoyment. My nightmare would begin soon.

THE FISCHER team arrived at the Balcony while we were there. They continued climbing up shortly thereafter. They probably wanted to get ahead and stay ahead of us. It's important for climbers to be spread out and not be too close together. We didn't want the two teams mixed together because after the Balcony we were climbing a ridgeline where passing could be difficult. This was the first time since two days before, when I first met a few of the Fischer team on the Lhotse Face, that the Fischer climbers entered my mind. And even then, I was so busy and focused on my own readiness that I didn't think beyond being aware of them passing through.

SO FAR, the summit day plan had worked. In looking at the big picture variables: the weather was good; wind was good; time was good; snow conditions were good; and people's health and energy levels were good (no altitude sickness or more than expected fatigue—as near as I could tell). Except for Beck, everyone was doing what was expected.

I didn't see any delays or other problems ahead. Most importantly, Rob said we were on time, which meant our timetable was still in place. With the six-weeks effort behind us, only a few more hours before it would be over. I was closing in on the final hours of the 59 hour long march.

"I can do this," said my inner voice. "I can do this."

I didn't think about the plan for fixing rope. I assumed the Sherpa rope team had left early. Nor had I thought about our concerns a few days earlier with Rob's decision to go to the summit on the same day as the Fischer team. Those concerns were resolved days earlier at Base Camp, and I hadn't thought about them again in the last five days. Each team would function separately, and as such, neither team would influence the outcome for the other. That was the assumption.

Rob's seven Everest expedition experiences also gave me confidence. "Mate, if someone gets this far physically, you can do the rest if you can manage your head to keep going." Managing my head was always one of my strong points. One of my favorite sayings from endurance athletics was, "Pain is temporary, but quitting is permanent."

"I can do this."

I was glad to get going when the group started to move. I climbed somewhere in the middle of the pack and Rob maintained his preferred position at the back. He had said earlier that on summit day he would lead from behind. I was puzzled by that idea, especially on the day when leadership counted the most. To me, it was counterintuitive and an important departure in conventional thinking. As leader and decision maker, Rob should have been in front, especially since he had untested assistant leaders. In our case, Andy was at the front, and he had never been on Everest. He also lacked high altitude experience, and more importantly, he lacked high altitude decision making experience.

If Rob led from the front, he could size up the situation while on the move, find the route, make decisions, communicate those decisions, and most importantly, set the proper pace and manage whatever complexities or problems arose. Mike or Andy could radio Rob about any problems behind.

We started to climb the Southeast Ridge. We were right on Rob's timetable. We were closing in on the mission. It looked like I would pull this off. Not much longer, and it would be over.

"I can do this."

We were getting close to outer space.

CHAPTER 21

UP THE RIDGE

THE SOUTHEAST Ridge was the last stretch before the summit, the final 1,400 vertical feet. I looked down for vast distances and saw ice capped mountains below my gaze. It was quite a sensation to be on that ridge, with Nepal on the left, and China/Tibet on the right. I knew the sun was casting my shadow far below into Nepal.

The early part of the ridge terrain required good balance and careful placement of my ice axe for self-belaying. The terrain flattened for a stretch and then started getting steeper. An occasional cloud came along and moved past below me. I saw myself getting close to outer space—on the summit of Everest.

I soon realized I had a problem with eye protection. The O2 mask, which I had put back on, had a strap that came over the top of my head and clipped on the mask at the top of the nose of the mask. This strap pulled my glacier glasses up a short distance off the bridge of my nose. As I climbed, the bottom of the lens was off my face just enough that I could see the snow on the mountain face below the glasses' frame. That was not good. If I lifted my head and looked forward, I had good eye protection. But when I looked down, which was most of the time, my eyes lacked protection.

I was not looking into the sun, but the sun's rays hit the snow and bounced back. This is how climbers get sunburned on the roof of their mouth, and why climbers are always careful to put sunscreen on the bottom of their nose. But I also remembered from high school physics that as the sun's rays reflect off the snow they refract and intensify. The eyes are vulnerable at high altitude, where the rays are so intense. It causes snowblindness.

As I climbed in the middle of the group that left the Balcony together, I felt the pressure to keep pace. Rob emphasized, "I've been here. I know how this works. Just keep pace." It had not been long since we left the Balcony. I was reluctant to stop and adjust my sunglasses, and possibly disrupt the flow of upward movement for others.

I had no fogging, which was good; but I was concerned about the reflection of the sun in my eyes under the gap. I tried to fidget with the mask strap and the glasses while on the move, or during a breathing pause. But nothing worked. I was still reluctant to make a bigger deal out of it. So I ignored the problem and hoped it would go away. Keep moving and keep pace was my priority. One foot in front of the other. Breathe. One foot in front of the other. "Climb smart. I can do this," said my inner voice. I used my mental techniques to manage fatigue. But by mentally ignoring my sunglasses problem, I was not climbing smart. My decision to ignore the problem for too long would be a mistake that I would pay for later.

Memorizing the terrain on the way up to help find the way down wasn't hard. I was on a ridge with 8,000 feet of air on both sides. There was not much risk of getting lost. Don't move too far left. Don't move too far right. It was simple.

Hour after hour after hour. I stepped, and I gasped to take four or five breaths of that frigid dry air that burned inside me like cold fire. Then, I shifted my weight to get into the correct balance position to make my next move, and I took another step. All my mental and physical strength focused on my next step. Nothing else mattered. I was getting close to the summit. But I wasn't happy or excited. I just wanted it to be over. Enough of the cold, fatigue, and not being able to breathe. I wanted to go home. Still, nothing could stop me from going up.

I wasn't having any particular problems that I hadn't expected. It didn't matter that I was dehydrated, malnourished, and could not digest food at this altitude. It didn't matter that I was oxygen starved. It didn't matter that I was fatigued from physical effort and lack of sleep. None of that mattered. After all, I was in the Death Zone. My body was literally dying. Another good reason to get it over with.

Sheer will kept me going. Nothing could stop me. This was summit day, and I was getting close.

"I can do this. I will do this."

Again I felt very alone. I was isolated. I couldn't talk with anyone. All I heard was the wind and my own breathing. The terrain got steeper and steeper. But step by step I was going to the summit. Five breaths, a step. By sheer will, each of us, a weaker force, was overcoming a greater one — Everest. Step by step by step. Just as small drops of water constantly dripping can hollow out a stone.

WHEN mountain climbers think of risks, their first thoughts usually go to snow avalanches, rock fall, glacial crevasses, storms, and altitude sickness. They pay less attention to the risks created by their own decisions, which can be just as deadly, and statistically more likely. When things go wrong, rarely is the cause a force of nature. Almost always the cause is climber error. Even what might appear to be the result of an act or force of nature can be traced back to a mistake in decision making that unnecessarily exposed the climber to nature's dangers. On Everest, this decision making risk was especially true on summit day.

And so — In Self We Trust.

Rob liked to talk about this, as he emphasized the role of individual decision making on summit day. None of the climbing members, except for Frank and Doug, had ever been in the Death Zone, much less close to the top, where the pressures and influences on good decision making, like everything else, were more extreme than anywhere else. The challenge was about the need for inner strength. The challenge was about "drawing the line."

On summit day, the inner strength needed as a climber is not just the sheer will to persevere to get to the top. It also takes inner strength to get back down alive. You need inner strength to resist the pressures to act and think *only* about getting to the top. You may not get down if you think only about going up. The top is only half way. And climbing down is frequently the hardest part of the climb.

Behind the powerful force of ambition resided specific performance pressures. For Yasuko, a world record was at stake. A world record was also at stake for Rob, along with the performance pressure to gain business promotion publicity from the presence of Jon Krakauer in the expedition.

Pressure. Pressure. Pressure.

Still, those pressures and the sheer will to persevere were powerful forces that each of us needed to control. We had serious responsibilities to others and to ourselves. If anything went wrong, people could die.

On summit day especially, the dilemma you face was to be ambitious, but not greedy; to be bold, but not reckless; to be confident, but not arrogant. Rob said, "To climb Everest, you must be pushy, but not too pushy." He knew there was a line a climber could not cross.

But, seeing that line was tough for people who wanted to climb Everest, who were now close to doing just that, and who were not quitters by nature. They are not accustomed to taking no for an answer, especially from themselves. These people were accustomed to winning. People who wanted to win. People who expected to win.

Ironically, it's crossing the invisible line that is the sign of weakness. Being "too pushy" is paradoxically not a display of too much strength, but of weakness. What's more impressive than ambition is the power to control it.

That was why we had a climbing plan to guide us, with safety priorities agreed to by everyone ahead of time. Someone long ago coined a great saying about mountain climbers: There are old mountaineers and there are bold mountaineers; but there are no old, bold mountaineers. If you gave everything you have to get to the top, or if getting there was the only thing that mattered — you might stay there.

Actually, our turnaround time was a line already drawn. There was nothing invisible about 1 PM.

SINCE leaving the Balcony, I kept pace with climbers above me, and there were climbers below me, including Rob. Staying on pace was one of my main objectives. I'd felt no better than earlier with the O2 system. I used more energy to get the system to work than I was benefiting from it. I finally found a place where I could move off to the side of the ridge to check on the system and change the canister. It was fairly tricky because I had to do it while propping my pack between my legs and the mountain face. Some people passed me, but I wasn't paying attention to who they were. I could see climbers below me, including Rob.

My O2 canister was still, just as at the Balcony, over half full according to the gauge. That told me the regulator or something else wasn't working. That's why I felt no difference. Others had told me that when it works and you run out, you know it instantly. But maybe the new canister will make a difference, I thought. I made the change, and gave the regulator a knock, as though that would fix whatever was wrong. I didn't think it would, and it didn't matter. As I learned a long time ago about life and climbing, if you don't have it, you don't need it. All I could think of at that moment was, "Okay, time to go."

I also spent time working with my glacier glasses and the O2 strap, and I thought I had corrected my coverage gap problem. But I was concerned enough about it that I took my ski goggles out of my pack and put them on top of my head. I could reach them from there without stopping to get into my pack. I didn't want to have to stop again. If needed, I could pull them down over my eyes. I also planned to quickly ditch the mask if connecting to the new O2 canister still made no difference. And that's what I did later, solving from that time on my glasses and strap problem.

When I stopped to change O2, I noticed something you would think was important. As I worked with my backpack and gear changes, I took off my gloves. My fingers were very, very cold and difficult to move. They were white and felt stiff. I thought it was probably frostbite. But I didn't even notice that until then. Worse yet, I didn't care.

So much for self leadership. How could I not know my fingers were freezing? How could I not care?

I started moving again. It was all about breathing and stepping. Five breaths, a step. Five breaths, a step. Shift my weight. Breathe. Breathe. Step. Small drops of water hollowing out a stone, as I continued to climb up the ridge.

I had no reason to think anything was going wrong. Rob said, "If you keep pace, all is okay." Climbers were above and below me. I saw no large gaps between climbers. Everyone was climbing up. Everything must have been okay. The pace seemed slow for quite a long time. But if it were too slow, Rob would have corrected it. He was the expert, and pace monitoring was part of his leadership and time management responsibility. My body felt about as bad as it could possibly feel, but I was still moving.

I heard a crackling sound. It was Rob's radio as he came up from behind me.

"Going up. Going up." He pointed. Rob didn't say any more, but he had a very serious look in his eyes. It was not the usual Kiwi twinkle. Rob moved quickly; he was in a hurry. He looked cold, mentally, physically, and emotionally. I'm sure I did too. I nodded, which was about all I had the energy to do.

We were very close to the South Summit. Andy and Mike would either be there or close. I assumed Rob had some leadership business to coordinate. I didn't know it was a big problem.

After Rob moved ahead, it was back to business. Five breaths, a step. At that point in the day on the ridge, my self confidence was up. I was going to the summit. Although I knew a lot could still happen, and difficult climbing was still ahead, my thinking was positive. Nothing could stop me. I was too close. This was summit day. This was Everest. "I can do this." Everything seemed to have worked out. "Lou, you actually pulled this off," came from my inner voice. "Yes, but let's get it over with," said the same voice.

One foot in front, breathe, breathe, breathe, gasp, shift my weight, and then move. Keep pace and climb smart.

It was impossible not to be dehydrated. Every breath I took was dehydrating as I inhaled the dry air, humidified it with body fluid, and exhaled the humidified air. In that extreme dry environment over 28,000 feet, and with air temperatures at 30 below zero, you need to drink more water than if you were in a hot desert. But that was not possible on summit day climbing Everest. The water I carried in my backpack was by then frozen into blocks of ice. I had a small thermos that I kept inside my climbing suit, but that was too inadequate to hydrate me. I just sipped from it occasionally to help my dry burning throat.

The ridge was never ending. It was always getting steeper. We got into and passed through some sections with fixed ropes. There were some old, ratty, and frayed ropes someone ahead had pulled up out of the snow. I had expected to find that. But some rope appeared new, and that I hadn't expected. The terrain was steeper but not a delay chokepoint and not technically difficult. I did not see any need to take the time to fix new rope in this area. But I welcomed the rope. And, as always, I climbed with concentration as though I weren't clipped to a rope. I did not want a false sense of security. I also had to be careful in handling those ropes, not knowing which could be trusted. I could not make any mistakes here. I knew if anything went wrong at that extreme altitude, I would be in big trouble.

In fact, things were going wrong above me right then, and were going to get much worse.

CHAPTER 22

I CAN DO THIS

I SAW climbers above, on the rise just below the South Summit. On the South Summit itself, a stone's throw away, a few climbers were standing. From where I was, I couldn't see how many were climbing beyond the South Summit, but I assumed they were still moving up. I had no reason to think otherwise. Some might have been sitting down, but I couldn't tell for sure. I didn't know why anyone would sit, or stand still for that matter. Maybe those that I could see were just taking a rest break. I really didn't care about *why*, and I didn't see any problem. I simply kept moving.

Based on where I was, it must have been around hour 52 of my 59 hour long march. In terms of time, that meant there was not much more to go to reach the top and to get back to High Camp. Soon it would be over—summiting the highest mountain in the world.

As I moved up, I saw that Taske was stopped ahead of me. He had his pack off and was adjusting the straps. As I came up from below, he said, "I'm going down." I don't recall if I said anything in return, because at that moment I saw Stu climbing down toward me. I made eye contact with Stu and climbed toward him. They were two of our team's strongest and smartest climbers.

"What's the deal?" I thought. After a short time, Stu said, "It's late. Too many people. Need to go down now or get caught out." "Caught out," is shorthand for being caught in the open after dark—a climber's worst fear at that altitude on Everest.

That hit me fast. I stood still. I had no emotion. It was more like disbelief, denial, or the tendency to not hear what I did not want to hear.

Stu looked me in the eyes. He knew what I did next was my decision, but his look said, "Don't get caught out," and was meant to persuade me to go down. Later, as I recalled that moment, I thought of the Buddha eyes Stu had sewn on his jacket in Katmandu. Eyes that symbolize compassion and watchfulness. Eyes that were present.

"I'm not ready for that," I finally said to Stu.

"If I keep pace, all is okay," said the inner voice I'd clung to and didn't want to let go.

Taske and Stu were good, tough, ambitious climbers, whom I respected and admired. Neither would go down so close to the summit without important reasons. They were among the few climbers who made life and death decisions in high tension situations in their careers, especially Taske during his tours as an SAS Commando in Vietnam. And they had just made a major decision, high on Everest. However, what they said didn't make any difference to me. I didn't even want to think about turning back. I was programmed for the last six weeks, and the many hours since leaving High Camp. The program was up. Sheer will was at work.

Rob was not far ahead. He was either on or close to the South Summit. I told Stu I'd talk to Rob. As leader, I assumed he would be at that strategic location, organizing and coordinating resources. And I could be there in minutes. "Why not just go talk to Rob?" said my inner voice.

Defer, and go talk to Rob.

In general, I defer important decisions as long as I practically can. I didn't think it was necessary to make that final and irreversible decision right then.

I Can Do This

Besides, I'm too close.

Besides, I don't like John and Stu's decision.

Besides, I don't even want to think about their decision.

I moved ahead. *I can do this,* again said my inner voice of ambition.

AS I climbed, I knew I was higher than any other mountain in the world, including the infamous K2. One of our Sherpa, Lhakpa Chhiri, was just ahead. I went up to him.

"How much longer?" I pointed up. I knew we were really close. I had a good idea about how much longer, but I still asked. Maybe it was less than I thought. Our Sherpa spoke a little English. He looked up and around and held up two fingers and said "Two—two hours. About 100 meters. Two hours." I looked at him for a few moments, even after he repeated himself. I knew where we were, so I didn't translate the altitude from meters to feet in my head. The only thing that mattered anyway was the two hours. "120 minutes," said my inner voice. That was longer than I'd estimated. Maybe to think in minutes made it feel shorter in time.

I unfastened the Velcro wrist straps on my climbing suit. I looked at my watch.

It was close to noon. I didn't expect that. I tried to be calm about the time, but I knew we were late. My mind raced to grasp the meaning and consequences. Almost 13 hours had passed since we started from High Camp. We were far behind schedule. This meant things were going wrong. Rob said we had to be on the South Summit at 10 AM or before. And on the main summit much earlier than now. About 11 AM was the plan. Rob planned to be coming down from the top by now, not still going up.

We were late. Very late. Why? I didn't know. But why didn't matter to me. My emotions were cold and calculating.

Late, yes, but was it too late? I asked myself that narrowly focused question.

I did the math in my head: two hours to get to the top, and two more hours before I could get back to here. To be where I was now standing, it would be about 4 PM, with 3,000 feet still to climb down to get back to High Camp before dark.

Based on Rob's summit day plan, I was too late. I was past the turn-around time. I was out of time. But others were still going up. Rob must think it's okay. So me too. I can do this. Just do it. Go for it. I've been climbing this mountain for six weeks, and today for almost 13 hours. I'm close—only 120 more minutes. Why not tough it out? And, besides, many others are still going. "Keep pace and stick with the others," said my inner voice.

I felt physically and mentally wasted from high altitude exhaustion. But I knew one thing that could make me feel even worse: regret. Regret later, if I didn't take the opportunity. In climbing, only one thing is worse than not reaching the summit. And that is, when others do—and you don't. That has never happened to me on any climb. And it was not going to happen here—on the biggest of all.

It wasn't hard to figure out what I should do. This was no longer about talking to Rob or about getting and processing more informa-tion. What to do was simple and came to me quickly. The only voice inside of me that I could hear at that moment was all and just about me—to go, to keep going to the summit. My goal. My desire. My hard work. My suffering. Me. *I am just too close. I can do this.* That's what that moment was about.

No internal debate. No inner struggle. No pros and cons to consider and weigh. Just 120 more minutes to the top. Do it. Get it over with. *That voice of ambition, the wind, and the thin air were determined to suffocate and drown out the sound of any other voice within me.*

Others were going. So I would too.

I chipped away the ice that had caked on my face so I could breathe what little oxygen there was six miles high. With my head down and gasping for air, I continued to climb up.

I can do this, said that first and only voice I heard within me.

When you only think about going to the summit, what else can you do?

I DIDN'T get very far before something frightening happened to me. My heart started to race and pound. Fast and hard. My heart seemed out of control. I could feel it jumping. I could hear it beating. I had never experienced anything like it.

I felt unsteady. I had an overwhelming urge to drop to my knees—almost a feeling of desperation. I put both hands on the head of my ice axe and jammed it like a stake into the snow directly in front of me. I pulled hard to secure myself. I buckled and fell to my knees. My heart throbbed and trembled. I heard it beating. I closed my eyes.

My God, what's happening to me? I knew whatever was happening was serious. I tried to settle my breathing. I felt that whatever was happening mattered.

I paused for a long time. I was empty of any inner voice. I'm not sure if I was trying to steady my breathing or just trying to breathe.

I prayed. I prayed, "God give me strength." It was an open-ended petition. I knew that I needed strength. But strength for what?

As I was on my knees gripping my ice axe, my breathing slowed. My focus shifted as I opened my eyes. I looked around. For the first time in hours, I looked at and talked through the big picture, in my usual self question and answer method. My center was no longer the myopia of one foot in front of the other. My perspective opened up.

I could reach the top. That I was sure about. I didn't even ask that question. But, I was past the turnaround time. That I was also sure about.

Based on the time of day, could I go to the top and get back down to High Camp in daylight? That was a question I asked. And I felt true doubt for the first time. My first impulse was, "I don't know. Maybe, not. Probably—not." But then my answer solidified, "No, I don't think so. I would be out of daylight on the way down. I would be caught out." And Rob had frequently said, "If you are not back in daylight, you might as well be on the moon."

I SAW climbers above me. Whatever went wrong concerning time didn't matter to them. No one was coming down. Only Stu. Only Taske.

My heart pounded in my ears and in my chest. I looked around and focused on the weather. Snow spindrift created by the wind swirled around me. The wind was stronger than even a short time ago. The sound became louder and louder. Looking up—things were fine. Looking down, the visibility was poor. I could no longer see the beautiful sights or the Balcony below. I felt the weather was changing, and not for the better.

I turned my focus to my physical condition. I took off my gloves. I saw my white and stiff fingers. Frostbite? Maybe. Probably. I was not sure. I already knew I had that problem, but then I hadn't cared. I didn't care much, even now. My voice of ambition deadened any concern or sense of the tissue in my fingers freezing.

I was fatigued and dehydrated. Dehydrated beyond belief. I desperately wanted water; but I knew the water bottles in my backpack were frozen blocks of ice. I scooped up some snow to put in my mouth. No matter how cold it was, I wanted the instant gratification of moisture in my dry throat.

My heart still pounded and pounded—ever harder, ever faster. It was racing, trembling. I felt it and heard it pound. The sound of the wind roared louder and louder.

I should turn around now. The decision for me to turn around was actually already made when I promised to the turnaround time. That should have ended the matter. In terms of right and wrong, I knew that. Promises made are to be kept. Nothing more needed to be decided. Others were counting on me to follow the turnaround time, the time set in advance for the safety of everyone—not just me. I had promised. I had also promised Sandy that I would only live a story I could tell. How could I take the added risks from continuing, and also honor my promises? All this came from a second voice within me—a voice that looked beyond myself.

For the first time, I actively engaged my situation as a decision dilemma about what to do. *I'm close—but I'm out of time. Do I turn around or keep going?*

The challenge to climb the highest mountain in the world now became a different challenge. Physical toughness and sheer will to face adversity and high risk to climb to the top didn't matter. I faced an even greater challenge than climbing a six-mile high mountain of rock, snow, and ice. My challenge was myself. I was now struggling with myself. Two inner voices were competing in a high stakes, human struggle with a hard call dilemma. I had to make a choice. I couldn't decide what to do. Back and forth I went in my struggle of two voices. And neither voice would let go. I kept looking up to make sure the others were still going. I hoped that somehow things would work out. If I turned around, all hope would be gone.

While I was on my knees, some climbers coming up from behind passed me. They didn't say a word. They were going up. I didn't pay any attention to who they were, but I felt their movement as more pressure to keep going. I even visualized myself moving up. But I

I can do this.

knew I had to make the hard choice. I faced the decision I feared I would not have the courage to face. The decision I hoped I would never have to make.

People were around me, but I felt alone with my feelings and my voices. I knew the right thing to do. But I didn't want to do it.

I can do this, said the first voice.

But what do I do? I again asked the question.

For the moment there was no answer. I was still on my knees, struggling within.

Suddenly, the sound of the wind vanished. Suddenly, everything went quiet. Stone silent. All I heard was my pounding heart. I heard no other sound—within me or around me. I no longer even heard my gasping for air. Did I stop breathing? I shook my hands to make sure I had not passed out or something else. I put an extra grip on my ice axe with both hands.

And then I felt detached, as though everything happening to me and around me was at a distance far away. Everything slowed down.

These were uncommon moments. I had never experienced anything like this before. Dead quiet, except for my pounding heart. But even the heart now seemed to beat in slow motion. I could see the spindrift snow swirl silently around me—also in slow motion. I heard no sound of the wind. I heard no sound of voices of struggle within me. I only heard the beating heart. Otherwise, only sheer silence.

WHAT would I hear—after the wind—when I listened to the sound of sheer silence? I didn't know. But I was about to find out.

What I heard saved my life.

CHAPTER 23

AFTER THE WIND

I DIDN'T move during those uncommon moments of silence and detachment. I was still. I just listened, for what seemed like a long time. I could only hear the beating heart. I then got up off my knees and stood. I was standing with my ice axe in hand, ready for my next move.

Not today. I can do this. I can climb to the top of Everest. But this is not the day. I'm going home. This is the story I can tell Sandy.

These were the words of the last voice — after the wind.

I looked up again. I visualized the moment of me standing on top of the world. A moment that would never happen. A place I would never stand.

Not today. I'm going home, were the lingering words of that last voice.

The invisible line I dared not cross was visible. I looked at it right above me.

I turned around.

I looked up again, one last time, at the climbers above me. They were still there in their colorful red, blue, and yellow climbing suits preparing to go the final short distance for their moment of celebration. I did not know what voices were talking to them. I did not know if any deliberate decision making process was taking place (it wasn't for me

177

until those past few moments). All I knew was that they went on — to live their dream of standing on top of the world.

I then started to climb down.

WITH MY first step down, my heart stopped pounding. I couldn't hear it beating or feel it throbbing anymore. But I again heard the wind, and my own gasping for air. I knew I faced great danger ahead, just to get back down. Ice axe in hand and feet pointed down, I felt strong and confident despite my ravaged and debilitated state. I was sure I could get back down. I was sure, even though I was in a very dangerous situation, with 3,000 feet of rock, snow, and ice to descend before getting back to High Camp.

As I was climbing down, the words still in my head were, *I can do this. But not today. This is not the day. I'm going home.*

Unlike earlier, I no longer felt alone. I could feel inside of me the presence of what I'd brought with me to Everest — to prepare me, to influence me, and to give me strength in those moments of decision. In preparation for Everest, much of who I am from my life came with me to help me face my challenges. But what counted the most was what resided in my heart. And that was Sandy's love and her presence in my life, my love for her and her influence on what I did, and those specific promises I made that bound us together in trust: to live a story I could tell her and to come back home. That was the key to my strength. That was the only story worth living.

I could not go to the top and back home and tell Sandy (or anyone) the story that I kept climbing to the summit past the turnaround time, that I knew I could not get back down to High Camp in daylight, that I chose to take risks that at noon rocketed far beyond the already high risks of just being there, that I was willing to jeopardize the safety of myself and others, and that I had broken my promises to her and my team. That was not the way I wanted to climb Everest. That was not who I wanted to be. That was not who Sandy wanted me to be.

And as it turned out, if I had kept climbing up, that would be how I would be remembered. I never would have lived to tell that story.

I felt at peace within myself. I said a prayer of thanks to God. I felt no regret or disappointment for saying no. I knew, early on, that turning around was the right thing to do. But just knowing was not enough. I must never forget that the first voice, the voice of my ambition, gave me the strength to go to the top—and almost killed me. And I must never forget that the last voice, the voice of the heart, gave me the greater strength to say no to the top—and saved my life.

I SOMETIMES wonder why or how I felt strong and confident when I started down. Before then I felt physically wasted. Perhaps it was just relief that I didn't have to climb up one more step. Or the knowledge that every step I took from then on was a step to go back home. Or, maybe, it was the sense of triumph and satisfaction deep inside that comes from doing the right thing when you don't want to. Either way, it was not physical strength I felt. I believe it was God's way of helping me to get home.

The lingering words of that last voice—the voice of the heart—again and again were, *Not today. I'm going home.* My thoughts went to Sandy. It was like so often in my everyday life, when I'd call her from the office to say, "I'm coming home." This time there was no phone call, but the image of Sandy and that inner verbal embrace was there. I'm coming home.

FIVE OUT of eight Hall expedition climbers had by then, at noon, made judgments independent of the leadership not to continue for the top. They were able to say no when they had to. These were the individual decisions Rob said he expected us to make. They stuck to the turnaround time, as promised. That left the leaders and three Hall climbers—Namba, Hansen, and Krakauer—still on the long march into the nightmare.

CHAPTER 24

BURNING DAYLIGHT

THE FIRST climbers had reached the South Summit at 10 AM. Only 85 more meters to go to the top. These climbers included Mike Groom. Their arrival was within Rob's timeline. But, remarkably, they didn't continue climbing.

These climbers apparently expected new rope to be fixed on the ridge traverse from the South Summit to the Hillary Step. Why was that an expectation? I don't know. But in any event, no Sherpa were ahead fixing new rope. Steadily, more climbers reached the South Summit, including members of the Fischer expedition and some of the Sherpa from both teams. But none of those continued climbing up either. In short order, the Hall and Fischer climbers were mixed together on the South Summit.

Rob was leading from behind, so he didn't know that his team had not continued to climb up.

Everyone knew the high priority on summit day was to keep moving and to stay spread apart to avoid delays. Stay spread out. Keep moving. But that wasn't happening, while they sat and waited.

The climbers and assistant leaders had clear and simple choices about what to do. The first and best choice was to continue climbing without fixing new rope on the short ridge traverse to the Hillary Step. No rope was needed. Just continuing should have been their first impulse.

In previous years, many (if not most) climbers had climbed the short traverse without a fixed rope. We all knew that. And in fact, about 24 hours earlier, the Yugoslavs that preceded us didn't see the need for a rope there either. No doubt the climbers would have welcomed the extra security of a rope if it was there, but they were fully capable of climbing that short traverse without it. The terrain was exposed, but straightforward and not difficult.

But, if they really wanted new rope, another choice to continue climbing was to fix the rope themselves. They didn't need to wait for any Sherpa to do the work. They could help themselves. They had extra rope, and the work to fix it on the traverse was not difficult or time consuming. And then, beyond the traverse, the only location where a short section of new rope should be fixed was at the end of the ridge traverse — the Hillary Step. All climbers, past and present, fix that section. And most climbers were capable of quickly fixing that short 40 foot section with rope. No Sherpa were needed.

The final choice was to not continue climbing — to wait for the Sherpa to do the work for them. And that's what they decided to do. They waited. They waited. They sat on their butts and waited. Waited and waited. But fixing the rope never happened. Five minutes passed. Then ten minutes. Waiting and waiting. Wasting time. Half an hour. Hour and more. Ticked away. Wasting time. Then, finally, *two hours* were lost. Wasted. By waiting and doing nothing, they were burning daylight — one of the most precious and critical resources on summit day.

How could that happen? How could so much time be needlessly wasted by waiting and doing nothing? What were those climbers and leaders thinking? Shouldn't someone at least be asking questions? Talking about it? These were experienced climbers. Jon Krakauer said he was sitting there with three professionals and lost track of time while waiting for the Sherpa to fix ropes. Did no one have a sense of leadership?

They sat and waited.

Because it's so basic, everyone had to know that waiting, by itself, was a very big problem. Stopping and waiting is something you *never do* in high altitude mountaineering, except in a major emergency. Waiting is never part of any plan at that extreme altitude. Waiting only leads to trouble.

Rob's summit day plan to keep climbers moving fluidly, on pace, and spread apart had failed. Soon after Rob moved ahead of me on the buttress just below the South Summit, where the terrain put him out of direct line of sight just beyond the South Summit, he was going to be shocked to find that 28 climbers were all piled together on or about the South Summit.

How could the plan for fixing rope to avoid delay actually create delay? Easy. By having a bad plan. Somewhere along the line, and for no good reason, Rob planned for the Sherpa of both teams to work together. But that didn't happen.

At the South Summit, Ang Dorje (who was the Hall team's Sherpa leader) was sitting with the other climbers and leaders. For almost two hours and until close to noon, Ang Dorje said nothing. And no one asked him any questions, until Neal Beidelman from the Fischer team asked him if he was going to fix rope. Ang Dorje flatly said no. He offered no explanation. Maybe he too thought no ropes were needed on the traverse? Maybe he too was as muddled as everyone else about why everyone was waiting? It was not his job to tell the others to get off their butts and get moving.

Mike was at the South Summit the entire two hours. He said that Rob had earlier given him strict instructions not to get involved with ropes. Before noon, Mike tried to reach Rob on the radio, but could not get through. Leading from behind put Rob out of touch with what was happening, and he was out of position to solve the problem for everyone sitting around waiting to be helped. It came down to the Hall team leadership again being a one-man band. Rob probably thought that such a thing could never happen — so many strong and experienced climbers, including professional climbers, waiting, burning daylight, wasting so much time, and doing nothing to help themselves. That could never happen. Right? But it did.

It seemed that the Sherpa first dropped the ball, but the other climbers watched it bounce around and didn't pick it up. The climbers' inaction and decision to wait was much more consequential to the outcome than the Sherpa failure. Lobsang Jangbu, the Fischer team Sherpa leader, who was slowed down by altitude sickness, said that it was ridiculous for the other climbers, including professionals, to sit and wait for him at the South Summit to come and fix rope for them.

If the climbers had continued climbing up after reaching the South Summit, either without a new rope on the traverse or by fixing it themselves (or if the Sherpa fixed it), they would have stayed spread apart, had fluidity of movement, and likely would have faced no delay all the way to the summit and back. There would be no 1996 Everest tragedy.

THE NEW rope everyone waited for on the traverse to the Hillary Step was, in the end, *never fixed*. At noon, Anatoli and Neal of the Fischer team left the South Summit to fix rope on the Hillary Step. While moving across the ridge traverse, Anatoli merely reached down and pulled up old rope that was buried in the snow. The climbers that followed then used the old rope.

No new rope was ever needed or fixed on the traverse. All that waiting was for nothing. Two hours lost. Burning daylight. For nothing.

CHAPTER 25

OUT OF TIME

BEFORE noon, Mike tried to reach Rob on the radio. Mike's focus wasn't about fixed rope. It was about whether it was too late to keep going up. Was there enough time? What about the weather? Were we "out of time"?

It was noon. As Rob stepped on the South Summit and looked around, everything was at stake in what he did next. The situation for Rob unfolded a short distance above me, as I just started climbing back down the ridge.

What happened next determined the outcome. What happened next *is* the 1996 Everest story.

At noon, 28 climbers were on or about the South Summit. This included three climbers from the Taiwanese expedition, which was not expected to be going to the summit on May 10. Up ahead for climbing was the short traverse along the ridge to the Hillary Step, then a climb up the Step, and then a final 15 minute or so stretch on the ridge to the summit. Not far to go. About 279 vertical feet. That should have been about one and a half hours of climbing time—if no delays.

Yet we were more than two hours behind schedule. Mike and Yasuko were waiting at the South Summit for Rob when he arrived. Mike did not want to continue until he talked to Rob about the weather and the turnaround time. Mike was concerned it was too late to continue. Rob had planned to reach the summit by about 11 AM.

Andy and Jon had left the South Summit moments earlier and were on the ridge traverse a short distance away. They were behind Anatoli and Neal of the Fischer team, who headed directly to the Hillary Step. Anatoli, belayed by Neal, fixed a new rope on the short 40-foot-high Step in just a few minutes.

But the needless and wasteful time loss at the South Summit had severe consequences. The most critical was that the climbers were then *bunched together* rather than spread apart. From where Rob stood, he could see that, within a few minutes, all 28 climbers would be moving close together on the short traverse between the South Summit and the Hillary Step. Then, in 35 to 40 minutes, they would again be at a stop and bunched together at the base of the Hillary Step waiting for their turns to climb the Step.

Looking across the traverse to the Hillary Step, with that large number of climbers close together, Rob could see the inevitable long delays getting *up and down* the Hillary Step. The Hillary Step itself is a natural chokepoint that stalls climbing traffic because only one climber at a time should be on the rope while climbing up or down that section.

Much additional time would be lost at the Step. No doubt about it. And the weather was changing. Clouds developed below and the wind increased, which was one of the concerns Mike wanted to discuss with Rob. When Mike raised the weather question at noon, Rob said, "It'll be all right, provided it doesn't get worse."

DELAYS climbing both up and down the Hillary Step would not be a surprise to anyone. This had happened before. The problem dated back to the late 1980s — long before professional expeditions came along. Coincidentally, and very importantly, it had happened on 10 May 1993, exactly three years earlier, and both Rob and Mike were there on different expeditions. Rob had summited that day for the third time, and Mike for the first. Mike was caught in a long delay as six climbers preceded him up the Step. And then he waited again on the way down. If six were significant for delay, what would you say about 28 — both up and down?

However, the situation in 1993 also made the point that the number of climbers on summit day, by itself, was not the problem. A record number of 40 climbers reached the summit on 10 May 1993. But the critical difference was that in 1993 they'd started to reach the summit by 9:30 AM, and ended at 1 PM. That was almost four hours earlier than now. So the time of day was more critical than the number of climbers. What mattered the most in 1993 (and now) was to be spread out and early enough when climbers first bumped into the Hillary Step chokepoint.

Until the waiting at the South Summit began late morning, the combined number of climbers from the Hall and Fischer expeditions was not a problem. Until then, the climbers were on time and spread apart on the route and fluidly moving along without delay. But as they bunched together to wait for ropes — ropes they didn't need — the combined number of climbers was a problem that would soon become much worse at the Hillary Step. Many more hours would then be lost, just waiting at an altitude close to the edge of outer space.

So many climbers had never before been jammed together on Everest so high and so late. This would be a new record in Mount Everest climbing history. But this was not a world record Rob was shooting for — a record that no one would want to be part of.

FROM WHERE they were in the crowd, with the inevitable major delay ahead at the Hillary Step, Yasuko, Doug, Mike, and Rob had absolutely no chance of reaching the summit by 1 PM, and for that matter by 2 or 3 PM. In addition, everyone's second canister of O2 would run out in another hour, before they could get to the summit and back to the South Summit for their third canister. There was not a worse place on the mountain to run out of O2. This was not a close call decision for Rob, as leader. And, that time calculation, focuses only on getting up to the top — not getting back down.

To get back down after reaching the top, they faced further delays from waiting in line to climb down the Hillary Step. All or most of the climbers, and certainly Yasuko, Doug, Mike, and Rob in the middle and at the back of them, would almost certainly be out of daylight, out of O2, and on the edge (if not over) of being out of strength and body heat before getting back to High Camp. The extreme risks of climbing down the final section to High Camp in the dark would be a nightmare scenario.

The time to turn back was right then — at noon — both as a matter of remaining faithful to the team turnaround time agreement and as a matter of mountaineering good judgment for safety.

AS AN astonishing coincidence, at almost the same time of day and place exactly 12 months earlier, on 10 May 1995, Rob had faced the same decision.

At 12:30 PM, he and his expedition of four climbers were on or about the South Summit. No other climbers were above or below. Rob's team faced no delays, up or down, at the Hillary Step, but they were behind the schedule Rob had set for the safety margin needed to get to the summit and back to High Camp before dark. That was the decision point. They were "out of time." One year ago almost to the moment, Rob stayed steadfast to the turnaround time and turned back. His demonstrated strength of leadership and good judgment that day were what led me to climb Everest with him. But last year's decision making pressures did not include an embedded writer for publicity or leadership competition with another expedition.

SO, TWO years in a row, Rob faced the same situation. Only 279 more vertical feet to go out of 29,000. So close. Everyone can get to the top. And everyone wants to. So, now what?

So close, but out of time. Turn around or keep going? That's the dilemma Rob faced at noon. What to do next was the question.

Rob decided to keep going to the summit.

Mike, Doug, and Yasuko followed Rob's lead.

At noon, of all the decision making pressures Rob confronted, the force probably most influential of all was the sight of the Fischer climbers going for it. All but Scott Fischer were just ahead on the ridge traverse heading for the summit. Rob saw that from the South Summit. That sight no doubt had a powerful influence, along with the sight of Jon Krakauer, Rob's expected publicity machine, also among those going for it. The only way for Rob to neutralize the leadership and business promotion publicity competition with Scott was to keep going.

At noon, was Rob a leader or a follower?

For Rob, the influencing forces were huge and powerful — the head-to-head competition with Scott; the competition for future expedition climbers; the ego and pride; the personal recognition from setting a world record for ascents; and the expected magazine promotional publicity.

For Rob, facing the possibility of not reaching the top two years in a row, when he was as close as the South Summit, would be difficult to explain, and especially so if the Fischer team reached the top and returned safely. If it all worked out for Scott and his team, even if by a miracle of luck, the mountaineering culture would treat Scott as a bold and courageous leader. And Rob, just the opposite if he turned back. That outcome would have a major adverse impact on Rob's expedition business.

When I made my decision to climb Everest in 1996, a major influencing factor was Rob's 1995 decision to turn back so close. I saw that decision as showing strength and character. I never could have imagined that Rob's 1995 decision could put him in a position of not being able to make the same decision in 1996, if he had to do that. A cruel irony.

WHOSE voice should have told Rob he was making the wrong decision? His assistant leader Mike? His assistant leader Andy, who had never summited Everest? Would the initially planned veteran leadership team of Hall, Viesturs, and Cotter have made a difference?

Several voices spoke up, but not in words. Voices spoke when some of Rob's strongest climbers turned around. Frank Fischbeck, with the experience of three prior Everest attempts, turned around because he didn't believe the day was safe. Stu and Taske turned around just before noon, a short distance below Rob because it was too late, too crowded, and past the turnaround time. It was no coincidence that Taske and Stu were seasoned decision makers, accustomed to making hard calls in their professional careers. They, as well as Frank, were independent, self-reliant thinkers. They needed Rob the least for judgment and decision making, and were not under the pressures of business, competition, publicity, and a quest for recognition. They were not there as part of their job and to advance their career, but only for the love of the sport. My voice spoke too when I was the last to turn back.

Finally, a loud and strong voice that Rob should have heard was that of Beck, still at the Balcony. Since sunrise, Beck had been left there alone. He was in trouble and needed assistance getting down. He waited for Rob's return. This unresolved problem should have been weighing on Rob's conscience. Under all climbing standards, Beck should have been helped right away at sunrise and should not have been left behind at the Balcony alone. His situation was a ticking time bomb.

Chokepoint

CHAPTER 26

ONE HOUR LATER

THE ILLUSTRATION opposite pictures the view from the South
Summit at 1 PM, one hour after Rob decided to keep going. It shows
the ridge traverse to the Hillary Step, and the ridge above and beyond
that leads to the main summit (just out of view). Seventeen climbers
are shown. Another three are close above, but out of view, and another eight are close behind, also out of view.

Since noon, over the last hour, Rob saw this unfolding. Rob himself
had not moved at all in one full hour. The foreseeable delay at the
Hillary Step had happened. Burning more daylight. There was no
more opportunity for denial, as 25 more climbers waited to take their
turn to climb the Step. It was already 1 PM. One climber said, "It was
so many people—like a line in a supermarket." And, after going to
the summit, all had to come back down the Step and face waiting in
line all over again. Burning still more daylight.

Without the delay of standing in line, it was about a one and a half
hour climb from the South Summit to the main summit. But the
picture makes it clear that because the climbers were so bunched
together there would be major delays of two or three or more hours
at the Hillary Step. Some would experience the delay on the way up.
Some on the way down. And some both up and down. Chokepoints
like the Hillary Step are a short distance. But, so frequently in climb-

193

ing, what's important is not distance. Instead, it's the time it takes to cover that distance. And that time varies depending upon the number of climbers involved. Scott Fischer arrived at the summit at 3:40 PM, followed by the final three others, with Doug last at 4:00 PM. As it turned out, four of the climbers who were close behind but out of the picture decided to turn back after reaching the South Summit. They were Sherpa. Looking at the picture and seeing what they saw on the ridge in front of them, it is clear why they turned back.

IN THE early afternoon, other expeditions on the mountain followed the climb. Among those were veterans Ed Viesturs, David Breashears, Jamling Norgay, Goran Kropp, and Sherpa Ang Rita. They either listened to radio transmissions at Base Camp or Camp 2, or watched the climbers on the upper ridge traverse through a telescope. (From Camp 2, you can see that area 7,400 feet directly above.)

These veterans thought the climbers were far too late, even at 1 PM. They became more alarmed when they heard radio reports and could see that climbers were still climbing across the traverse toward (not back from) the Hillary Step at 2:30 and 3:00 PM.

Jamling Tenzing Norgay, deputy leader of the Imax expedition, was one of those who watched through a telescope from Camp 2. After finally spotting climbers in the early afternoon, he thought at first they had reached the top and were on the way down. He found it unbelievable that the climbers were actually going up. He was convinced they would be coming down in the dark and into the bad weather that still raked the upper mountain every afternoon.

"Why aren't they turning around?" Ed Viesturs asked, while watching through a telescope. "I can't understand why they are still going on." "It's going to be 3 or 4 PM before they get to the summit," "Guys, turn around, turn around."

David Breashears was among those veterans at Camp 2 listening to reports and watching through a telescope. Referring to the climbers still forging across the traverse on the way up, he remarked that they wouldn't be back to the South Summit until at least 4 PM and were willfully giving away their small margin of safety and ability to return to High Camp in daylight.

Ang Rita, the most experienced Sherpa on the mountain in 1996 (he reached the summit nine times) was quoted at Base Camp as saying, "This too late, too late." Ang Rita was a Sherpa on the Goran Kropp Swedish expedition. Goran himself was at Base Camp on May 10 and, while listening to the radio for news, said that he expected Rob to turn around soon because he knew how strict Rob was about the turnaround time. A week earlier, when Goran had turned around at the South Summit, Rob praised him for his decision and told people at Base Camp, "That showed incredibly good judgment on Goran's part. I'm more impressed than if he had continued to the top."

Our paths would never cross again.

CHAPTER 27

CROSSING PATHS AND INTO THE CLOUDS

ONCE I turned around, I never thought again about my decision. I had a new focus. I had to get down. And climbing down can be the toughest part of any climb. Accidents are more common on the way down because so many variables work against you. Fatigue, dehydration, energy depletion, and hypoxia had been accumulating over the past 52 hours of my 59 hour long march.

The visual sensation of climbing down is much different from climbing up. When going up you are facing in, looking at your feet and frequently a rope. The mountain is close in front of your eyes. But when going down, most of the time you are facing out into space. As you look down, everything is far away.

The biomechanics of climbing down are also technically more difficult. On the climb up, your front foot is planted before you shift your weight to it. But coming down is the opposite. You shift your weight before the front foot is planted and the surface is further away, making for a less stable situation.

The initial sections coming down were steep. After a while, I saw another climber in a blue suit climbing up toward me. As the climber came closer, I realized it was Scott Fischer. I had known Scott for a long time, but only casually. Scott spent part of his youth growing up in Michigan, so we always reminded each other of our common link. Michigan is not known for many people interested in climbing.

Over the years our paths had occasionally crossed in the mountains. Scott was gregarious and charismatic and everyone who met him seemed to like him, me included. Now we were both close to the top of Everest. As we met, we had a short conversation. I said, "It's too late, Scott. I'm going down." Scott looked right at me, with a little new snow on his blonde hair and a twinkle in his eye, and without hesitation he said, "Good decision, Lou. Good decision." I was not emotional about it. And neither was he. It was just a matter of fact. Neither of us acted as though we had any concerns. It was more a moment of climber fellowship. We chatted for a few minutes about what a beautiful, but hard, place Everest is. And then our paths literally crossed—Scott climbed up, and I climbed down.

It didn't strike me then that while he thought my decision to go down was good, he continued up. I wasn't thinking like that. Nor did I sense that Scott was physically struggling or ill. Being legendary for his strength and power as a climber, if he were having a problem I probably wouldn't have believed it even if I saw it.

As it turned out, Scott was right about one thing. It was a good decision. It was too late—even for Scott. He summited at 3:40 PM, but he couldn't make it back down to High Camp and froze to death just below the gully leading to the Balcony.

Our paths would never cross again.

AS I CLIMBED down the ridge, I saw two people at the Balcony. I was glad to see someone. I tried to pick up my pace in order to catch up before they left. As I got closer, I could see that one was standing and the other was sitting on the snow on top of his red backpack. The standing climber looked up and I saw that it was Taske. That felt like good news. The one sitting down was covered with a dusting of snow. "My God, it's Beck," said my inner voice as I got close. That did not feel like good news. I had forgotten about Beck. I had forgotten he was in trouble. I had forgotten he was left alone all this time.

"Beck, how you doing?" I asked. He was cold. So was I. But Beck never complained about anything. Taske and I told Beck to come with us and we would help him down. We discussed how best to assist him. Did he need short roping for protection because of his blindness? We did not have a rope. Beck finally declined our offer. He had promised Rob he would stay and wait for Rob's return.

I didn't recall what Taske said to me earlier on the ridge when he was turning around. But I now learned that he, like Stu, thought it was too late. Taske was concerned about losing daylight and facing much colder temperatures without O2 before getting back down. I asked him if he had any water because mine was a block of ice. He did. I was thankful for the drink, but reserved in the amount I drank because he didn't have much.

While we were standing with Beck, Sherpa Lhakpa Chhiri joined us, after his delivery of O2 at the South Summit (his job for the day). We asked him if he had a rope, and he said no. With the resources of three professional climbers and three Sherpa coming down behind us, Taske and I had no reservations about getting going. In fact, it seemed best and safest for us to keep moving: we needed to move to keep warm and the weather was worsening. The wind was getting stronger by the minute. Snow was swirling around. Visibility was poor and getting poorer.

We bid our farewell to Beck and started down. The Balcony is at the top of a steep gully full of dry, sugar-like snow. Taske went first, and Lhakpa and I followed. The technique for descending the terrain was to face outward and climb down in sort of a plunge step with your ice axe hand held off to the side. You can move quickly and securely, even on steep terrain like this gully.

Suddenly, the snow gave way under Taske and he disappeared from sight. My heart lurched. I scanned the terrain. Then I caught sight of him falling down the mountain. He was on his back, face up with his feet below, racing downhill. Unless Taske self-arrested the fall—and quickly—he was on a runaway toboggan slide a couple of miles into Nepal.

Lhakpa and I glanced at each other, with our eyes bugged out in sheer terror. I slammed my ice axe into the snow like a stake. I dropped to my knees as I turned my body around facing the mountain, all while looking over my shoulder at the crisis unfolding below me. Lhakpa did the same. For the moment, there was simply nothing we could do but hang on and watch.

The only way Taske would survive was to get his body weight over the pick of his ice axe and force it into the snow. Since he was face up on his back, he first brought his ice axe across his chest, and then he rolled over toward the pick and dug it firmly into the snow, and came to a stop. It was textbook. He kept his cool and applied mountaineering skills that saved his life. This was what you want to see in your fellow climber. This composure and skillful self-arrest came from Taske's experience, guts, and cool head. No wonder the guy had been an SAS commando in the Australian Armed Forces.

Taske looked back up to us with an expression on his face that said, "Be careful." You bet I would, I said to myself. Even before Taske came to a stop, Lhakpa took off. I assumed he was going to give Taske assistance, but Lhakpa whizzed right by him. If Taske had needed assistance, I have no doubt Lhakpa would have responded. But the Sherpa stay very focused on doing only their assigned job. He must have assumed nothing more was needed. John was safe.

John waited as I caught up. "That one made me nervous," I said to him. He gave me a dismissive shrug, to tell me he was okay, let's get going, and we can talk about it later.

By now, it was clear that we were moving down into a bad weather system. The snow intensified. The wind grew stiffer. New snow covered the footsteps made during the ascent. The route was harder and harder to read. I felt a rising sense of dread.

"Let's try to keep up with Lhakpa, or at least keep him in sight. He has been here before and he knows the best way back to the barn," I said. Keep up with Lhakpa? Not a chance. Keeping him in sight, yes, but not for long. He was too fast, and clouds rolled up and visibility shrank by the minute.

It appeared that Lhakpa had also figured out it was too late. In total from various teams, four Sherpa turned back at the South Summit around noon. Perhaps it was because they had done their job for the day delivering O2 canisters. But, more likely, they knew they were out of time. On May 10, no Sherpa died, none had to be rescued, and none were injured.

I never thought about the climbers above me. Everyone had to get down—on their own. All my mental energy was devoted to my next step. "Make no mistake," said my inner voice.

As we climbed down, Taske was right in front of me. Looking down, I saw only clouds. I couldn't tell if we were climbing down into a storm or if the storm was moving up to engulf us. But, with every step, we were getting more concerned. More dread. At one point Taske stopped and asked me to put his O2 mask inside his pack. He had run out long ago. For both of us, intense concentration on each step ruled over all other adversities. "Make no mistakes," said my inner voice—over and over. I wore large, expedition weight gloves and in the rush to get into John's pack I took them off and jammed them at the point where a fixed rope was anchored to the mountain face. A climber never sets his gloves down because it is so easy to lose control of them, especially in high winds. The wind will blow them or they just slide away. I rarely made that mistake. In this case, I thought my gloves were secure, but something else intervened.

Rocks tumbled down from above. My first concern was getting killed from falling rock. Then my concern shifted as I saw rocks hit the exact spot where my gloves were, dislodging them. I watched them slide down the mountain face. Taske looked at me. I looked at him. This was not good.

Actually, we were concerned more about the falling rocks than the lost gloves.

"How did that happen?" Taske said. "Somebody must be climbing down above us," he replied to his own question. Sure enough, a short time later, a climber moved very quickly past us without saying a word. It was Anatoli Boukreev of the Fischer expedition. Someone later said he was cold from not using O2 and needed to quickly head back to High Camp.

I wore a pair of fairly heavy glove liners, but in 30 below zero temperature they didn't help much. I had back-up expedition mittens in my pack, but they were more difficult to work with when using climbing hardware on a fixed rope. John felt responsible for the loss of my gloves and wanted to give me his. But I was getting very anxious about the weather and I just said, "Go, go, go, let's go. We've got to move."

The section fixed with rope ended. Finding the way from there was much more difficult. We were in a full storm. Visibility was down to a few feet. With no definition, I had vertigo and felt unsure about every step I took. I was not sure what was below and even what direction to take. Countless stories are told of climbers coming down in bad visibility and walking off the side of an overhanging cornice and plunging thousands of feet into midair. In bad weather like this, it is sometimes difficult to distinguish the mountain edge from the sky beneath you.

We were now on the steep ice bulge section above High Camp. As we climbed down we didn't want to get off line to the camp, even by a few degrees. If I moved too far off line to the left, I would fall 7,000 feet off the Kangshung Face into China. Or if I moved too far off line to the right, I would fall 4,000 feet into Nepal. Where was the line? Through the passing visibility, one second I saw it and the next I didn't.

Then we got a break. I noticed the crampon marks we had made in the ice on the way up. The wind blew new snow horizontally across the ice, and the snow did not stick to fill in these marks. Following the spike marks was like following a bread crumb trail. But the ice bulge was steep and tricky—hard, blue ice. Because of the lack of visibility, climbing down facing out didn't work. I needed to get visually closer to the ice to see the marks. Moving diagonally allowed for a hunched-over position, but then I lost track of the marks. So I turned and faced into the mountain.

Normally this technique leads to less visibility and more difficult route finding, but it was perfect for this situation. I simply looked at the ice in front of my face. With the palm of my hand over the adze of my ice axe, I pushed the pick into the ice, looked between my legs, and backed down the mountain on the front crampon points on my boots following the old marks.

After the ice bulge, we were on easier terrain, but visibility was almost zero. All I saw was snow swirling and dancing before my eyes. The roar of the wind deafened and disoriented me. The roar of rage. Suddenly we spotted the shapes of our tents. We moved faster. Really fast. Faster than I thought possible. I don't know where that strength came from. But we knew this was our shot at survival. We didn't want to lose visibility before reaching the tents.

Finally. Relief. Taske went to his tent.

I then found my tent. I took my crampons off and, along with my ice axe, I set them right next to the tent door. I crawled inside. I was on my knees. My first priority was to drop my head into my trembling and freezing hands and say, "Thank you God for giving me the strength I needed to come back home." I had no idea at that moment that I wasn't even close to being back home. I had no idea that this very place could be my eternal home. I fumbled to take off my climbing suit. I crawled inside my sleeping bag. I don't know if I fell asleep or collapsed unconscious from exhaustion, but I think it was the latter.

On the way down, I never doubted having enough physical reserves. But that was an illusion. My body now told me that nothing was left. Nothing. My last molecule of energy was gone.

It was about 5 PM May 10.

CHAPTER 28

SANDY BACK HOME — MAY 10

A SHORT TIME after I turned around, Rob reported to Base Camp that "Lou turned around at the South Summit." That was the message then sent shortly later by Base Camp to Rob's New Zealand office by satellite phone, and from there to Sandy in Michigan. Within minutes, Sandy reported the news to our friends in her May 10 Everest Update. Based on the details Sandy had received from Base Camp, here is what she wrote:

Friday, May 10, 1996

6 AM (4 PM Nepal time)

Everest Update from Sandy:

The call came at 5:30 AM. Rob Hall reported to Base Camp and Base Camp to me, that Lou climbed to within 100 meters from the summit. At the time of the call, Lou was on his way back to Camp 4.

Everest is 29,028 ft. high. Lou climbed to 28,700 ft. Turning back 100 meters (328 feet) from the summit must have been a very difficult decision for Lou, as well as a disappointment. He did say that he planned to lose no fingers or toes and would only turn back for reasons of safety or frostbite. Hopefully the decision he made was timely and all is well.

I should hear from Lou in a few days. I will pass on more information at that time.

I have a feeling there is more to Lou's story.

Sandy

This Update was written in Michigan at the exact time I was climbing down into the clouds on the Triangular Face above the South Col. It was sent about one hour before I reached High Camp. Sandy's Update was sent three days before I could even talk to her about what happened. Still, Sandy intuitively spoke to the essence of the story.

Time and decision making: indeed, that's what this story is all about — and not just for me. Making a decision — about time, and on time. A story about running out of time.

Sandy knew from the report she received that I made the difficult decision to turn around. But what she didn't know was that, at first, from the driving force of my ambition, I'd made the reckless decision to keep going. That, at first, I was not strong enough to turn back. That I made the wrong decision, which put me on a path to an eternal grave of Everest ice and snow.

But the best part of Sandy's "more to Lou's story" intuition was that, without her knowing so at the time of her report, she was a main actor in the part of the story when I was given a second chance.

What's so special to me in this story is how that second chance came about.

How can I explain that racing, beating heart? And, after the wind, the sheer silence and the feeling of physical detachment? And then, after the wind, the voice that led me to turn back?

Here is what I believe.

It was all about the heart. The heart has a voice. The heart spoke.

Since the beating heart was the only sound I could hear in those uncommon moments of decision, that voice was the voice of the heart. But, that voice within me telling me to turn back was not my inner voice. It's not possible for me to say that my unassisted thought and decision process led to my survival. That would also not explain the mystery of the beating heart, the sheer silence, and the feeling of physical detachment. The explanation of the source of that voice goes deeper into personal and spiritual places.

The voice of the heart was Sandy's voice. That beating heart—which may even have been Sandy's heart—was crying out to be heard. And the sheer silence made sure I heard that heart give voice.

All this may sound mystical, but I have known for a long time that I don't hear only my own voice within me. From the depth and strength of our relationship from 28 years of marriage and love for each other, Sandy's voice has been embedded within me. I'm sure most of the time Sandy's voice speaks below my level of awareness; but sometimes, such as 10 May 1996, I can, and do, become fully aware of its presence, especially when words of promise are involved.

At close to noon on Everest, a short distance below the summit, it was Sandy back home, through the influencing voice of the heart, who spoke about my promises to live a story I could tell her, and to come back home. That voice—to live that story—won the struggle within me, and led me to turn back, and saved my life.

If I had not heard Sandy's voice during those moments of sheer silence, at about the same time she was writing her Everest Update to our friends, she would likely be getting different news—the news that I would be staying on Everest for eternity, the news that I would be leaving her back home alone—with a broken heart.

But, as it turned out, Sandy was there within me. She was "living my story" with me. I believe the heart was the sound of sheer silence—a still, small voice from God, spoken through God's gift to me of Sandy's love.

Alone and Blind

CHAPTER 29

BLINDED BY LIGHT

I WOKE to the roar of the wind. Of rage. I bounced around inside the tent—terrified. I was alone, disoriented, and for a moment I could not mentally comprehend what was happening. My eyes would not open. They were sealed shut. I couldn't see.

I yelled "Beck! Andy!" No one—if anyone was around—could hear me over the roar of the wind. My eyes stung with sharp pain. Was it totally dark or what? I suddenly realized what had happened, but with an even greater sense of panic mixed with dread. I was blind, snowblind from intense sunburn of the cornea. No wonder my eyes were stinging sharply with pain. The feeling was like a welding torch had been put to my eyes. I had been concerned during the day about snow blindness when I had problems with eye protection. Now it was real.

By now the wind was in full hurricane force. It was the wind bouncing me around inside the tent. It felt like one of my tentmates was shoving me. The wind got under the floor of the tent, and was picking me up in my sleeping bag and slamming me back down on the ice. The sound and the feeling were like a freight train rolling over on top of me—rumbling, thundering, and bouncing me around underneath. A roar of rage.

Nobody? Where is everybody? Why am I here alone? How long have I been unconscious? What day is it? How am I going to get out of here?

"I am going to die." So this is what it feels like to know you're in your final moments. I felt helpless, because I could not see. It took me a few minutes to finally comprehend that I was at High Camp, after returning from my summit attempt. The weather was bad when I returned. I remembered that. But now it seemed worse. Or at least the wind was worse, from what I could sense from the sound. A roar of rage. I couldn't see what else was happening. And I was cold. Really cold.

I had to do something. I knew I had few options. But I felt compelled to act. Something bad was happening to me, and I couldn't just lie there.

So, I unzipped and crawled out of my sleeping bag and groped around in the tent—trying to do what, I was not sure. Just something. But I soon figured out this was a bad idea because it was too cold, and I was going no place anyway. Earlier, when I had returned to the tent, I took off my climbing suit. Now I was in just my thermal underwear. I was very cold. I was in a tent designed for four people. But after groping around blind, I could not find my way back to my sleeping bag.

I was at 26,000 feet and lost in a small space. I was hypoxic, blind, and freezing to death. The intensity of the noise and the wind compounded the hunt for my sleeping bag. A roar of rage.

I wasn't technically blind. But I might as well have been because I couldn't open my eyes and keep them open. Eventually I found my sleeping bag and crawled inside. I tried to calm down. The idea seemed pretty weird—being disoriented and lost inside a tent.

The roar. The unbelievable rage of the wind. I can still hear it today. I zipped into my sleeping bag and lay like a mummy, with only my face showing. Water poured out of my eyes, which is the body's natural response to protect the injured cornea. I wanted to blot my eyes. But my hands and arms were zipped inside my sleeping bag. It was too cold to unzip and bring them out. But I knew I had to blot my eyes, or the cold air would freeze my eyeballs into blocks of ice. The thought and visualization of frozen eyeballs lingered in my head. I tried to keep down the feeling of panic.

I lay there, shivering, gasping for air, and wondering what to do next. There I was, in my tent, alone, high on Everest, deep in a hostile place where human life can't be sustained for very long. My body and my brain were dying, minute by minute, from oxygen starvation. I decided the best thing to do was to stay with my sleeping bag, but I was worried about the wind. The rage. I was in a tent. How long would it hold up in a hurricane?

"I am going to die." This is what it feels like. Knowing. I always wondered what it would be like. What will it be like to be dead? I thought. My life didn't flash in front of my eyes, and I didn't have images of Sandy. Instead, my focus was myopic. I needed a plan. One step at a time. Be methodical. I rehearsed my steps. Unzip my sleeping bag. Blot my watering eyes. Figure out if the wind was tearing up the tent. Keep warm. Find water to drink. The tent could not possibly withstand for long the intensive torture from the hurricane force winds. What would I do if the tent tore up — or, worse yet, blew away with me inside? It could blow me into China or Nepal. I would surely die if I got caught out in the elements at 26,000 feet in a hurricane force blizzard without my gear on. I better be ready. The wind. A roar of rage.

Where was everyone else? Andy, Beck, Doug?

After completing the first steps of my plan, I got back into my sleeping bag. I lay there planning my next move. I decided to put my gear on. I needed to put on my climbing suit and boots. Forget the harness.

I wouldn't need that, and it would be too complicated to try to get on. I needed to find my ice axe and crampons. I needed to be ready to fight. But where was my stuff? How could I put it on if I couldn't open my eyes? I just lay there in my mummy bag. Gasping for air. Rehearsing the plan of what I was going to do. Rehearsing step by step. My eyes were in intense pain. I tried to crack them open, like a squint, but that didn't help. They automatically slammed shut. The wind. A roar of rage.

I finally unzipped my sleeping bag and felt around to locate my gear. Fortunately, I had put everything in a neat pile in the corner of the tent when I arrived earlier—an old habit of mine. I started to put it on—as best I could. The hardest part was putting on my boots. It took forever. I first needed to decide which was the right and the left foot. I could only tell the difference because the right had a special insole that I could feel. I needed to stop and rest several times from the physical effort of putting them on. Your feet don't just slide into those things. I then found the tent door and unzipped it, and reached outside to bring my crampons and ice axe inside with me. I thought about putting the crampons on my feet. I decided not to because I wanted to be able to crawl back inside my sleeping bag. With crampons on, I would tear the bag into pieces.

Now I was ready for the worst. Or at least I was as ready as I could be. I got back into my sleeping bag, after having done all this blind. What next? I decided there was nothing more I could do, or should do. Sit tight for now. In this wind, without eyesight, this was not the time to leave where I was. My eyes, the wind, the roar. The rage. The unbelievable roar. I just laid there, seemingly forever, in the dark. Alone.

Am I really going to die?

Now the matter of dying became a question, and not a conclusive statement.

But how would I ever get out of here? I was at 26,000 feet. In one of the most hostile places on the planet. In a storm. And I was blind. Where were Andy, Beck, and Doug? Why were my tentmates not here? The wind. A roar of rage.

THE ZIPPER of the tent door was opening. I could hear it. I'll never forget that moment, that sound. Someone crawled inside. I knew then that I wasn't going to die alone, at 26,000 feet in the Death Zone.

CHAPTER 30

DOWN INTO DARKNESS

NO WONDER I was alone. Andy, Beck, and Doug, my tentmates, didn't make it back. Getting to the top of Everest was one thing; but as Rob said, "The trick is to get back down alive." Over time, the puzzle pieces of what happened to them fell into place.

Delay at the Hillary Step wasn't limited to those waiting at the bottom to climb up. Climbers on the way down from the summit had to wait at the top of the Step before climbing down it. They had to wait until all the climbers lined up below were up the Step before they could use the rope anchored at the top of the Step to rappel down.

The supermarket line went in both directions. Some at the bottom of the Step were waiting to go up. Some at the top were waiting to go down. As the number of climbers at the bottom shrank, the number at the top grew. Wait and wait.

At the top of the Step on the way back from the summit, Jon and Andy were among those who had to wait. When going up the Step, for those at the front of the line like Jon and Andy, the 24 plus climbers close behind them waiting to climb were of little concern. But coming down, those in front had to switch places and now face the tensions and troubles of waiting in line.

Because of the stalled traffic in climbing up and down the Hillary Step, Jon, Mike, Yasuko, and Andy didn't make it back to the South

Summit until between 3:00 and 3:30 PM. Rob and Doug were on their way much later.

On the way back to the South Summit, Jon's O2 ran out, and he was unmoving on the ridge. Luckily for Jon, Mike came along and selflessly gave Jon his O2. Mike was willing to take the risk that without O2 he would not have the same immobilizing response as Jon. Mike made a major sacrifice to help Jon get moving. Jon was then able to continue until they reached the O2 cache at the South Summit.

By the time Andy reached the South Summit, he was also out of O2 and extremely hypoxic. He was so debilitated from the high altitude that he couldn't distinguish full O2 canisters from empty ones. Andy thought they were all empty, and he gave that misinformation to others. Andy was clearly beyond normal hypoxia, and he was in big trouble from the high altitude.

DOUG WAS caught in the traffic logjam of climbers waiting to climb up the Hillary Step. At that time, no specific red flag showed that Doug was in trouble. Doug moved along at the pace of the other climbers ahead of him. He was in the parade, and marching in time. But since everyone moved at a creeping pace, no one could tell much about Doug's real physical reserve condition.

The Everest veterans following the climb at Base Camp and Camp 2 said the time was "desperately late" for all climbers. About 2:30 PM, Mike radioed Rob, who was on the summit waiting for Doug. Mike and Yasuko were coming down from the summit. Mike told Rob that Doug was just above the Hillary Step. Rob was only a few minutes of climbing time away, but because of a hump on the ridge, Doug was out of Rob's line of sight.

Rob then waited an unbelievable one and a half hours — until 4 PM — for Doug to climb a distance that the other climbers were climbing in fifteen minutes or so. To wait that long, at 29,000 feet, is unthinkable. Doug obviously couldn't keep pace with the climbers ahead of him. His inertia should have put Rob on high alert that Doug was in trouble. This would be so even without the other circumstances to consider—Doug's decision to turn around earlier in the day because he was feeling bad, his not being part of the same acclimatization adjustment process as the others, and his problem at high altitude the year before.

Doug was in serious physical strength deficit, and probably out of O2. Rob knew that Doug had changed his O2 canister just after sunrise, which at the normal flow rate would be out by about 1 PM. It was possible the canister lasted for another hour or so, depending on the flow rate and if Doug turned off the flow while waiting in line. But it's more probable that by 4 PM Doug had been out of O2 for three hours.

When Doug finally arrived at the summit at 4 PM, three hours past the safety turnaround time, Rob radioed Base Camp with the "good news." Then, shortly after 4 PM, Rob and Doug started climbing down. On the summit ridge, just above the Hillary Step, Doug collapsed. At first he could barely move, and then he couldn't move at all.

All the other climbers were by then below Rob and Doug. Rob radioed for help. He wanted a fresh canister of O2, hoping it would help Doug get moving. Andy came on the radio and said there were none. Full canisters were, in fact, at the South Summit cache site, but Andy still believed they were empty. Rob then tried to get Doug moving without new O2, instead of climbing down the Step and going the short distance to check the supplies himself. It would not have taken long for Rob to do that, but he didn't. And trying to get Doug moving was to no avail.

What does Rob do next? At 4:30 PM, Rob and Doug were on the summit ridge just above the Hillary Step, only minutes below the top. Doug can't move. As Rob said many times, "If you're not mobile—it's over. If you are in trouble that high, you might as well be at the moon." If Rob didn't do something quickly, he would be out of time to do anything at all.

AT NOON and later, Rob may have been in denial about the consequences of his leadership decision to disregard—by a large margin—the safety turnaround time. But at 4:30 PM, there could be no denial. Rob could see Doug—right in front of him—and Rob had to know how horribly bad his decision at noon had turned out. Rob also had to know that by waiting so long on the summit for Doug, in practical reality, he had encouraged Doug to continue so desperately late. Rob even moved down a short distance from the top to assist Doug in the final stretch.

Rob could no longer deny his bad judgment. His only hope was to somehow get away with it. But how? What to do next? What would "getting away with it" mean? Rob survives? Doug survives? Both survive?

Rob brought upon himself a true dilemma of two hard choices. One choice was to keep going down, leave Doug behind to die, but try to save himself by surviving the 3,000 foot climb down. Without daylight on the final part of the descent, that would be a big challenge even for a veteran professional climber like Rob. With that choice, if Rob survived, he would face harsh criticism as a professional climber and expedition leader. The record would show that Rob had led Doug to his death. Rob would take a major, perhaps unrecoverable, blow to his standing as a professional. Rob would know that, as part of that choice.

The other choice was for Rob to stay behind with Doug, and do his best to get Doug mobile again. And if that were possible, to then hope for a miracle to get himself and Doug down the Hillary Step and then down another 3,000 feet to High Camp before freezing to death in the dark. It was already 4:30 PM. That was a choice for which a good outcome was almost impossible.

So, Rob was either condemned as a professional or dead.

He had to choose.

Later, Mike told a story about a leadership meeting at Base Camp before the summit push. Referring to a career as a professional climber, Rob told Mike that if a climber dies under your leadership "you might as well be dead."

Rob chose to stay behind with Doug.

They froze to death.

WHY WAS Andy still at the South Summit at 4:30 PM?

Andy, Jon, Mike, and Yasuko arrived back at the South Summit together. The three others then left Andy there at about 3:30 PM, an hour earlier, for the climb down. Andy was seriously hypoxic and in trouble when they arrived at the South Summit. But the assumption was that he would recover once he connected to fresh O2. With all their individual mental and physical struggles, anxieties, and the pressures that climbers feel so high, such an assumption was probably easy to make. Jon later said the seriousness of Andy's trouble simply didn't register with him. He also partially attributed his lack of recognition of Andy's trouble to the "guide illusion," which postulates that professional climbers never need your help. This illusion leads others to neglect to recognize when a professional climber actually does need help.

Andy did need help, but no one was there to help him. Andy stayed behind at the South Summit. Again, why? At 3:30 PM, Rob was above Andy, along with Doug and two Sherpa, leaving no reason for

Andy to stay behind as an added resource. Why did Andy stay at the South Summit?

That's still a mystery. One view is that he just could not get going again. Another is that Andy did start down from the South Summit, but intuitively knew Rob might need help and returned. I like to think the latter.

At that early stage of the desperately late descent, things were already going terribly wrong. About 3,000 vertical feet of demanding descent was still ahead of all the climbers. But the physical climbing was not the only problem they faced. By being so late, more serious problems would come from the already lost body function, body heat, strength, O2 supplies, and the magnification of the ever present effects of hypoxia, dehydration, sleep deprivation, and malnutrition.

And they were running out of daylight. The loss of daylight meant more than a loss of visibility. Additionally, the air temperature, which in daylight was about 30 below zero, would get much colder when the sun went down. Maintaining body heat in the dark would be almost impossible.

While moving, the body's engine is revving and generating body heat. When you stop moving, heat production from movement stops, but heat loss does not stop. Body temperature then plunges. When the brain senses the body is cold, it sends warm blood flowing to the brain, heart, and lungs as the priority. The brain also slows down the warm blood flow to the hands and feet. The cruel irony is that, to keep the core alive, the brain sacrifices the hands and feet—the very things needed for a climber to survive. A climber who can't move his hands and feet will die, especially in the dark.

At 3:30 PM or so, Mike, Yasuko, and Jon left the South Summit for the long climb down. Mike stopped at the Balcony to assist Beck, who was still waiting there because of his impaired vision. Jon and Yasuko continued down from the Balcony, with Mike and Beck

Yasuko was found alone.

following. Mike had to assist Beck down with a rope, a technique known as short roping. It was slow going as the storm closed in and daylight faded.

The bad weather, especially high winds, snow, and poor visibility was getting increasingly worse. Along the way, and by then in near whiteout visibility, Mike found Yasuko lying in the snow. She was alone. She couldn't move.

Yasuko had continuously climbed in the Death Zone for over 18 hours. She was extremely fatigued, dehydrated, malnourished, hypoxic, and cold from the 30 below zero temperature. And, now, perhaps afraid. Like all of us, she had been without food, water, and sleep for a long time. She had only one-third of the oxygen available at sea level to breathe.

To make Yasuko's situation even more desperate, she was caught out in a whiteout. A whiteout occurs as clouds cover the white snow and ice surface. The sky and the ground combine to form the illusion of one. Yasuko was in a featureless landscape. She had no sense of depth and distance. She couldn't see, so she didn't know how far she had to go, or even which direction to go. She couldn't tell if her next step should be up or down. She couldn't tell if her next step would be over the edge into oblivion. Disorientation is not just physical. The mind and emotions become disoriented as well. Disorientation leads to fear. Yasuko faced a dilemma. She could not safely continue to move. She had to stop moving to avoid trouble. But, at that extreme altitude in the Death Zone, moving was something she had to do to generate body heat to live. If she stopped for too long, she would never get moving again.

On top of all of this—Yasuko Namba was alone.

A major factor, and perhaps the most dominant factor, leading to Yasuko's collapse was the mental effect of finding herself alone and disoriented by the whiteout. Behavioral science has well established, in circumstances like this, the profound and adverse compounding consequences of a person being alone in a hostile environment, especially in an almost broken physical and mental state. The fear, disorientation, cold, and feeling of hopelessness lead a person to give up and become immobile. It was over for Yasuko unless she got help.

Hall expedition Sherpa passed Yasuko a short time earlier, so she must still have been down climbing at that point, or they would have offered assistance. Jon Krakauer was a faster climber and would not have known she'd collapsed.

Mike was still short roping Beck and couldn't help both Beck and Yasuko. No one was available to help her. Then, Neal Beidleman from the Fischer expedition came along. At much personal sacrifice, Neal heroically and humanely came to her aid. While Mike assisted Beck, Neal helped — practically carried — Yasuko down the remaining about 500 vertical feet to the South Col.

The weather became increasingly worse as the climbers moved down into the storm. The same storm I'd climbed down into. Jon was the first among this group to make it back to High Camp. But even Jon, who was a strong and fast climber, could not make it back to High Camp before dark. He was incredibly lucky to find the safety of his tent.

Mike, Yasuko, and Beck were further behind as darkness fell and the storm got worse. Even though they too reached the South Col, they were unable to find the camp site in the zero visibility. By now the storm was raging around them. The three had little choice but to stop moving or risk plunging over the edge into China or Nepal. By then, Mike, Beck, and Yasuko were mixed together with most of the Fischer climbers. Collectively, they became known as "the huddle." They literally huddled together in a pile in a desperate attempt to keep warm as they waited for clear visibility to find camp. Their odds of surviving the night out in the open were small.

CHAPTER 31

SOME ARE DEAD.
MOST ARE MISSING.

STU HUTCHISON unzipped my tent door and quickly crawled inside. There was no mistaking his deep voice. "How are you doing, Lou?" he shouted over the roar of the wind. Stu had crawled from his tent to mine. He said, "I came to see if you made it back."

Until that time, the idea that some of the others were in serious trouble, missing, or dead had not entered my mind. I was too focused on myself, the tent shredding to pieces, and the wind. The rage of the wind. All I knew was that my teammates were not there; I was snowblind, cold, and thirsty; and the wind was trying hard to kill me. I said, "I'm snowblind. Nobody is here. Where are Beck, Andy, and Doug?"

Stu was the first and only person I talked to on May 10 after arriving back to High Camp. Rather than answer my questions, Stu felt the priority was to evaluate my snowblindness. He explained that the cornea and other parts of the eye can be damaged as they absorb ultraviolet radiation, just like the skin. The symptoms develop six to twelve hours after a burn is sustained. Based on his experience as a high altitude climber, Stu was confident my condition would improve in 24 hours or so.

I, too, have had the experience of being with others who were snow-blind. I wanted to accept his positive prognosis. But my own experience with others was limited to lower altitudes, where the ultraviolet rays are less intense and damaging. Here, the damage occurred from the sun's rays while I was between 28,000 and 29,000 feet. Does the same prognosis apply in such a case? I decided to try my best not to worry about something I could not control. Besides, I had other greater and immediate threats to my life at that moment. The wind. A roar of rage.

Stu had a radio in his tent, and said that there were big problems. Rob and Doug were caught out up high and Mike, Yasuko, Beck, and the entire Fischer team were missing. Stu guessed 20 people in total were missing. I don't recall what he said about Andy's whereabouts.

High Camp was fairly large, but when you come down the mountain you have to see it and head right at it to get there safely. If you miss, you could go off the edge, either into China, or into Nepal, depending on which side you miss. Stu said there was zero visibility and the snow was blowing horizontally. This sounded like it had been as I was coming down a few hours earlier. Stu said he couldn't stand up outside without getting blown over by the wind. "The winds feel like hurricane force," he said. My thoughts exactly. Adding the wind chill to the 30 to 40 below zero temperatures, any exposed skin would freeze instantly. He said that as soon as he could, he would search for others. Stu crawled back outside, saying, "Take it easy." He was gone. I was alone again.

I could do nothing. I wondered if I would ever see or talk with anyone again. Stu popped in two or three more times over the next few hours. That alone was a great feeling. He had been trying to go out looking for the others, but the storm was too intense and there was still no visibility. Stu could not find anyone in camp able to assist him. He was alone in his rescue attempts of Hall climbers. On one attempt, he couldn't find his way back until a brief lull in conditions gave him his bearings. He took very high personal risks to rescue others. The whiteout is one of the scariest and most dangerous situations to be in.

I also heard noises—yelling and banging. At first, I didn't understand it, but then I realized it was Stu's effort to signal the others who might be within hearing distance of our camp. What we didn't know was

The rage of the wind.

that the lost climbers were huddled a couple hundred yards away on the South Col. But they couldn't hear or see anything.

May 10 drifted into May 11. Time was meaningless. All I sensed was the wind hammering my tent. The rage of the wind. And being cold. Very, very cold. And unbelievably thirsty. Sleeping was out of the question, even if I wanted to sleep. Not being able to breathe didn't seem to be much of a priority. I was prepared, as best I could be, to survive the wind.

My thoughts focused on my spiritual relationship with God and Sandy. I prayed I would see her again. I prayed I would hold her hand. I prayed I would hear her voice. Nothing else mattered.

At some point in the early morning on May 11, Frank Fischbeck came into my tent. I must have been dozing at the time because I didn't realize when he came in. All of a sudden I heard someone inside.

"Mike made it back to camp and is now in our tent with Taske, but he's unconscious and in big trouble." When Mike arrived covered with a sheet of ice, he found Jon and Stu's tent and did the best he could to give information about the location of Beck, Yasuko, and the others for possible rescue. Stu was the only one from our expedition able to try, but he was unsuccessful in the fierce storm. Apparently, Anatoli Boukreev was making his own attempts to locate the Fischer climbers. Taske was now caring for Mike, but thought he could be dying. Frank left his tent to give Taske more room to assist Mike to get stabilized. At that time, neither Frank nor I knew anything about the huddle.

Later in the morning, Frank reported that the Fischer expedition, except for Scott Fischer, had made it back to camp in the early morning hours of May 11, but Beck and Yasuko were found dead.

I asked Frank if he had any water and he said no. I asked Frank if any of the Sherpa were missing. He said no. I don't know how he knew that, but we didn't discuss it further. My focus was on water. I wanted

water more than anything. The Sherpa had all of our stoves and supplies. Everest can't be climbed without Sherpa logistical assistance,
but I was always insecure about giving up control of my own stove for
melting snow and ice for water. By now, I had no food and little water
for almost two days. And I had no real sleep since three days earlier
at Camp 2. But even if I had a stove, it would be hard to think about
actually melting ice while the wind was taking a pretty good shot at
blowing me into oblivion.

Todd Burleson and Pete Athans, the two leaders of the Alpine Ascents
International expedition, came into my tent in the afternoon. I was
surprised they were there, but glad because they were really strong
Everest climbers. They had come up from Camp 3 to help. I told
them about my snowblindness and Pete crawled out and back again
shortly with eye drops. My eyesight felt a little better by then, and Pete
said the drops would help even more. As Pete crawled out, he said that
they were preparing to launch an attempt to rescue Rob. Apparently,
there had been radio communication with him. He was still alive. It
was remarkable that he'd survived the night in the open. Scott and
Andy were also missing. But we didn't talk about them. Everything
was happening quickly.

As I lay there in the tent, I was cold to the bone, even though I was
wearing my down climbing suit. I was part way inside my sleeping
bag, but my body weight compressed the down in the suit and sleeping bag against the cold ice surface under the tent floor. So I gathered
the extra sleeping pads and the sleeping bags of my missing tentmates
and stuffed them underneath me.

I didn't think about it when they first arrived, but as I then lay there
alone, I couldn't stop thinking about the sacrifice Pete and Todd
were making. The human spirit, humanity, that sense of compassion and compulsion to help others overcame these men. For them
to climb from 24,000 feet to 26,000 feet in those weather conditions

was unbelievable. It meant total selflessness. For all practical purposes, using their strength and resources to help us would mean giving up any personal attempt on the summit. It could also mean that their entire expedition might have no later opportunity to go to the summit. Although Pete and Todd were much stronger than most climbers, it would be nearly impossible for anyone to physically climb from Camp 3 to Camp 4, attempt further rescues, and still have enough strength to go back down and up again later.

As the day progressed, my eyes felt better. I could open them and they didn't hurt as much. The eye drops from Pete had helped. I saw more than just blurry images. But my vision was still hazy, and I kept wanting to blot my watering eyes.

In about mid-afternoon on May 11, my concern started to focus on our lack of leadership and team organization. As for our leaders, Rob and Andy were probably dead, and it appeared Mike was close to that. I felt that whoever was left needed to fashion an exit plan. I crawled out of my tent and over to Mike's tent. I looked inside and Mike was in a sleeping bag zipped up close to his chin. Taske was kneeling at his side. Mike appeared to be barely breathing. Taske looked at me and gave a shrug—as if to say, "Who knows?" There wasn't much more to say.

Before I left Taske, we took several long moments to look each other in the eyes. This was the first time we had seen each other since we'd struggled together to get back to High Camp from the ridgeline at the Balcony. We'd shared something special—incredible moments neither of us would forget. When all hell was breaking loose the day before, Taske and I climbed down together through the storm to High Camp. We'd worked together finding the route when the visibility was close to zero. We'd helped each other. I couldn't imagine having done it alone. I still can't.

I then went to Stu's tent. Jon Krakauer was there, tightly pressing an oxygen mask to his face, sitting in the corner of the tent with his legs crossed, and slightly rocking back and forth. He didn't say a word, but his eyes spoke of the dread we all felt.

I said to Stu that we needed an exit plan. I suggested that he function as the leader. At that moment, Stu appeared the most capable. Up to then, Stu was the only one at High Camp physically and mentally able to attempt rescues. We agreed that with rescue efforts still underway for Rob, nothing would happen until morning. We should talk then. I crawled back to my tent.

At one point in late afternoon on May 11, someone outside my tent door yelled, "Do you have an extra sleeping bag?" He offered no other explanation and talked as if he was in a hurry. I didn't ask what was happening or why he needed it. I partially unzipped the tent door and stuffed a sleeping bag through and said, "Yes, take Beck's bag. He won't be needing it." I remember using those words, and it now seems like such a cold, heartless thing to say. But my emotions were as cold as my body.

As it began to get dark, I checked the status of my headlamp. I didn't want to go through the night without it in case problems developed from the wind or otherwise. The headlamp didn't work. I had an extra battery in my pack. The Petzl headlamp used a single 4.5 volt alkaline battery. To change the battery, however, was more complex than just dropping a new one in place. Wires had to disconnect from the old and then reconnect to the new. I had great difficulty doing this with my impaired eyesight. I tried holding it close to my eyes while squinting. I thought maybe I had it, but the headlamp still didn't work. I assumed I didn't get the connections right and took it apart, and tried again. It still didn't work. I then decided to change bulbs. I had a spare in my tool bag. Now it worked. I clutched the headlamp close.

Hillary Step
Doug last seen on ridge above Step.

South Summit
Climbers waited 2 hours for ropes and caused critical delays at Hillary Step. Rob's body found. Andy last seen.

Balcony
Beck left alone at sunrise. Mike assisted him down at 5 PM.

Scott Fischer's body found.

Yasuko found by Mike collapsed and alone just before dark at 6 PM.

The "Huddle"
Mike, Beck, Yasuko, and Fischer climbers can't find camp in dark and weather and huddled together.

High Camp

Beck and Yasuko found dead.

Some are Dead. Most are Missing.

CHAPTER 32

END OF DAY — MAY 11

DOUG WAS dead. Rob was dead.

Doug collapsed above the Hillary Step during his descent. He never moved again. Doug and Rob were together. To generate the body heat needed to live, they had to keep moving. They had no chance otherwise.

Rob and Doug's deaths were confirmed for me on May 12. But I knew within me the outcome on May 11. Two weeks later, Rob's body was found near the South Summit. By the time Rob made it that far, it was too late. He froze to death.

Doug's body was never found. All I know about what happened to Doug was what Rob reported on the radio: "Doug is gone."

Andy was dead. At first, some thought, he had made it back to High Camp, but was hypoxic and fell off the South Col and down the 4,000 foot Lhotse Face. But that was not what happened. Andy was still at the South Summit late on May 10. He just couldn't get going again after reaching that far on the descent. Andy needed assistance, as evidenced by his seriously hypoxic behavior and confusion. But no one was around to help him.

Two weeks later, Andy's ice axe was found next to Rob's at the South Summit, suggesting that at the end he was near Rob.

Andy's body was never found.

Beck and Yasuko couldn't make it back to High Camp from the huddle. They were found in the morning on May 11. They were in a dangerous location close to the edge of the steep Kangshung Face that falls into China. Both were dead. It was apparently too risky in the then adverse weather conditions to do anything with the dead bodies. And the Sherpa would not even go near them. The Sherpa believe it is bad luck to touch, or even see, a dead body on the mountain.

No wonder I was alone in my tent. My tentmates were dead. I recall well the moments on May 11 when I was told that Beck and Yasuko were dead. Frozen to death. I felt paralyzed for a long time. But my emotions were quiet, as I felt nearly frozen to death myself.

What about Mike Groom? Would he survive?

LATE IN the day on May 11, Rob was patched through from his radio near the top to his seven-month pregnant wife Jan in New Zealand. Rob and Jan talked and decided on the name Sara for their unborn child. Rob's last words were that he loved Jan and Sara, and not to worry too much. Rob was never going to see Sara born.

QUESTIONS filled my mind about the dead. Days later I learned some answers, but I would never learn all the answers.

What is known is that all of them were climbing far too late, became immobile, and couldn't make it back down. For 17 hours, of a planned 18-hour round trip, Rob and Doug were still climbing up. They should have started climbing down four or five hours earlier. Yasuko got caught out in the open, in the dark, in a zero visibility whiteout, alone, and out of strength.

Yasuko almost made it back to High Camp before she became immobile. Only a couple hundred yards to go. She almost made it. In better weather, she could have been rescued. But Rob, Doug, and Andy were immobile 3,000 feet above High Camp. They had no chance of being rescued.

WHAT WERE Doug and Yasuko thinking at noon, a short distance above me at the South Summit? We will never know. Nor will we ever know if they talked with Rob about continuing. Did they even know that noon was a decision point? Did they even know what time it was?

Rob was our chosen leader because he had specialized expertise in Everest risk management, especially safety judgment calls. Rob had an unmatched record in leading professional Everest expeditions. But at noon and every moment after that, it was Rob who made the leadership decision to keep climbing to the summit after it was far too late.

Even at the desperately late hour of 2:30 PM, it was Rob who made the decision to wait at the summit until 4 PM for Doug, rather than make the leadership decision for Doug and himself to go down. Rob was in control of the life and death direction he and Doug were headed. Waiting left both of them with no chance of getting back down in daylight. I have no doubt that if Rob had advised Doug to go back with him at 2:30 PM, Doug would have followed Rob's lead. Doug could say no to the summit. He'd done so earlier in the day when he decided to turn back (although he later changed his mind).

Doug and Yasuko were with Rob and Mike, whom they respected and trusted to make good decisions. My sense is that at noon and every moment afterward, Doug and Yasuko were just following Rob. They were simply thinking, "Rob and others are still going, so it must be okay." Actually, I can say that—with authority. I was there. And I thought the same thing at about just the same time.

It's true that Doug and Yasuko could have and should have said no—and not followed Rob's lead. They had plenty of time and opportunity during all the waiting to think about the situation and to make that decision. If Doug and Yasuko had followed the safety turnaround time—instead of Rob—they would be alive today. My heart aches.

LEADERSHIP and teamwork failed big time. It was a mess. Just look: Beck Weathers was left at the Balcony. He was left alone. Yasuko Namba was found collapsed in the snow 500 feet above the South Col. She was alone. Andy Harris didn't climb down from the South Summit with Jon Krakauer, Mike Groom, and Yasuko Namba at 3:30 PM when they were all together. At 4:30 PM, Andy was still at the South Summit—alone. At 4 PM, Rob had waited one and a half hours on the summit for Doug, who was only 15 minutes away. When Doug arrived, Rob was alone. Doug Hansen climbed above the Hillary Step, clearly in trouble. For one and a half hours Doug barely moved. He, too, was alone.

QUESTIONS. Questions. So many questions.

Were Rob's decisions at noon and at 2:30 PM in the service of Doug's interest? Of Yasuko's interest? Of Beck's interest? Of Andy's interest? Or were those decisions in the service of Rob's competitive and business promotion and publicity interests? Were concerns for safety suffocated by the quest for a magazine story and publicity?

Were Doug and Yasuko victims of Rob's unbridled ambition?

Was Rob a hero (as some later said) at 4:30 PM for staying with Doug and trying to help him down? Or was Rob just trying to put out a fire he'd started? Can you be a hero for that?

Did embedding a writer in the team light just one of the matches of the performance pressure bonfire, or soak it with gasoline?

Would there be any victims if Rob had stuck to the safety turn-around time?

Is it fair to say — after the fact when it's easy to say — that Doug and Yasuko should not have placed their trust in Rob, the leader? For me, it hurts to say that. I may be the only person who was there who can say how close I came to making the same decision they made.

Whose job was it to tell Rob to stick to the turnaround time? Whose job was it to tell Rob he was using bad judgment by continuing to climb to the top, at a time when by all measures it was too late?

By noon, five out of eight of the Hall climbers made the decision, in-dependent of Rob, that it was not wise or safe to continue. They said no to Rob. How much louder did those voices need to be to tell Rob that his judgment was wrong?

Victims? Who were they? Were there any?

CHAPTER 33

MY DEEPEST DARKNESS

I JUST lay there. We had no leader and no plan. Tomorrow we had to do something. That was my plan. Do something. We had to start climbing down, no matter what. Slow death at 26,000 feet was rapidly approaching.

My opponents were weather and altitude—more specifically no visibility, not enough oxygen to sustain life much longer, and the wind. If the wind didn't kill me, it would drive me insane. I wasn't thinking at all about the technical climbing challenges that lay ahead in trying to climb down.

I didn't think, with a certainty, that I was going to die. At first I did. But dying, for certain, had receded from those earlier thoughts. Sometimes denial can be good. I would call it acceptance. The best, but twisted, face I could put on my situation was that a good outcome was less likely than not.

I had never thought about what I would do, or what it would be like, if I had the time or opportunity to accept that I was at the end of my life. And then, to reflect about dying and life before it actually happened. But that was the position I found myself in that evening.

It was dark now on May 11. Everything was out of my control. The storm still pounded. The wind still roared. I lay in my tent waiting, hoping, for nothing to happen. I was overwhelmed with loneliness at the thought that I might never see or talk to Sandy again. *I may never hold her hand again. I may never feel the warmth of her presence again.* I wanted to talk to her one more time — to say I love you. I wanted to hear her voice — the real one and not only the one in my head and heart. I wanted her to know that just before dying I was thinking about her. I wanted to write her a note about my feelings for her and about how she'd given rich meaning to my life. She would value something tangible like a written note to hold. I still had in my pocket the faxes that she sent to me. They were in my shirt pocket in a Ziploc bag. They gave warmth to my body and my heart. I thought about writing on the back of them, but I couldn't find a pen. At least she would know I had her messages of love covering my heart when I died.

What would happen to Sandy? It looked like I was breaking my promise to come back home. Sandy would suffer the most from my death. I'd broken her heart. Thinking that was my deepest darkness.

"You, Lou, will have no problems. You will be dead. All the obligations about living will be on me," Sandy said over the years as she expressed her concerns about me dying on a mountain.

I wondered if Sandy would forgive me for dying here. She always said she would not: "I will never forgive you. And don't wait around in heaven for me to get there. I'm going to find someone else."

Sandy knew we were going to the summit on May 10. She was probably waiting to hear from me. She always hated the waiting. Many years ago, after being a week late in contacting her while climbing in Alaska and caught in a storm, I told Sandy to always wait an extra week before she started to worry. But that would not work in this case. Unlike most other climbs, we had too much communication from Everest.

What was Sandy thinking about right then?

I knew the answer. As I lay there, in my inner speech, I had a conversation with her. I could hear her voice. What overwhelmed both of us was regret.

Among all my feelings when I thought I was about to die, nothing was worse than the feeling of regret for breaking the heart of the person I loved the most. My ambition would leave her alone in life with a broken heart.

I said that in our conversation. Sandy said nothing about it in response. And then we expressed the mutual regret that we would not share more of life together. I cried. Sandy did too. And then she said that she did forgive me.

I had kept one promise, to live a story I could tell. As for the other promise—to come back home—I didn't. But I did the best I could. She said that she could not ask from me more than that. I knew she would forgive me. Sandy loves me. And she knows, even if I'm dead, that it would be important to me to know that she forgave me.

IN OTHER close call situations in the mountains, I asked God for help. I even promised I would be a better person if He got me out alive. But those promises were soon forgotten.

I wasn't concerned now about myself—after death. I was secure, from my faith, in what would happen to my soul—my everlasting life. But I wanted another chance at life. "Give me another chance. Get me out of here. I promise to be worthy of another chance," said my inner voice.

It sounds like I was trying to negotiate a business deal. The problem was that you don't negotiate with God. Besides, since I had defaulted on my earlier promises to God, why should I be trusted to follow through this time?

I believe in prayer. I believe it has power. So, I prayed hard and bold. The Bible tells me to pray. You must be able to change the outcome by praying. What would be the point otherwise? My friends at the Last Supper said they would pray for my safe return. They had better get on with it. I believe in the community of prayer.

I WAS a passionate climber for a long time. I was a serious student of the sport. I went to Everest knowing it was a dangerous place. I knew all the risks and all the statistics. Everyone else knew I was in high danger of losing my life just by being there, even without being trapped in a storm at 26,000 feet for days. Everyone else knew. But not me. I didn't believe that. I was in denial that it could ever happen to me.

But, not this time. This time it was happening — to me. How could I be such a fool — to fool myself?

WHAT I did not think about, in those moments, was wishing I had reached the Everest summit and gotten away with it. I didn't think about climbing the rest of the mountains on my climbing wish list. I didn't think about my career or any other of my future life goals or things I enjoyed doing. I didn't think about what I, before then, considered my life achievements.

I wanted to say "I love you, Sandy" one more time. I wanted to say to my sons, "I love you, Doug and Gregg." I wanted to have more of life together. I wanted to hold Sandy's hand. I wanted to feel her presence.

CHAPTER 34

THE ROAR OF RAGE

IT WAS early morning. The storm. The wind. The roar of rage. Then, the unexpected happened: Mike Groom crawled inside my tent. I was surprised because I'd feared he was dead. Even if he survived, I had written him off as a functioning leader. But there he was, seemingly the same as always. Mike was one tough guy. He spoke softly, slowly, with reserve, as though not much had happened. There was no tension or frenzy in his voice or manner. The same old Mike. We didn't spend any time talking about his condition or about what had happened in the past. He said he was "just making the rounds in the tents to talk to people to see how they are and what they think." We got right to the heart of it: *what are we going to do next*?

All of us were students of mountaineering history and familiar with a similar situation 10 years earlier, when climbers were trapped on K2 in a storm. They were at an altitude lower than we were. Although highly experienced, the climbers waited too long for the storm to subside before making an attempt to escape. By waiting, their bodies broke down so much from slow death, oxygen starvation that they lost their physical capacity to climb down, and they died. Frank and I had talked about that case the night before. We, too, faced the body's deterioration from the combined effects of hypoxia, sleep deprivation, dehydration, malnutrition, and extreme cold, hour after hour since May 9.

Mike and I discussed the situation as though we had two choices. But we knew we had only one. Which meant no choice at all. We could make a run for it and possibly live, or stay and wait for the weather to improve, and probably die from waiting. I said, "Let's go." I didn't know if I could have beaten slow death for another 24 hours in the Death Zone, and I didn't want to die in a tent waiting to find out. If this was the end, let it be while trying to escape.

Mike stuck his head in the tent again a few minutes later. No discussion. He said, "Let's go." The decision was made to run for it. Abandon everything, except for what we absolutely needed to climb down. Leaving everything else behind meant that if we didn't make it to a lower camp we would die for sure. But we needed to be light to move as fast as possible.

"Be ready to move in 20 minutes or be dead like the guy in the tent next door," Mike said. He quickly zipped the tent door shut and was gone. I understood part of what he said. Be ready in 20 minutes. The other part I didn't understand: "Or be dead like the guy in the tent next door." I had no idea what or whom he was talking about. But I never gave it another thought. This was no time to find out. How could it not matter who was dead in the tent 25 feet away? How could my emotions be like frozen blocks of ice?

My three tentmates were dead. I sorted through their gear, with no thoughts or feelings about them. I put my pack together, including Andy's extra expedition gloves. I strapped on my crampons inside the tent, which was something I otherwise would never do because the sharp points tore the tent floor. That didn't matter. Without me inside to hold it down, the tent would shortly be taken by the wind and would be bouncing around 100 miles away in China or Nepal. By then, my eyesight had sufficiently restored. The fact that my vision was blurry didn't matter. All that mattered was to get out of hell.

I crawled outside my tent in well under 20 minutes. When Mike and I discussed our escape, it was understood that each of us was on his

241

They faded away through the cloud.

own. We might start out together, but I'd make it or not—on my own. I knew that, but still felt there was no way I was going to miss being part of the team starting out. I needed to be ready—and early.

I stood up. And I buckled right back down to my knees. I stood up again, and once more fell to my knees. I tried and tried, but I could not stand up. I had no strength. I was on my knees as I heard someone yell, "Ready, ready, moving, moving," and the others started to move. I saw them fade away through the cloud.

Even though the wind still roared, for me it had stopped. All had gone quiet. It was once again—"after the wind." I felt alone. And helpless. I had no physical strength. But I didn't want to die just because I couldn't get up. My inner voice asked, "How am I ever going to get down?" I answered my question by praying, "Dear God, please help me. Give me strength." I knew no one on the mountain could help me. I either move on my own, right now, or die. My physical body was broken down from four days with no food or sleep, and from oxygen starvation.

My memory of what happened next is gone. I don't think I ever knew what happened next. What I do remember is the sound of sheer silence and the image of being on my knees, without the strength to stand up. I felt alone, but clearly I was not. I didn't have to get up on my own. The spirit instilled in me by God was not broken. My spirit—that non-physical part of me provided the strength. I got up and started down.

Weak and dehydrated, I wanted water more than anything. No doubt severe dehydration and malnutrition were the biggest factors contributing to my lack of strength. Of all the days on Everest, that was the most difficult. Step by step. Move. Try to get down. This was much more difficult than climbing on summit day. And I had a long way to go in the storm. The wind. The roar of rage.

Go slow, no mistakes.

From the beginning of the climb down, my inner voice repeated that mantra. Over and over to myself. Sometimes, even out loud. Every move I made. "Go slow, no mistakes. But keep going."

Most climbing accidents occur on the way down, and usually from a momentary loss of concentration. The biggest danger was to make a mistake by moving too fast. I had to keep a good pace, but make no mistakes. Keep my head down. Keep going. Keep moving. My inner voice helped me concentrate. Get down. May hell be over. Keep going, but make no mistakes. Winston Churchill once said, "When going through hell, just keep going."

Climbing down is always more difficult than climbing up. Up or down, in both cases you're fighting gravity. But down climbing requires different muscles and skills, and working against you is fatigue, dehydration, hypoxia, and the absence of performance enhancing adrenaline. I'd had no food or water for days. As you de-hydrate, the blood thickens and makes it more difficult to transport oxygen and energy to be burned from the fat cells to your muscle tissue. I needed water.

I climbed off the South Col and started up the rocky Geneva Spur. Slow, but steady. I was climbing through much new snow on the Spur. As I climbed up and over to the other side, the weather was materi-ally different. The wind didn't calm. It just couldn't get to me there. It felt like I had come inside and bolted the door shut behind me. I felt incredible relief and protection. The constant, unrelenting battering by the wind had torn my spirit to shreds. The deafening roar had been never-ending torture. The roar of rage. Technically, either I had climbed below the storm, or I was simply isolated by the rocky spur. From the absence of the roar, I felt paroled from an insane asylum.

I headed toward the Yellow Band of rock, which required a couple of short rappels. Ordinarily, these would not be difficult, but this time they were difficult because of my ravaged physical state. No matter how simple and easy something may be, it becomes hard to do when you know you will die by making any mistake. My frostbitten fingers struggled with the ropes and the hardware. I had to rig my figure eight descender with the climbing rope, which required taking off the expedition mittens I had worn since leaving High Camp. The climbing rope was frozen stiff. I tried to bend it to thread it through the descending device. I couldn't. Dread rose within me. I had to find another way. I tried an old basic method to rappel, known as the dulfersitz, by wrapping the rope around my torso to apply friction between my body and the rope. I inched down. I prayed I had enough strength to make it safely.

AFTER THE Yellow Band, I traversed the Lhotse Face to where the climbing route goes fairly straight down to Camp 3 at 24,000 feet. About halfway across the Lhotse Face, our team Sherpa came behind me. I was glad to see someone up close. I let them pass. This was the first time I had seen any Sherpa since summit day — two days ago. I hadn't even thought about them, except when I thought about the stoves they had for melting ice into water. From the looks on their faces, they had gone through as much fear and anguish as I had. They, too, had hunkered down on the South Col, hoping the tents would hold together. As it turned out, the Sherpa with the stoves were sick with carbon monoxide poisoning from cooking inside the tent.

I asked, "Any new word about Rob?" The Sherpa just looked at me with blank stares and were speechless. Maybe they didn't understand me. I don't know why I asked that question. I already knew the answer. But it didn't matter; their look gave me the confirmation I may have been looking for. One of the Sherpa finally said, "Go slow. Go slow, very, very careful." He understood English. I later learned that Kami and Ang Dorje had made an unsuccessful attempt to rescue Rob.

After the traverse, I started to climb straight down the Lhotse Face. Camp 3 was my destination, and I knew I was getting close. I looked forward to a rest. Maybe there would be water there. Maybe food too. Because of the terrain features, I wasn't able to see the tents off to the side of the climbing route until I was fairly close. Finally, I saw the tents and started to move in that direction. I was nearly there. I had left some climbing gear at Camp 3, and I thought about it for some strange reason. Who cared about gear? What I needed was water.

Go slow. No mistakes.

A short time later I looked further down the Lhotse Face and saw Stu and Taske sitting on an ice ledge at the Imax expedition campsite. I negotiated my way through the lines anchoring the tents to the mountain face, and I sat next to Stu.

It felt so good to sit down. But the best was yet to come. Someone from the Imax team handed me a liter of water. At that moment nothing else mattered. The water was like a miracle drug. I'll never forget the feeling of the liquid flowing down my throat. I am forever indebted to the Imax team for their generosity. It takes a lot of time, effort, and fuel to melt ice for just one liter of water. But I was yet to learn the full scope of their thoughtfulness and generosity—their unbelievable efforts to help other people in their time of need.

CHAPTER 35

THE DEAD GUY
IS STILL ALIVE

WHILE at Camp 3, I talked to some members of the Imax expedition. As I drank and rested, I answered questions about who was dead. I included Beck Weathers on the list. The day before I was told that Beck and Yasuko were dead, and I had never heard otherwise. Then someone said, "No, I just heard on the radio that Beck is alive."

I said, "No, Beck was my tentmate. He didn't make it back. Beck has been out in the open above 26,000 feet since the ninth. He is dead."

I didn't say any more about it. No one did. I was mostly interested in drinking water. Besides, I still had serious business to take care of. I was at 24,000 feet and I had been told that a medical treatment tent was set up at our Camp 2 campsite at 21,300 feet. Almost 2,000 vertical feet of difficult down climbing on the wind-packed ice of the steep Lhotse Face still lay ahead before I would reach the Valley of Silence leading to Camp 2. I might be out of the Death Zone, but I was not in a safe zone.

Sitting on that ice shelf at 24,000 feet, and hearing "the dead guy is still alive," was the first piece of the complex puzzle surrounding Beck's miracle survival. But at that time, I had little motivation to ask questions or think about what might have happened. As we left the Imax campsite, I was told that some of their climbers were preparing

Beck refused to die.

to climb up to assist Pete Athans and Todd Burleson in Beck's rescue. I still denied to myself that Beck could be alive. Solving the Beck Weathers puzzle wasn't high on my list of priorities at that moment. All that mattered was getting down to Camp 2.

ACTUALLY, two other Beck Weathers puzzle pieces related back in time. One piece related to the late afternoon on May 11. I was asked from outside my tent, in an anxious and hurried voice, if I had an extra sleeping bag. I said yes and quickly pushed Beck's bag through the tent door. I had been lying on top of it for extra insulation from the cold below. Not another word was said after that about the bag. As it turned out, Beck's bag was for Beck. Beck, apparently not as dead as everyone thought, had walked into camp by himself from the huddle location.

Another puzzle piece related to the morning of May 12, as we prepared to make a run for it from High Camp. I now realize that Mike's reference to "the dead guy next door" was to Beck. Beck had evidently died a second time, back at camp. But, again, as it turned out, Beck was not dead.

Still another puzzle piece came days later, when I was asked why we didn't make a run for it and climb down from High Camp a day earlier on May 11, when there was a break in the weather. My first answer was we didn't want to leave camp knowing Rob was still alive. But that was never a good answer because Rob was beyond rescue. Now I know the real answer. I know why. It was clear and simple: if we had climbed down on May 11, Beck would have had no one at High Camp to come back to from the dead. The dead guy then really would have been dead.

AS WE started to climb down to Camp 2, I let some of the other climbers clip into the fixed rope ahead of me. For me, this was good. Everyone moved slowly, yet they were faster than me. Go slow, no mistakes. No point in changing the plan that had gotten me to 24,000 feet. The next target was 22,000 feet, the base of the Lhotse Face. The weather was good. I didn't see any point in pushing faster than I felt safe.

I overheard Mike in a conversation with Lhakpa. Mike asked Lhakpa if he would go the short distance back up to Camp 3 and retrieve some of the gear we had left behind. Lhakpa nodded in agreement and started back up. I started to climb down, with Mike following. About half way down, between Camp 3 and the bergschrund at the bottom of the Lhotse Face, another climber came toward us. It was Mal Duff from Scotland. He was the leader of a British expedition, who had come up to help out. Again, I was in a bit of disbelief that someone would give so much of himself to help others he didn't even know. This was a huge physical undertaking and sacrifice for him.

Mal continued down with us. There wasn't much he could do to help while climbing down on the rope, but his presence was important for my peace of mind. I was very weak, and something going wrong was not out of the question. If I made one mistake, I would have a long fast ride down the Lhotse Face. Mal was exceptionally helpful when we reached the bottom of the Lhotse Face and had to cross the bergschrund. The bergschrund was physically demanding down climbing, especially under the circumstances. Once over the bergschrund, as we sat down, Mal gave me water, a candy bar, and glucose tablets for quick energy. I was ready to eat anything and drink everything I could.

My memory of Mal and his presence have always been important to me. It was with profound sadness that I learned Mal died a year later on Everest.

After a steep section at the base of bergschrund, the terrain to Camp 2 leveled off. For the first time in days I felt safe. I even felt strong. The best in days. No doubt the psychological relief of being off the Lhotse Face played a big part in that feeling. But I had 5,000 more vertical feet of difficult climbing to get back down to Base Camp. All I cared about now, however, was Camp 2, more water, and sleep in a tent that wasn't tearing to shreds in hurricane force winds.

Along the way, some of our Sherpa from Camp 2 greeted us with hot tea. I drank the tea. I was happy to see Tendi, the Sherpa cook from Camp 2. Arriving at Camp 2 was like checking into a luxury oasis in a cold desert. Just a week before, breathing at 21,300 feet was uncomfortable. But now it felt like a haven, lush with oxygen. A haven far from the hellish nightmare above. I knew I could get off my feet and get more water to drink. And maybe even get some sleep. I went to the tent that was previously my Camp 2 home with Beck. I found things that he and I had left behind. I sat still for several moments, just looking at them.

I set up my gear and moved to the eating tent, which was converted into a medical tent, Mash style. Dr. Henrik Hansen, from Denmark with one of the European expeditions, and Dr. Ken Kamler, from New York with the Alpine Ascents expedition, treated me. I had frostbite on four fingers. Ken bandaged me and said it was not serious, as long as I didn't get an infection. This meant letting the body do its natural thing, which was the blistering process. The bandages were just to protect the blisters, so that if a blister broke no infection could get in.

I overheard the doctors preparing for Beck and the Taiwanese climber, "Makalu" Gau Ming-Ho, who were coming in later. This was the first I heard anything about Makalu Gau, which was another complicated puzzle yet to put together. Henrik and Ken requested that Frank Fischbeck, an experienced photographer, stay available to take photos of Beck and Gau's treatment.

After I was treated I decided to go to my tent and sleep, my first sleep in five days. First, Tendi offered me food. I ate some and it would have been smart to eat more, but all I wanted was sleep. I remember lying in my sleeping bag and desiring only to sleep, but it was fitful. I kept hearing voices. I was only a few feet away from the Mash tent, where the doctors prepared to treat Beck and Makalu Gau.

Voices inside me were also active. Voices reflecting. It was not about what went wrong resulting in tragedy, but about what went right since then. We had lacked the teamwork needed to avoid the tragedy. Many bad personal and team decisions were made because people were too focused on themselves. But over the last two days, I witnessed sacrifice, selflessness, overwhelming concern for others, and compassion by people who were not even part of our expedition. People from every direction came together to prevent further injury and loss of life. As I looked at some of what happened, it made me stand in awe:

Stu Hutchison for all the high risks he took in the rescue attempts. Pete Athans and Todd Burleson for their decision to climb up from Camp 3 to High Camp in the storm to offer help and rescue aid. The Sherpa in their expedition refused to climb up to High Camp in those conditions. So Pete and Todd did it alone. Although I doubt they thought about it, the rescue meant giving up any summit attempt for themselves. In late morning of May 12, Pete and Todd were also the climbers who assisted Beck from High Camp and down the Lhotse Face, to where Ed Viesturs and Robert Schauer of the Imax expedition then assisted in the rescue down to Camp 2.

The Imax expedition also offered O2 and radio batteries from their supplies at High Camp. These supplies were critical for their attempt on the summit. Mal Duff and two others leaders from the British expedition climbed up to assist. Henrik Hansen climbed up from Base Camp to Camp 2 and offered his services as a doctor to treat those in need. Ken Kamler climbed down from Camp 3 to give medical care. Before doing so, he radioed Base Camp for someone to bring certain medicines he needed up to Camp 2. Ken was camped at Camp 3 and prepared for a summit attempt. He gave that up to help us.

Frank Fischbeck spent almost the entire evening of May 12 helping in the medical tent, while Henrik and Ken treated Beck and Makalu Gau. Jon Krakauer helped organize Beck's helicopter rescue and the descent to Camp 1.

All this selflessness, compassion, and concern for the benefit of others.

I only hope that one day I am strong enough to do what they did.

AFTER eating, drinking, and resting at Camp 2, I felt pretty good. But I was concerned about getting down the 5,000 feet to Base Camp. Dangerous climbing still lay ahead. And I had seen how fast things could go wrong. I was also concerned about the leadership in our team—what was left of it. Mike did the best he could after his ordeal on summit day and with the further damage done to his already impaired feet. Fortunately, Jon had already been planning the logistics for Beck's arrival and his departure the next day.

I was in my tent talking with Frank about his readiness to photograph the medical treatment of Beck and Makalu Gau. Photographs of their condition at the outset were important for their later treatment. We had no idea at this time about Beck's condition.

The story of Beck's survival is almost unbelievable. Beck had been left for dead higher up on the mountain—not once, or twice, but three times. (At least three, depending on how you count.) The first two times were during rescue attempts. Both times Beck appeared to be dead—or, as one person said, "as good as dead," referring both to his physical state and the adverse weather that made it nearly impossible to deal with someone immobile. But Beck, believing that the news of his death was greatly exaggerated, decided to rescue himself. Almost blind from damage to his face, and with arms frozen into blocks of ice, Beck regained consciousness and slowly picked himself up and then walked into High Camp in the late afternoon of May 11 on his own.

A walking dead man.

Beck was put in an empty tent. Few climbers were aware he was there. Based on his condition, it was assumed that he would die before morning. Wrapped in his own sleeping bag for his coffin, his presumed corpse was left in that tent. As we made our run for it from High Camp the next morning, the presumed corpse screamed for help. Beck, again, had refused to die. That's just like Beck. By then, I was already climbing down. But as the last of our team to leave camp, Jon Krakauer heard him. Surprised that Beck was still alive, and at Beck's request Jon notified Todd and Pete, who then launched Beck's rescue. Earlier that morning, when Mike referred to the "dead guy next door," his reference was unknowingly to Beck. Mike had been told by a Sherpa there was a dead guy in there. But Beck was again not as dead as everyone thought he should be. The dead guy was still alive.

Beck is the best example I know of the virtue of perseverance. He simply got up one more time than he fell down. Jack Dempsey, former world heavyweight boxing champion, once said, "A champion is someone who gets up when he can't." That's Beck. He is testimony of the depth of strength we each have within us when we reach inside and find it.

WHEN BECK and Makalu Gau arrived, Frank left the tent to take photographs until his camera froze. I looked over to the medical tent and concluded there was so much going on that I should stay out of the way.

The next morning, May 13, I felt pretty good physically. But before I had the usual morning fare of oatmeal and hot chocolate, I went to the medical tent to see what was happening and to say hello. I looked inside and saw two people on cots, but not Beck. I didn't recognize either of them. Then a voice came from one of the cots and said, "How you doing, Lou?"

"Beck? Is that you?" I looked right at him and didn't recognize him. Beck had been my tentmate for six weeks, sleeping inches away, but now I couldn't recognize him. I wanted to find Beck's face in the one in front of me, but I couldn't.

Until then, the situation regarding Beck was just words and images in my mind. For the first time, I could combine the words and images with my own eyes. It was a feeling I still haven't found the words to describe.

But the sight was one I'll never forget. I can speak about that part concretely. Beck's face was covered with a pitch black crust. His face was huge, swollen to another half size. Beck's hands and his right forearm were deep purple in color from being frozen solid. One of the doctors said, "They were the hands of a dead man."

I guess there's dead, and then there's dead.

The dead guy got up when he couldn't.

The dead guy is still alive.

CHAPTER 36

BLINDED BY TEARS

WE HEADED to Base Camp on May 13. One more day of serious climbing. The last day of climbing for me—ever. Never again. *I won't do this again. It's over for me.*

First, we climbed down through the Valley of Silence. Moving through the crevasses in the glacial terrain was very risky, and it's important to assist each other with the ropes. Several climbers on our team departed Camp 2 at the same time, including Pemba Sherpa. I liked Pemba. We had one thing in common not shared with the other Sherpa. We were the same size—height and weight. The other Sherpa were much smaller. Pemba was 25 years younger than me, and under the adverse circumstances he offered to carry my pack. It was thoughtful of him, but I declined his offer. "The pack always goes with me, but thank you," I said. This was mostly for practical reasons. I never want to lose sight of my pack. It was also important for me to at least feel self reliant.

Climbers talk much about the important mountaineering value of self reliance. We give good speeches about self reliance. But reality is another matter. The last few days had proven there is no such thing as pure self reliance—in climbing or life. Your goals are not just about you. Climbing a mountain is not just about you. Whatever you do in life is not just about you. You always need others, no matter what you do. To climb Everest, others must also. It's a team endeavor. It can't be done alone. Then, when tough times come in climbing and in life, you need the strength that can only be drawn from other people — and from a power greater than any of us. On Everest, to survive, I needed strength from Sandy and from God to make the right choice in facing my dilemma at close to noon on May 10. That strength came from within and from prayers. That strength came from the heart.

As it turned out, Sandy knew about the adversity we faced at High Camp — almost as it was happening. The information communicated by radio from High Camp to Base Camp was relayed to her from Rob's office in New Zealand. Many friends also knew what was happening from Sandy's Everest Updates. Here is what she wrote on May 11:

Everest Report - 5/11/96

From Sandy K - 5/11/96

Dear Friends:

The latest Everest Update is not good news. I received another call from New Zealand this morning. Three members of Lou's expedition are dead, one more is dying, and one more is missing. Lou is still alive.

If anyone hears any news, or comes across something on the Internet, please fax it to me at 810/644-8967.

Most important at this time is our trust in the Lord and prayer.

Thanks,

Sandy

I wasn't alone up there. Sandy and my friends were with me. They prayed with and for me. On the following day, Mother's Day Sunday, several friends asked for prayers in their church services. Phone calls poured in to Sandy from many people, including some we didn't know — calls to say she and I were in their prayers.

Self reliance? There is no such thing. Declining Pemba's offer and carrying my own pack was a mere outward symbol of self reliance. Real strength resided inside me from my relationship with Sandy, family, friends, and God.

WHILE climbing down in the Valley of Silence, Jon came up from behind. "Lou, you won't believe this. Beck is only a short distance behind. Climbing down on his own power," Jon said with pride and respect for Beck.

Once again, Beck astonished everyone. Jon had stayed behind at Camp 2 for a short time after the rest of us departed to help organize Beck's rescue. Jon had shown leadership in these last two days. Until then, while climbing, Jon had been a loner. For six weeks, I don't recall talking or interacting with him while climbing. That was unusual for me because one of the joys of climbing is doing it together. On May 12, Jon was one of those stepping up to fill a void in organization and leadership. He looked physically beaten up and emotionally shaken at High Camp, but he now looked strong and solid when we needed him.

In the area of Camp 1 at 19,000 feet and the top of the Khumbu Icefall, people were organizing the possible helicopter rescue of Beck and Makalu Gau. They studied the crevasse-ridden terrain and figured out the best place to land, if the pilot was willing to risk it. They took red kool-aid and marked the landing location with a big x. As a rule, helicopters cannot fly that high because the air is so thin the blades have too little air to grab for aerodynamic lift. The only open question was whether the pilot was willing to try. If it could be done, the rescue would be the highest in aviation history.

To pull this off called for a heroic act by the pilot—a Nepalese man named Lieutenant Colonel Madan Khatri Chhetri. But if the helicopter crashed or could not lift off again—and again, this had never been done before — it would probably be fatal for Colonel Chhetri. Even if he didn't die from a crash, he would die (after his O2 ran out) from the effects on his body of exposure to the thin air at 19,000 feet, after having flown from 4,000 feet without acclimatizing.

I was in the Khumbu Icefall when I heard the throb of the helicopter's rotor blades echoing off the walls of Nuptse and Everest. Thump, thump, thump. I stopped climbing and watched as it passed. I then watched it land, pick up Beck, and take off. It was impressive. But I was still in a survival mindset. Even though people died and suffered around me for days, my emotions were as frozen as my body. All my mental and emotional energy was focused on getting through the Icefall. And passing over the crevasses on the precarious ladders. These had challenged me when I passed through in better health and physical condition. Now the task felt much greater.

Go slow, no mistakes.

I had to play Russian roulette one last time to get through the steep and unstable blocks of ice in the Khumbu Icefall.

AS I climbed down the Icefall, a doctor specializing in high altitude medicine from the Himalayan Rescue Mission in Pheriche climbed up to help those coming down. He offered me a candy bar. I ate it and we talked. The doctor said he needed to keep going because our team doctor at Base Camp was concerned about the mental condition of some of the climbers. I didn't know who he referred to, but I guessed it wasn't me. Physically, I was a wreck. Mentally I was holding it together — for the moment.

As I climbed through the last section of the Icefall, I saw people ahead from Base Camp with food and water. I sat down. I couldn't go on. Suddenly I started to cry. I cried and cried and cried. The frozen emotions from the last four days had been stored up for that moment.

Cry I did. It had a loud and anguished tone. Tears ran out of my eyes. At High Camp, tears flowed to heal my injured corneas. Now the tears flowed to thaw my frozen emotions. So that I could feel again.

No one talked. Spoken words were not needed. Conversations came from the look on the faces. Sorrow. Grief. Heartbreak. These were some of the words spoken from the expressions on the faces. Also, disbelief. That was all there was to say. I sat on a big rock—eating and drinking, but mostly holding my head in my hands and crying.

Jon arrived a short time later and he, too, was crying. That was the first time I had seen any emotion from his otherwise cool exterior. It didn't surprise me. How could anyone escape those emotions at that particular moment? Many friends were dead. Beck and Mike were seriously injured. Did Sandy know what happened? Did she know I was alive? Those were my thoughts. I needed to hear her voice. I needed to call her and tell her, "I'm coming home."

Then I knew, but not until then, that I had survived Everest. My journey into nature, to experience the grandeur and spirit of the high Himalaya, had been a nightmare. All I could do at that moment was cry. I survived. Now, I could feel again.

While I was sitting on that rock, filled with emotion, and as I was about ready to get up and walk to Base Camp, a climber I had seen before at Base Camp approached me. I recognized him as a climber from the British expedition. We had never spoken to each other before, but I recalled from earlier days at Base Camp that he was a friend of Doug. In his thick British accent, he said, "I am very sorry about Doug and everyone else, and all that's happened." We embraced each other and held on, almost like we were old friends. He had tears in his eyes. And then he asked me, "Do you think it would be okay if I used some of the climbing gear Doug left at Base Camp for my summit attempt?"

I didn't know what to say. People had been dying around me for days. I was almost one of them. After what had happened, this was a question—for me?

I looked at him and finally said, "I don't know if Doug cares."

What kind of answer was that? I later remembered that occasion and my use of the present tense — cares. I often thought about whether the dead care or not. Is it too late, after you are dead, to care? Or do you care forever?

I remember so well at High Camp in the storm, when I thought I was about to die, that I cared about what would happen to Sandy after I was dead. And I felt an overwhelming sense of regret for my actions in breaking her heart by dying and not coming back home. And I felt it mattered to me to know, even after I was dead, that Sandy loved me and forgave me for breaking her heart.

I learned from those moments at the bottom of the Khumbu Icefall that I want to live my life in such a way that when I die I have no regrets. I haven't figured out yet for certain if the dead care. But I don't want to take any chances — of the possibility of being dead and still feeling regret, especially for such a long time.

Now, I can feel again.

CHAPTER 37

SANDY BACK HOME — MAY 13

IT WAS a half hour walk over the boulders of the glacial moraine at the base of the Icefall to Base Camp. One of Rob's friends from New Zealand, who had been climbing Pumori nearby, grabbed my pack before I stood up. I let him carry it. I didn't need it for security any more. I finally felt secure. I had survived Everest. I lived the story to its end. Or at least the part that ended on the mountain.

I walked into Base Camp. I hope I never have another experience like that. Grim is the best word I can use to describe it. The first thing I came to was Rob's tent. This brought a familiar image from Base Camp—Rob holding court in the mess tent. And then another image. A frozen corpse surrounded by blowing snow. Then I came to Yasuko's tent. Then Doug's tent. Then Beck's tent. Then Andy's tent. Each brought two images. One I wanted to see. And one I didn't. My heart ached. I felt sick to my stomach. I felt disbelief and wonder. Helen Wilton, our Base Camp manager, was sobbing. I hugged her. "Is the satellite phone working?" I asked. She said, "No, not at the moment." It was hard to keep eye contact with Helen. Her heartbreak was visible. But I could tell how happy she was to see me and to see for herself that I was okay. At that moment I didn't want to talk to anyone else. I quickly went to my tent. I set my gear down outside. I crawled inside.

I desperately needed food, fluid, and sleep. But first I had something more important to take care of. I needed to talk to Sandy. I needed to let her know what happened and that I was okay. The satellite phone wasn't working yet, so the next best thing was to talk to her inside myself and to express my thoughts in a note to be sent by fax as soon as possible. And for that, I needed to be alone to talk inside myself to Sandy. I lay there for a long time. I was still fully dressed in my climbing gear. My inner voice was talking to Sandy. I told her I loved her and that I was coming home.

I then gave thanks to God. I said I had not forgotten my promise to be a better person. I asked for help in never forgetting to keep that promise. I started to cry again—softly and quietly. I didn't want anyone to hear me. I wanted to cry in silence. I wanted to feel the tears on my face. I don't know why I didn't want anyone to hear me, except that it was not a cry in anguish, as it had been after getting through the Icefall. It was a personal cry of love and thankfulness.

I then wrote a note to Sandy for Helen to fax, which she did while I was sleeping and when the satellite phone became operational. I later forgot writing the note and what I said in it. A year later I found it as I was going through some Everest papers Sandy had saved. Reading that note one year later was deeply revealing about what I actually understood about my own survival, before having an opportunity to think about it.

Here is the note:

Fax to USA   810/644-7406

May 13

To Sandy

Just arrived back to BC. The sat phone is out for now. I don't know what you know. But I'm OK. I'm alive. I survived. Don't worry anymore. All I want now is to hear your voice, to see you, to be with you, forever. It was so bad. People dying. We were close to the top. The summit was lost. Everything seemed OK but late. Then everything went wrong. It will take me some time before I'm able to report on the details about what happened. Suffice to say for now: I survived, but among the 10 others, 4 died in the summit attempt and 2 were severely and permanently injured. *God's will and the strength of our love for each other turned me around a short distance from the summit and saved my life.* I have frostbite on both hands. I'm told by treating people that if careful and lucky my fingers will be okay. I was snowblind for 2 days and I still can't read, but my vision is improving. I hope you can read this note. It's hard to write because of my bandages. Make an appointment with Dr. Magnel and Dr. Stevenson ASAP for my hands and eyes. I know this may sound clichéd or trite, but I feel like a different person than the one who came here. Same physical body but different. Probably everyone does and it may wear off. I hope I can forget the violence and suffering on summit day and the storm days that followed. I hope I can forget the wind. I came to live a story I can tell, but I almost didn't live and I don't know if I'll ever find the words to tell. The strength that it took to get down on the 10th and 12th came from beyond all human understanding. It came from beyond me. This probably didn't make the news in North America because our expedition was New Zealand based. But a doctor I passed in the KIF said it was big news in Asia. Tragedy. That's what happened. I just want to come home and be with you. Nothing else matters. You came with me and you brought me home. Scott Fischer died. Beck is a whole other story. Beck wouldn't die. As I write I have to stop and rest every few minutes because my fingers hurt. I'm going to try to sleep now. I wrote this in case the sat phone starts working while I'm sleeping. I want you to know I love you and I'm coming home. I don't know if I will ever understand this. It will just have to stand at that. All I want now is to come home and be with you, Doug and Gregg and friends and I will never, ever climb mountains again. The direction of our lives is a product of our experiences. I just want no part of climbing again. I'm giving away my climbing gear to the Sherpa. This will be better than collecting dust in the basement. Right now, more than anything I want to hear your voice. I love you very much and our love for each other and God's will are bringing me home so we can spend the rest of our lives together. I want to hear your voice. In case I can't get through earlier, I'll call you when I get to the Garuda about flight arrangements. It's difficult for you to get through here because of the cold.

Love, Lou

I'm coming home.

The satisfying and revealing part of the note that spoke to what I did and why at noon on May 10 was this:

"God's will and the strength of our love for each other turned me around a short distance from the summit and saved my life."

AFTER my time alone, I changed out of my dirty and stinking climbing clothes and went to the mess tent for food and drink. I first washed, one by one, the fingers not covered with bandages. My first priority was to drink. To my delight, there were soft drinks. I didn't have to endure another cup of tea. Chumba, our cook, must have stashed away the soft drinks for our return to Base Camp. Not a joyful return, but a return nevertheless. I drank everything in sight. I could not get enough fluid to satisfy my body's needs.

Nobody in the mess tent was celebrating a return to safety. Eat and drink. Not even much talking. Mike looked in really bad shape. I bet I did, too. Oddly, strangely even, there was almost no discussion about the events up high. And certainly no judgments or criticisms about what happened. Mike never said a word. Not a single word. It was like he couldn't verbalize words. I could see he was in significant physical pain from his frostbite injuries. Someone later told me he was on morphine for the pain. Mike was also clearly hurting inside. I doubted any morphine could have helped that pain.

My heart was heavy for Mike. I walked to where he was sitting. He was alone. I told him I was proud of him. He never said a word in response. He did the best he could on the way down when things were going wrong. What more could you ask of someone who had done all that he could? Besides, Mike saved Beck from certain death at the Balcony when he tied a rope to Beck and held him from falling as he assisted Beck step-by-step for 1,500 vertical feet back down to the South Col. No one else could have done that. Mike also saved Jon Krakauer's life above the South Summit. He selflessly gave Jon his O2 when Jon's ran out and Jon was unmoving. Mike deserved plenty of thanks.

Another community medical tent was set up. I went over to have my fingers looked at and re-bandaged. The bandages put on at Camp 2 had taken a beating from the climb down. I knew from past experience with frostbite that the blisters needed special attention. Eventually, they would turn black—really ugly—and the dried skin would fall off. But for now the idea was to keep the blisters intact to stay free from exposure to infection.

Before long I wanted to go back to my tent, to be alone, and to again talk to Sandy with my inner voice. I walked over the glacier. Because we camped on moving ice, the path had changed since I was last there. As I lay inside my sleeping bag, I felt overwhelmed with loneliness. I just wanted to go home. I wanted to see Sandy. I wanted to hear her voice.

I started asking myself questions: What will happen to Beck, to Mike? What about the bodies of Rob, Andy, Doug, Yasuko, and Scott? I didn't like those concrete questions. I moved to the more abstract. What did all this mean? Did it mean anything?

I didn't see it at the time, but it's now clear that those moments—the questions I asked myself—were steps in my journey to understand. But sometimes I think that maybe the first steps of that journey were those taken close to noon on May 10—the first steps that faced down the mountain.

I KEPT checking on the satellite phone, which worked off and on, and finally it was operational to place a call. My hands shook as I followed the call procedure. When Sandy answered the phone, I lost it. I broke down. I was overwhelmed with emotion and started to cry. I have no memory of what I said or what Sandy said. None. But Sandy told the story of those moments in her update to our friends. Here is what she wrote:

3:45 AM

Lou called. He was very emotional. It was difficult for him to speak. He said it wasn't the time to talk about what happened. He said he called to say "I'm coming home" and that he loved me. That was all I needed or wanted to hear at that time. He also said his usual "I'm OK. Don't worry." He's always worried that I worry too much. And then he asked me to do all the talking. He said he just wanted to hear my voice. The words didn't matter. So I talked and talked about anything.

I heard other people crying in the background. Probably other people waiting to use the satellite phone. Even though this Update doesn't have much news to report, I still wanted to share Lou's call with you. It meant so much to me.

Sandy

After talking to Sandy, I again wanted to be alone. To return to my tent. To savor the sound of her voice. I felt relief. I felt safe. I was going to be okay. It meant so much to know that she knew I was coming home. She would be waiting for me. We'd still have our life together. Tension flowed away, and I felt the freedom to think about other things.

Sometime later Helen came to my tent and handed me a fax from Sandy. Here is what she wrote:

To: Lou Kasischke   May 13, 3:45 AM

Dear Lou –

I know you've been to hell. You're on your way back now. It will take a long time for your wounds — physical, mental, and emotional — to heal. Don't worry, Lou. I will be with you every step of the way. I will help you. I will be there to hold you and comfort you. I will take care of you. You promised me you would come back home. Even when everything was looking very bad, I believed you. It got me through 3 days of anguish. My mom and dad were either here or calling each day to find out news. I don't think I could have gotten through this without their support and comfort. You have many good friends who did everything including offering to fly to Katmandu. I have been in contact with the American Embassy in Nepal. Their rep was looking to find out about you. News was hard to come by. New Zealand did a good job but so much was conflicting. You are a strong person and I love you very much.

Love – Sandy

Later I received another fax. This is just like Sandy.

To: Lou Kasischke   May 13 8:30 PM

Dear Lou – I hope you are beginning to feel better. Soon you will be home. I'm sure you are suffering in many ways. I wish I could be there to help you, take care of you, and comfort you. You were so smart to make the right choices. I'll never let you go away without me again. This whole ordeal has been awful. I can't begin to imagine what you have been through. I've had to stop answering the phone — and the door. People want to know what's happening. Thank God you are coming home. I've never prayed so much in my life. You said you had problems with frostbite on your hands — what about your feet? Just come home. I love you with all my heart.

Love – Sandy

I remember these notes, and I am happy Sandy kept them. Discovering and reading the notes one year later meant much to me. The first note mentioned her days of anguish and the strength she received from my promise to "come back home." The bad days of anguish she referred to happened during the period of uncertainty about my wellbeing. At first, Sandy was told I was alive and on my way back to High Camp. She reported the news to our friends in her Everest Update. She later heard that Beck was dead. And still later that he was alive. Sandy knew Beck and I were tentmates. These incomplete and conflicting reports made her insecure about whether I was dead or alive. That was her time of anguish. It's also meaningful to me, as she said in her note, that my words of promise got her through those days. We both see words of promise to each other as a well from which to draw strength.

I included her second note because it refers to her thanks to God for answering prayers. And it closes by saying she loves me "with all my heart." Indeed. And her heart gave voice at close to noon on May 10. And I heard that voice of the heart and came back home.

They wept as they spoke.

CHAPTER 38

THE EVENING AND
THE MOURNING

I TREASURED my time alone in my tent. But I had serious physical needs that required attention: food and fluid. I'd lost about 25 to 30 pounds since I arrived on Everest. My body was crying out for nutrition and hydration.

I went back to the mess tent and voraciously consumed food and fluid. When the soft drinks ran out, I drank boiled water mixed with kool-aid (please, no more tea). No smiles, no jokes, no laughter. We talked, but not much about the events up high. That seemed strange—then and now. It's not like we were in denial and expected Andy, who was never accounted for, to walk through the door. It was like we were somehow detached from the disaster.

The most frequent remarks were disbelief. "I can't believe what happened," was a common expression. Much of the time we sat in silence. I believe all of us, to ourselves, wanted to discuss what happened and what went wrong. But it felt uncomfortable or unseemly to do that openly. This was because it would require honestly acknowledging what had really happened. We knew. But people were hurting. So we wanted to put a nice face on things. But we knew.

This was not about a climbing accident. It was not about a storm or any force of nature as a cause of what happened. It was not about bad luck as a cause. Instead, it was about decisions made at noon — 279 vertical feet from the top. There was no life or death story until then — at noon.

In leading up to noon, the story was about how and why we ran out of time. How could that happen? We had planned so carefully. But still, in the bigger picture, the consequence of being out of time at noon was only about a lost summit. It was not about lost life.

The big story was what happened next. Being out of time at noon presented a high stakes dilemma. Everest was no longer a mental and physical toughness challenge to climb the highest mountain in the world. The challenge then was about making a difficult decision — a choice. To turn around or keep going. And, it was about the forces that influenced that decision.

And then, finally, the story was about the choice made — to keep going to the summit, and the nightmare that followed as a consequence. No one would have died if the summit day plan were followed. It was a story about bad judgment. At noon, it was too late to continue climbing up under both the agreed, predetermined turnaround time and real-time mountaineering good judgment. To continue so late meant climbers ran out of strength and daylight. Before getting back to High Camp, all who continued to the summit, except Mike and Jon, became immobile and beyond rescue. When Rob set the turnaround time, he said, "If you are not back to High Camp in daylight, you will die." He was right. Rob had also said, "If you're not mobile, it's over." He was right about that, too.

Everyone in the mess tent on May 13 knew all that. But no one wanted to say it so unequivocally. But we knew.

DURING the evening of May 13, Mike came to the mess tent for a while. He had not been around all day. He still wasn't speaking. Not a word. Not one word. He was hurting too much physically and mentally. Through his silence he sent signals to the rest of us to ease off on any discussion of what went wrong. Still, one of the pivotal issues was the major loss of time from climbers waiting at the South Summit for fixed rope. It seems hard to believe that such experienced climbers were so muddled about what to do. If that waiting had not happened, there would have been no tragedy. And, for answers about how that happened, Mike had been right there up front when it occurred.

Furthermore, none of that loss of time (and resulting tragedy) would have happened if Rob had known climbers were waiting and doing nothing. Why had Mike been up front where the leader should have been? Why did Rob lead from behind? How could leading from behind possibly be a good idea? I wanted to ask Mike those questions. But I didn't. I couldn't. The time wasn't right. What's especially sad is that the critical loss of time between ten and noon was for nothing. Two hours of waiting—burning daylight—all for the momentary effort it took to pull some old ropes out of the snow.

Frank was invisible during the day, which was not uncommon for Frank. But he appeared in the mess tent that evening. We talked privately for a while. I liked Frank. He was easy to talk to, and always thoughtful. Unlike the rest of us, Frank didn't hesitate to express himself about what went wrong. He wasn't around earlier when the "no discussion" tone was set. This was Frank's fourth attempt to summit Everest. He brought a very experienced perspective to the conversation and post-mortem analysis. Frank felt things had started going wrong early. The weather wasn't right on the evening of May 9 when we started for the top. The late afternoon winds were still too high. We faced the likelihood of another afternoon storm the following day, on May 10. "We should have waited," he said.

Interesting, I thought. This was the argument we waged in our tent on the early evening of May 9 at High Camp. Three of the four of us (Beck, Doug, and myself) argued and supported that position. Andy, being an assistant leader, and the fourth in the tent, didn't disagree—he just wouldn't argue against Rob.

Frank's position cracked open two issues for discussion. One was why did Rob anchor to May 10 and not let go? There was no evidence the weather window was open. But the second issue was more important: Did that weather decision really matter? Was the weather irrelevant—as a cause—of the outcome? By focusing on weather, it was easy and convenient for climbers involved and those later commenting to get distracted about the real causes of what went wrong.

Two of Rob's four summits were on May 10. Rob said it was his lucky day. But this was never seen by me, nor do I think by others, as a serious influence. Rob was too smart and too professional to make such a major decision based on superstition. Still, for some reason none of us understood, Rob had anchored to May 10. Ed Viesturs, who had assisted Rob in the past, said Rob fixed his sights a little too rigidly on an arbitrary calendar date. So, Frank and I were not alone in our assessment of this point.

As it would turn out, we had bad weather the following afternoon. Still, bad weather was not a cause of the outcome. However, the weather was a significant factor in measuring the consequences of the cause. More than anything, Rob's high risk-taking decision on the evening of May 9 was a precursor of an even higher risk-taking decision at noon the next day. Rob's decision making on May 10 should have leaned in the opposite direction from May 9. As the leader, if he was going to be aggressive on May 9 in terms of the weather risk, he should have been conservative on May 10 in his plan to get back down, such as by setting an earlier turnaround time as a safety cushion. On the evening of May 9, the risk was encountering bad weather while coming down. At noon on May 10, the risk was not getting down at all.

After dinner, climbers from other expeditions and some of our Sherpa joined us in the mess tent. A few things struck me about that time. First, a member from one of the European expeditions asked if *Outside* magazine had any legal or moral responsibility for the added risks from having embedded a writer in an already highly dangerous situation. The consensus was that only time would reveal the answer.

One of the Europeans, who could not have known Rob's advance planning calculations, also asked if 2 PM could possibly have worked as the turnaround time. The answer was no. We knew that 2 PM was not, and could not be, the predetermined turnaround time. But, to speculate that it could have been, was for some a means to cover up and put a better face on the actions of the late climbers. It's easy to obscure the true story by raising distracting questions. When you looked at the total picture and did the math, 2 PM could not have worked in our situation. That time put climbers coming down in the dark and out of O2. When you plan to leave at 11 PM, a turnaround time of 2 PM would put you 15 hours into a planned 18 hour round trip climb. The O2 supplies were only enough for 18 hours. No one would plan to come down in the dark, into bad weather, and out of O2.

Dr. Henrik Hansen was also in the mess tent for the discussion. He had assisted in Beck's medical treatment at Camp 2 and had more knowledge and insight than others about the huddle aftermath. There was discussion about Beck being found dead, but later walking around and finally walking into High Camp. Henrik then raised a question about Yasuko, who was also part of the huddle and found dead. Henrik said he understood the weather was calm at the time Beck walked in camp, and he asked if it occurred to anyone to go back to check and see if Yasuko was walking around too. Interesting question. No one responded. We moved on to another topic.

The final thing from the evening that struck me came from my conversation with Norbu, one of our Sherpa. He was part of our summit team. He told me that he, along with Ang Dorje, went to the summit with Rob. There was a long pause after he told me that. I had to let that sink in for a minute.

I didn't say this to Norbu, but I thought: if you were with Rob, did you and Ang Dorje help Rob with Doug? And if not, why not? Why was Rob left alone with Doug? And what about Yasuko on the way down? What was she doing when you passed her? Was she okay? What was Beck's situation when you passed him? At any time did you see Andy? And if so, was he okay? Do you have any idea what happened to Andy? You, Norbu, may have been the last person to see him alive on your way down.

I could have asked those questions, but I didn't. The questions were right there in my head. But I know why I didn't. I wasn't conducting an investigation. And we were so close in time to what had happened that I didn't want to seem, nor did I feel, argumentative or confrontational about events so hurtful to those involved.

I also had to keep things in perspective. The Sherpa do what they are paid to do. The Sherpa's only job on summit day was logistics. It wasn't their job to stick around to see what happened or to provide climbing support beyond logistics. They were not a rescue team on stand-by duty. We knew that, and we didn't expect otherwise. Besides, the Sherpa also had physical limits. Climbing down together in the dark and in the storm, Lobsang eventually had to leave Scott Fischer behind, 1,200 vertical feet above High Camp. Makalu Gau's Sherpa left him behind as well, in about the same location as Scott. They had to do whatever it took to survive. On May 10, no Sherpa died or were injured.

I also should have asked, on the subject of logistics, why Norbu didn't help to fix rope on the Hillary Step to avoid the deadly delays. But on that point, I didn't know enough about who on our team was supposed to do what, and who didn't do his part. As it turned out, the

Sherpa failure was of small consequence compared to the capable climbers sitting around and waiting for hours for someone to fix rope for them and doing nothing to help themselves.

After our time in the mess tent, I went back to my tent to sleep. I did not sleep well that evening. Too many things were going on in my head.

I GOT up late on Thursday morning, May 14. Once I fell asleep, my body wanted to stay that way as long as possible. My body cried for rest. But it was now time to resume my recovery with food and drink. So back to the mess tent. Eat and drink.

The word spread during the day that a memorial gathering would take place at 4 PM at the Fischer expedition campsite. Fifty or sixty people gathered for about two hours. Most faces I had never seen before. Several people had bandages on frostbitten fingers. The afternoon was cold and dark.

The Sherpa lit a fire at the base of the lhap-so's stone altar. The smell of the smoke from smoldering juniper had become a familiar one whenever the Sherpa were in a serious moment with their Buddhist beliefs. The smoke was accompanied by the monotone chanting of Buddhist scriptures by a lama. During the chanting and amid the smoldering juniper, some followed the lead of the Sherpa to place candy bars, energy bars, crackers, and other offerings on the lhap-so's stone altar, arranging them around a photo of Scott Fischer. I brought a packet of powdered energy drink to offer. I sat on a big rock with one hand gripping the other. I was deep in thought and sorrow and grief. I couldn't bring myself to move to the lhap-so to place my offering with the others. I wanted to stay in that moment. Later, the articles on the stone altar were distributed to the attendees as a kind of communion.

Several people spoke. Neal Beidleman went first. He wept as he spoke about Scott and his effort to help Yasuko. Some told stories in remembrance. Charlotte Fox recited a poem. Charlotte is a tough athlete and a good climber, but you could also see in her a heart as big as they come. More crying and sobbing. Anatoli, with his thick Russian accent, found it difficult to find the right words in English. Lene Gammelgaard, Guy Cotter, John Taske, Lobsang. They all spoke. It was very moving. Not always eloquent, but always from the heart.

Some spoke philosophically. Others about specific people and specific moments and memories. One climber said that those who died, "died doing what they loved best. Climbing made them feel alive inside." I'd heard several say the same during the last 24 hours, and I have read those expressed thoughts frequently about climbers who die while climbing. Climbing is the only sport I know where the magazines and journals have a standard obituary feature. Before Everest, whenever I heard or read things like that, I never thought much about it. It always seemed like just a nice thing to say.

At that moment, however, I tried to understand how that explanation should make a difference. "Dying doing something he loved." "Climbing made him feel alive inside." True enough—certainly. And nice enough to say. But hardly something that could or should have softened the blow to others affected by the outcome. Also, at this moment in the memorial service, I thought of Sandy's agonizing concerns about my climbing. "How can you justify taking these risks? Are you being fair to me? Where is your sense of responsibility to those who need you and depend upon you?"

I can now answer her verbal interrogatories:

Through the years, either I didn't know, was in denial, or was unwilling to be truthful. And maybe all of the above. Now, perhaps for the first time, I was honest, even if only to myself. My answer: *I can't justify taking the risks. I was wrong. I was reckless. I was irresponsible. I was selfish to take the risks and to leave you alone if I didn't come back. I'm sorry. I feel shame.*

My head was hanging at the memorial, not just out of sorrow for those who died, but also out of regret and lack of self respect for my own recklessness for even being there. I have a wife, two children, a mother with Alzheimer's, and a brother with special needs. Because of my responsibilities to my family, climbing Everest was plain wrong. I should not have been there. When you have so many people that need you and depend on you, you can't think only about what you want and your passions. Your goals and actions are not just about you. Life is not, and never will be, just about you.

I again thought about whether the dead care — forever carrying shame and regret. I'm still not sure about the answer. But even that question puts the focus in the wrong place. Even that question focused on me — the dead me.

What I am sure about, and where my focus should be, is that for others still living, my death would matter. The hole left behind. The broken hearts. The shattered lives and dreams. The loneliness.

So, I am sorry.

Too bad it took getting caught to be sorry. Too bad I had to learn the hard way. Maybe — no, not maybe — I will make up for it by being a better person, as I promised God.

It occurred to me at one moment that most of the people who attended the memorial service, and almost all who spoke, were connected in some way to the Fischer expedition. The only climbers from the Hall expedition who spoke were John Taske and Jon Krakauer. That made sense. Most of our expedition was dead, or lying in a hospital or tent with serious injury. I couldn't think of anything to say that hadn't already been said, so I didn't speak. If Beck were there, he would have had something to say. Beck always had something to say. Beck? He should have been there—not lying in a hospital bed in Katmandu. The dead guy is still alive. He got up when he couldn't. I'll never forget Beck.

Someone during the memorial made reference to "heroic actions" by Rob. I knew that was not true. But I wanted to believe it was true. Maybe there was something he did that I didn't know about? At that moment, I didn't see any heroes, except for the rescuers. But in the remarks, everyone tried to put a nice face on the tragedy. Blaming the storm was frequently mentioned. That was an easy way to make everyone feel better. After all, by blaming the storm we didn't have to talk about human error. But we all knew better. The late afternoon storm wasn't a cause of the outcome. The storm came after the causal mistakes and set the price to be paid for those mistakes.

Later, after the memorial, we had more discussion in the mess tent about the storm, and its role in the outcome. We asked ourselves, if there had been no storm, would there have been different results? That framework for analysis revealed the storm was not relevant at all to the outcome for Rob, Doug, and Andy. They couldn't get down before freezing to death because they were immobile from the cold and hypoxia. Weather had nothing to do with their immobility. For them, being 3,000 feet above the South Col, being rescued in time was not possible—storm or no storm.

But there would likely have been a different outcome for Yasuko, Beck, and Scott Fischer. Like the others, they could not make it back to High Camp because of immobility, a product of being out too late and not the weather. None of them could have made it back without being rescued. But unlike the situation for Rob, Andy, and Doug, they were close enough to High Camp that if there had been no storm, they likely could have been rescued.

I PRAYED several times while sitting on that big rock at the memorial. My praying was mostly in a conversational style. My favorite formal prayer is the Lord's Prayer. "Our Father who art in heaven … thy will be done. On earth … ." Thy will be done. God's will?

I didn't think about it at the time, but now I remember the note I wrote to Sandy after arriving at Base Camp: "God's will and the strength of our love for each other … saved my life." I wrote that during a moment of high emotion and at a time when I lacked any material understanding of what had happened and what went wrong. But somehow I knew in my heart that inner strength was manifested through Sandy's love.

God's will?

I'd chosen the journey to climb Everest. But perhaps God chose for me a different journey—one to experience the bond between my heart and Sandy's heart, and to guide me in my purpose on earth. For what purpose did God's will have for me to live? This question I did not have to ponder long before getting an answer.

CHAPTER 39

THE HEDGE

AFTER the memorial, several climbers from different teams gathered in our mess tent. More discussion was on their minds. The European climbers were especially forthright and analytical. After all, climbers from Britain invented the sport of mountaineering, and they were serious about understanding how things went so wrong.

It was evident to all that the mother of all bad decisions that led to the tragic outcome was what I earlier thought of as the "same day" decision—Rob's decision for the Hall team to go to the summit on the same day as the Fischer team. We knew at the time that this decision did not serve our individual climber or team interests. But because we didn't understand the real reason for the decision, we also didn't see it as a safety threat either.

The real reason to go on the "same day" explains several things — most importantly, why Rob continued to push to the summit after it was too late and past the turnaround time.

The real reason had nothing to do with climbing. The real reason had everything to do with business, competition, and an aggressive quest for publicity.

Rob and Scott Fischer were friends, sometimes climbing partners, and even had planned to climb together after the Everest climb. But they were also competitors in the business of leading professional Everest expeditions. Each felt the pressure and tension of competition from the other. Each was aggressive and ambitious. The outcome this year was vital for future expedition business.

Rob wanted success for himself, but he also wanted success for Scott. Even though competitors, they were not rivals who wanted to beat each other, as in one the winner and the other the loser. There was no one prize in the competition to be claimed. Rob said there was enough room for both in leading Everest expeditions.

Both also knew the importance of publicity about the outcome on summit day and was aggressive in promotional publicity pursuit. Rob planned for and expected powerful publicity on his summit day success.

Rob and Scott each wanted the summit day record of an expedition leader with climbers on top. But more importantly, neither wanted to *lose* the summit day record and promotional publicity competition to the other. And so, to protect against loss, Rob and Scott hedged the business and publicity competition by deciding to go to the summit on the same day, with the likely result of a draw—a shared outcome in which both expeditions would get to the top or neither would.

Conditions on the mountain and weather are unpredictable. One day can make a big difference. If each team had gone to the summit on separate days, weather, climbing conditions, or something else outside their control could have been different, and made one a winner and the other a loser of the competition. With a shared outcome, neither would gain nor lose an advantage to the other. A draw was acceptable.

While in that sense the decision served the business interests of Rob and Scott, it was a bad decision for the individual team climbers. It was a misplaced priority. Safety of the climbers should always be the decision making priority for the leader. Going on the same day in no way fostered safety. There was no upside, and all downside. Going on the same day fostered future business, but at the cost of added, immediate risk. The downside complexities and pitfalls of mixing two teams together were self evident when you looked at what happened on May 10.

Unfortunately, at noon on May 10, when things were going wrong because of delays, Rob stuck to the hedge plan. He looked across the ridge traverse from the South Summit and saw the Fischer team going for the summit. Even though it was too late, in order for the plan to produce a shared outcome, Rob decided to follow. The key adverse consequence of the "same day" decision was the influence each leader had on the other at that critical decision moment at noon.

The plan did produce a shared outcome, with climbers from each team reaching the summit. But five memorial monuments now also share the trail to Base Camp.

The hedge didn't work as planned.

If Rob had stuck to the major expedition leader's plan to keep climbing teams spread out on separate days, there would have been no delays, and climbers would have reached the top and been back to High Camp before bad weather. No one dying. No tragedy.

CHAPTER 40

ON MY WAY BACK HOME

MAY 15 was the day of departure from Base Camp. A new morning. My physical journey into nature had ended in a fight for my life. Now I was struggling to understand what it all meant—a journey of the heart and soul. And searching to discover if and how it would reshape my life. So many deep questions and a quest for answers. But first, I had to finish my physical journey back from Everest.

Before leaving Base Camp for Katmandu, I asked Ang Tshering, the Base Camp Sherpa leader, for one of the prayer flags that flew at the site of our lhap-so in Base Camp. As part of their Buddhist beliefs, the Sherpa believe that the wind takes the prayers written on the flags and sends them to the gods. But this year the wind didn't blow the prayers high enough or the gods didn't hear these prayers. Ang Tshering was thoughtful enough to take one down for me. He said the rest were still needed. A few Sherpa would be going back to Camp 2 to take down the camp.

Today I have that prayer flag, ragged, faded, and withered from the wind and sun, hanging on the wall at home. I wanted a prayer flag to be the keepsake of remembrance of that time in my life. As it turns out, I have never needed to be reminded.

Before leaving, I also wanted to give the Sherpa my climbing gear. I told Sandy I wouldn't need it again. I was done with climbing. I gave my gear to Ang Tshering because he was in the best position to allocate it according to needs. I made one suggestion. Pemba should have the boots. Pemba was tall and had big feet, just like me.

MIKE and Taske flew out of Base Camp by helicopter in the early morning with members of the Fischer expedition who had serious frostbite. Mike's frostbite was severe. He had previously lost about 30 percent of his feet to frostbite. If he lost any more, he might never walk on his own feet again. Taske, who was a friend from Australia, went along to help Mike get treatment in Katmandu and to get back home. The rest of us were happy Mike was getting prompt medical treatment. We were also envious because we had several days of trekking ahead before getting to Katmandu. "Let's get out of here," was all I thought.

We finished packing and our gear was loaded on yaks that arrived the night before. Frank, Stu, Jon, and I turned our backs on Everest and started the trek down the Khumbu glacier towards the village of Gorak Shep. Our destination for the day was Pheriche.

As we exited the glacier and started on the trail, I saw up ahead a sole traveler approach and talk to Stu. Stu walked away as the man kept talking and motioned with his hands. The man then approached Frank, who gave him similar dismissive treatment. I picked up my pace to see what was going on. The man talked to someone else on the trail. "Photos of the dead. Photos of bodies. Pay money for photos," he was saying. "Photos of the dead. Pay money." I inquired and found that he was a journalist. Yes, he wanted to buy photos of the dead. The facts of the story didn't matter. The priority was photos of the dead. This episode was emblematic of the future shallow and misleading journalism and movie making to follow, when storytelling was shaped more for sales than truth.

IT WAS a quiet night in Pheriche, with few people around. Stu and I stayed up late talking. He, along with Beck, was my closest friend on the expedition. Until heading for the dorm room, we spent most of the evening eating omelets, yak steak, and fried potatoes, and drinking beer. It felt good to be eating different food. It felt even better to be away from Base Camp, or more precisely, Everest.

Stu and I agreed that it was time to go home and try to never think about Everest again. But that was wishful thinking. All the questions and replay of events in my head would not go away any time soon.

THE PLAN on May 16 was to continue our trek to Lukla, but because of the good weather, we had the opportunity to catch a helicopter part way to the village of Syangboche. When we landed, we were swarmed by members of the press, mostly Asian. Included with the group was Yasuko's husband from Tokyo, Kenichi Namba. How did he get there so fast? He wanted to find out what happened to Yasuko. I could see the pain in his eyes. The answer was short but hurtful: she reached the top too late and couldn't make it back to camp. Of course, it wasn't that simple. Why wasn't she rescued with the others, since she was so close to High Camp? What would happen to her body? Kenichi raised good questions. What are the answers? Who had the answers?

Jon volunteered to handle the media, along with Stu. They volunteered, but without enthusiasm. Jon and Stu had a radio at High Camp. They knew more than anyone about what happened and why. It was quite a scene with everyone in the media talking at once, while the rest of the climbers pointed to Jon and Stu in the middle. We then ducked aside and headed for a lodge for food and drink.

WHILE IN a tea house in Syangboche, a young man came to our table, looked at me and said, "Is your name Lou?" Astonished, I said yes. He gave me his card. He was part of the staff from the U.S. Embassy. He told me the Embassy had arranged for a small plane to fly around Everest.

Small plane? What in the world was he talking about? How did my government know about me or where I was? He said the Embassy was involved in the helicopter rescue of Beck.

"That's great, thank you very much," I said, and he walked away. That was it. I looked around at the others at the table and gave a big shoulder shrug.

A woman, who didn't introduce herself, was with the Embassy staffer. She had called Sandy at one point and offered to help with any logistics in Katmandu. This was unbelievable. Why were they in Syangboche? Where were they going? Even I hadn't known I would be in Syangboche until an hour earlier.

We luckily caught another helicopter flight to Katmandu. That saved a lot of trekking time, and accelerated the process of getting home. It was a 45 minute flight through the valley to Katmandu. We landed at the airport in late afternoon, and again were swarmed by the media, mostly the Asian press. That made sense. We were in Asia. The rest of us pointed at Jon and Stu as spokesmen, and we ducked away to a van for a ride across the runway to the terminal. We collected our duffels and headed to the Hotel Garuda. As we drove away, the journalists and photographers were all over Jon and Stu.

David Schemstead of the U.S. Embassy met me at the Garuda. Again, I shook my head in wonder. He said he had been in contact with Sandy and told her what he knew. Sandy was already tuned in, but knowing he made the effort was satisfying. He asked me a lot of questions and wrote down the answers on a printed form. I was happy to answer them, considering my government was there on my behalf and concerned about my wellbeing in a time of tragedy. This was something I never expected. Fortunately, I did not need any assistance on or off the mountain. But I was impressed my government knew and cared.

Now for a great moment at the Garuda: a shower. My first real shower in almost two months. Of course, the hotel had no soap. Fortunately, I had a small bar with me. Since I'd spent most of the time in the same clothes, the hot water was black as it ran down the drain. I wanted the soap and water to remove every part of Everest from my body. I scrubbed and scrubbed. I stood in the shower as long as the water stayed hot. The bar of soap had little left to it when I was done.

I received a call to come to the hotel front desk. I was handed a fax that had arrived earlier from Sandy telling me about flights she had arranged. As usual, Sandy was looking out for me. Helping me. Her message also said I couldn't call her because she was on her way to meet me in Bangkok. I had no idea she was going to do that. I didn't see any need for that, but I was happy to see her as soon as possible. She said I would recognize her as the "woman with the bags under her eyes." I knew what she meant. I knew this had put her through much adversity.

Ed Colosimo, Sandy's father, encouraged Sandy to travel to Asia to be with me. To bring me home. Sandy was with her mother and father on Mother's Day, May 12, shortly after receiving word that I was making my way down the mountain. Ed was extremely concerned for me during the tense and uncertain days of May 10 and 11. Sandy said it was the first time she saw her father cry.

CAROLINE Mackenzie, our expedition doctor, Frank, Jon, Stu and I had dinner together that evening. We all wondered if we would see each other again. In a way, I hoped we never would. What would be the point? To reminisce? No thanks. If we did see each other, it certainly would not be climbing. I would never climb a mountain again. That was for sure.

I knew Jon was a good writer. That evening I encouraged him to write the story. He said he couldn't even think about it at that time, and he didn't think he could ever write about what happened. I said that I hoped in time he would change his mind. By then, I knew what went wrong and could understand Jon's reluctance.

Jon did write the story and did so with respect for the privacy of those who were not central figures in the tragic outcome. For that, Jon received my respect. I, in turn, have tried to follow his good example in these pages.

That evening I learned *Newsweek* and *Time* magazine had scheduled interviews for the next morning. *Newsweek? Time?* Wow, I thought, this must be big news here in Asia. I was thinking of their international editions. It never occurred to me that it was also a big story in America — or even a little story.

WHEN I arrived at the Katmandu airport on May 17, for the first time I felt I was on my way home. Sandy had the airline schedule worked out. I was fortunate to have a window seat with no one next to me. I wanted to be alone. As the plane took off, I closed my eyes. I wanted my inner voice to say, "The nightmare is over." I wanted to hear that voice. But I didn't. The entire flight was a constant replay of the events. Over and over. And over again.

I sat with one hand holding the other, looking out the window over the Himalaya. I didn't move until the plane landed in Bangkok. I went to Everest to live a story. I expected a story of high adventure. Sandy asked me to live a story I could tell. But the Everest story turned out to have nothing to do with something for me to tell. It had everything to do with something for me to learn. It had everything to do with guiding and influencing me to live the rest of my life in a way to become the kind of person I now know I wanted to be. And Sandy wanted me to be. Life is about making choices and knowing where to go for the strength to make the right choices. Sometimes the hardest choice in life is to say no. Sometimes the most important choice in life is to say no.

As I flew over Everest for one last look at the top, those words from the voice of the heart that I'd heard close to the summit returned to me: Not today. I'm going home. Not today.

Not today. I'm going home.

CHAPTER 41

BACK HOME — MAY 18

I STOOD in lines in the Bangkok Airport, waiting for immigration and customs. I carried one duffel bag. In front of me, I also pushed with my foot my large climbing gear duffel. It took forever. The lines, the looks from the officials, and the stamping of several pieces of paper. I wanted to see Sandy, but all I saw were the double doors leading to the public area. People ahead of me went through the doors. But the doors quickly swung shut. I could get just a quick look to the other side each time. I could see her in the front of the crowd of people waiting. My heart was beating. I heard it give voice, speaking in our private language of love and verbal embrace. "I'm home."

As I passed through the double doors, I had one of the most joyful moments of my life: holding Sandy in my arms. This was the first moment of joy I had felt in two months. Yes, there she was with bags under her eyes. I hugged her and wouldn't let go.

"You kept your promise," Sandy said. I hugged her again. After we walked for a few minutes, Sandy looked down at the climbing gear duffel bag I pushed ahead of me with my foot, as if it was too heavy to carry. Was the bag still full of gear? Sandy had a suspicious look. I heard her voice before she spoke. "What's in the big duffel? You said you gave away your climbing gear." All I could do was grin. I couldn't hold it back. This was such a happy moment. I'm home. Nothing, absolutely nothing gets past Sandy. For fun, I paused before responding. "I did. What's in there stinks pretty bad." She smiled.

Sandy had a room for us at the airport hotel. Shortly before I arrived, she called home and talked to her father and our son Gregg. She told them everything was on schedule and we would return on a flight the next morning through Tokyo to Detroit. In our room, Sandy handed me a stack of U.S. newspaper clippings about the tragedy. I was dumbfounded. Only a few days earlier I wondered if the U.S. media had picked up the story. Now I saw that it had been a non-stop media avalanche. Sandy said the local media was all over it, and my involvement. Again, I was astonished. I'm from Michigan. Who in Michigan cares about mountains? Sandy said, "Rob's radio call to his pregnant wife triggered the media avalanche."

We were so happy to be with each other. The summit of all the mountains in the world put together meant nothing compared to those moments. To this day, nothing means more to me than feeling the warmth of Sandy's presence. After 46 years of marriage, having Sandy next to me when we go to sleep at night is the best part of the day.

Later that evening I read the newspaper clippings. I quickly saw from the reporting that the world-wide attention was driven by the confluence of certain factors. I agreed with Sandy that the top of the list was Rob's radio call—a man freezing to death at the top of Mount Everest calling his pregnant wife. Then there was the miracle survival of Beck after being left for dead. And his heroic helicopter rescue at 19,000 feet, the highest in aviation history. Another was the historical record set from the number of climbers (eight in total) dying in a single day's events. This included the five I was involved with on the south side, and another three on the north side in similar circumstances. This was also the first time that climbing Everest was followed on the Internet. Last, of course, it was about Mount Everest, the most famous mountain in the world.

In Dallas, Texas, Beck had much of his right arm amputated and he lost all fingers on his left hand. The doctors also cut off what remained of his nose and constructed a new one for him. Beck has many scars today for the times he was left for dead. Makalu Gau lost large portions of his hands and parts of both feet.

ON THE long flight home on May 18, Sandy brought me up to date on what had happened over the past six weeks. The only things that really mattered were about Doug and Gregg and the rest of our family and friends. The small, everyday life things that aren't really small. Actually, the things that enrich life. "How is Baby doing?" I asked. Baby, our cat, usually acts like she doesn't even like me very much. Sandy and I held hands and looked at each other through the entire flight. People around us probably thought we were newlyweds.

WE FINALLY landed in Detroit International Airport. It was good to see our son Gregg at the terminal. He was quiet. I thought he would have many questions when we met. As we walked to the car in the parking lot, Gregg stopped. He had tears in his eyes. He turned to Sandy and said, "Papa died a few hours ago." Gregg called Sandy's father papa. She stared at me in disbelief. A few hours ago? This can't be happening. Sandy was devastated, fell to her knees, and broke down and cried. We all did, right in the parking lot. Sandy hugged Gregg and me. None of us wanted to get in the car. We didn't want to face reality.

How could this be? Now what? Sandy and I were so joyful over the past 24 hours, just to be together after the nightmare on Everest.

Sandy was exceptionally close to her father. I mean—very, very close. Ed Colosimo was an extraordinary man, a wonderful man, generous to everyone, and deeply loved by Sandy and all of the family. He was the kind of man I wished I could be. He always stood up straight. He walked and used his hands with grace and class. He spoke succinctly and softly. He treated everyone with respect. He knew when and how much humor to use. He never lost his temper or used foul language. Ed was a better role model for our sons than me.

I remember Sandy telling me on the airplane about being with her father and mother on Mother's Day, a few days earlier. That was the last time Sandy saw her father alive. The last time they spoke, from the hotel in Bangkok, Sandy's father was caring about me, and happy I was coming home.

In the same clothes I had worn in Asia, we drove straight to the funeral home in Royal Oak, where Ed's body had been taken. Our son Doug, who lived in California, asked Sandy to call him as soon as we arrived at the airport to tell him I was home. On the way to the funeral home, Sandy called him from the car. She told Doug I was home safe, but Papa had just died. Sandy was crushed. The grief of Ed's death overshadowed everything, even the joy of my survival and return.

The story at that moment was Ed's death — not Everest. While television satellite trucks were parked in my driveway, waiting to hear from a man who survived tragedy while climbing in the Death Zone of Mount Everest, Sandy's father had died nearby while strolling in his garden. I lived; Sandy's father died. Sandy's heart brought me home; her father's stopped beating. The television news had to wait. Some things needed attending to that were more important than news about Everest and me.

DURING the visitation at the funeral home the evening before Ed's funeral, I saw my friends for the first time since I returned. With my bandaged fingers, people weren't sure about shaking hands. Under the circumstances, I also sensed that people didn't want to ask me too much about Everest. The moments were not about me, but about mourning for Sandy's father. Besides, I didn't know what to say. "Good to see you, Lou," some said. "Yes, thank you, good to be seen." That was about all. I'd travelled half way around the world from the graveyard of Everest directly to the graveyard in Royal Oak, without unpacking a bag.

One of my golfing friends said, "Lou, just because you have those bandages on your frostbitten fingers, don't figure on getting any additional handicap strokes." He smiled. I smiled. That really felt good. That made me feel home again.

While in church the next morning for Ed's funeral, I looked at Sandy as she cried for her father. I watched her suffer through the grief and sorrow. I could see into her soul. I couldn't help but think about how close I'd come, by my own selfish recklessness, to adding my death to Sandy's broken heart. This could have been a double funeral. How could Sandy have endured the death of her father and her husband at the same time? I tried not to think about myself. The day wasn't about me. But I couldn't help search for meaning. My survival as God's will? A purpose on earth? I asked myself those same questions a few days earlier at Base Camp. Perhaps the answer was there, as I stepped off the airplane and learned that Sandy's father had died. Did Ed's death explain, in part, my own survival? I needed Sandy to "come back home." And now, back home—she needed me. Sandy and I walked out of church, holding hands.

NOT LONG after Ed's funeral, I went to the mailbox to get the mail. I sorted through it and came upon a large postcard of Everest. I turned it over and saw it was addressed to me. The writing on the back only said: "Welcome home."

It was signed, "Cheers, Rob Hall."

I sat down on a bench outside my house and put my head in my hands. I was alone. I sat for a long time. The postcard was just one more step in my journey to understand. What did it mean? Did it mean anything? Those were questions in my head.

Welcome home?

Yes, thank you, Rob. I did come back home.

I didn't see anything mystical about the card. It was immediately evident that putting the postcard in the mail system was something Rob did just before we left Base Camp for the summit. Even so, I sat and held my head in wonder. Something spiritually powerful was at work. I knew that if the dead do care, Rob was happy I was here to receive his welcome.

But Rob is still there. He didn't come home.

I walked into the house and handed the card to Sandy. She looked at it, looked at me with tears in her eyes, hugged me, and walked away. She didn't say a word. We never talked about it. We didn't have to. We both thought the same thing—I came back home. Indeed, there was a powerful force at work to bring me home, and even Rob knew that, I thought. The card made that point.

The postcard again raised the question: Why did I live through Everest? I still struggle with the "purpose in life" question. The card was another occasion for that struggle to come into my mind. In 54 years of life, I had never thought much about purpose or any of the big, life questions. God, please help me to understand this.

Why did Rob send the card? What did sending it, and what he wrote, say about Rob? I noted he didn't extend congratulations for reaching the top. He wasn't confident about that when he wrote the card. But he was confident I'd come back home. Safely getting back down, the highest of all climbing priorities and ideals, was something he was sure about.

THE TELEVISION satellite trucks were back in the driveway. The phone rang off the hook. Endless requests for interviews came from radio, television, newspapers, magazines, and on and on. I was mostly silent. Dealing with Ed's death came first. But after a week, I took the calls. As expected, almost all the questions were about the big story. Little was asked about my personal story. I answered the questions. One memory of that time was about a producer in New York for one of the national television networks. He called to thank me for my assistance on a program he was working on about the Everest tragedy. He told me the completed program focused on the exciting stories, and then remarked, you were "just there."

Just there. True enough.

But by being *just there,* this is a story I can tell.

CHAPTER 42

THE LAST CLIMB

11 years, 62 days later

All I can see is the mountain facing my feet—one slow step, then another. One more, and another. Beyond the beam of light cast by my headlamp, all is darkness. I reach up to turn it off, as I have done so often this evening. I look up in the sky. It's full of stars. No clouds. No wind. A perfect evening. What an incredible evening to be climbing here. Of all places in the world.

I am close to the summit. My senses are on full alert. I feel higher than the highest mountain in the world.

I keep climbing. The light from my headlamp moves up to a new point and at the same time measures my effort. I step to a rhythm with my breathing, which is the only sound I can hear. A mysterious feeling wells up inside me. I am ascending to a place more than exceptional. My inner voice frequently asks, "Am I really here? Is this actually happening?" Being here is nothing like any other mountain I've climbed.

A mountain in the darkness and in the cold of night can be a dangerous and forbidding place. But not this one. Not this time. I feel invited and welcomed. I cannot see its beauty. But I feel beauty in its form, with my feet as I step and with my hands as I touch the mountain face.

I finally stand on top. I feel great excitement. Not from being on top. But from anticipation: What story am I about to live?

I look around with my headlamp to find the right location—a ledge with enough space. I take off my backpack and put on my down parka to keep warm. I situate the pack on the ledge. I lie down on my back and stretch out, with my head resting on my pack.

It is 4:30 AM. I made it to the top on time—before sunrise—and the beginning of a new day. The timing is important.

I gaze up at the star-filled sky. The stars feel so close. And one of the biggest shoots across the sky. For centuries, stars have guided people to what they were looking for, and on a spiritual level, have guided people searching for a new beginning. For me, that shooting star is a good sign on both counts.

Again, my inner voice asks, "Am I really here?"

I lie on the rocky ledge surrounded by the cold air. I have the comforting feeling of warmth from the rock beneath me, warmth retained from the 120 degree heat of the sun during the day before. I am at peace. I fall asleep. Sleeping is the last thing I thought would happen at this moment. After all, I haven't slept well for 11 years and 62 days.

I awake as a thin line of light appears on the horizon. I watch the sun slowly rise, minute by minute. Ever more light is cast over the landscape of desert sand, barren and jagged mountain peaks rolling off into the distance, sculpted by wind and sand. The rocks turn different shades of red, pink, and black as the sun rises.

All I hear is sheer silence.

In the distance: Arabia, the Gulf of Aqaba, the Red Sea, the red sand and mountains in the desert. A place untouched by time.

Mount Sinai in the Sinai Desert, Egypt, is 7,498 feet above the level of the Red Sea. The most sacred mountain in the world.

When the sun is fully up, the spirit of Mount Sinai finds a place within me. Until now, I didn't want to think about anything. I wanted my mind and heart to be fully open. I just wanted to experience whatever comes my way. I have chosen most journeys in my life. But I feel this journey—this journey today—has chosen me.

This is the best moment I've spent on top of a mountain. But it is also the worst moments in my life that sent me here. It's been 11 years and 62 days since I was climbing Mount Everest, when my dream of climbing the highest mountain in the world became a nightmare of death and horror. It was 10 May 1996. It's still known as the worst tragedy in Mount Everest history.

Many years have passed since those dark days on Everest. Many nights have passed with that darkness still living within me. The life and death events were complex, yet simple on the surface. But for years I could not stop thinking about my survival and the meaning of it. My journey finally brought me to this mountain top. This was not for a climbing challenge or adventure, but to experience the place itself for specific reasons.

MY PERSONAL story on Everest provides me with the same warmth I feel from the mountain rock beneath me. Surviving Everest made it important for me to embrace my personal story on a deeper level. By now I have resolved most of the questions about my survival. I have found some meaning. To be here, on top of Mount Sinai, is an important part of my journey to understand and embrace.

First, I am here to experience the new day.

At sunrise, I stand and slowly look around. I embrace the unique feeling, when standing on a mountain top, of being at the center, where I can see for great distances, see the horizon, see the new day as a circle spread out before me and around me. Since surviving Everest, every new day is part of my second chance in life.

Mount Sinai

I AM also here to remember.

Rob Hall, Andy Harris, Yasuko Namba, Doug Hansen, and Scott Fischer. They didn't come back home.

I remember, with a deep sense of friendship: Rob's excitement on becoming a father. Andy's thoughtfulness for others. Yasuko's soft smile. Doug reading aloud letters from home. Scott, the man everyone liked. Memories of good people. Memories that don't fade away.

I'm also here to remember the incomparable Beck Weathers, who was left for dead on the mountain, but got up when he couldn't, and lived—and still lives a rich life.

I AM also here to never forget.

I am here to recall and relive, as I often do on sleepless nights, how close I came to making a decision on that fateful day that would have left me forever entombed in Everest ice and snow, along with the others.

I didn't always see it this way, but I now accept those decision moments—the endless recall of them and the sleepless nights that followed—as everlasting. And I embrace them as a healthy reminder to never forget.

I must never forget the unbridled ambition that almost killed me.

I must never forget the voice of the heart that saved me.

I must never forget, in making my future choices, what Everest says about how to live a story I can tell—to not just follow what others are doing, to keep my promises, to look beyond myself with care and concern for others, to stick to priorities, and to listen to my heart.

On Everest, to have forgotten, would mean to still be there.

FINALLY, I AM here to give thanks and to listen.

For this, after experiencing my moments on top, I climb down to a small plateau about 500 vertical feet below the summit. I get there by following an untraveled rocky route. Growing in the center of the plateau is a cypress tree, said to be a thousand years old.

I want to be here, at this specific historic site called Elijah's Basin, where thousands of years ago a story was lived. A Biblical story that helps me to understand my own. A man named Elijah was on this plateau. He faced and struggled with a dilemma about what to do, and he was about to die. The story is about finding, in the inner voice, the strength needed to do the right thing when you face life's difficult decisions. Elijah heard that voice, found that strength, and turned back down the mountain and lived to fulfill God's purpose.

Elijah's story is most remembered for the spiritually powerful Biblical reference to the "still, small voice" that was heard — after the wind.

When I arrived at Elijah's Basin, the cypress tree looks a thousand years old. And this makes my being here feel all the more real.

My story is also about facing and struggling with a dilemma about what to do, as things went wrong, and a decision that meant my life or death. It happened close to noon on 10 May 1996 near the top of Everest. My story, too, is about how and where I found the strength I needed in my internal struggle. For me, it's a story about listening and hearing — the voice of the heart. A love story.

As I sit on a rock ledge across from the cypress tree, I give thanks to God for the gift of Sandy's love and for the love story that saved my life. This moment is why I am here.

I then sit, alone, and listen to the sound of sheer silence, to hear the unheard, and to hear — after the wind — the still, small voice of the heart.

A READER'S GUIDE

MOUNTAINEERING EXPERIENCES

THIS IS a partial list of my mountaineering experiences. I included this because people sometimes ask about my experience. On the list are the names of mountains many people are familiar with, some that were a special joy for me to climb because of their history or public prominence, and even some that are not important as mountaineering challenges to expert climbers.

This list gives only basic information. To understand the true nature of any mountaineering experience would require more detail, such as route climbed and time of year (summer or winter). I have climbed some of the mountains listed more than once by different routes and at different times of the year. In each case the challenge was significantly different. As much as anything, this list just shows the scope of my climbing interests and history.

Mount Vinson	Antarctica	16,067 ft.
Denali (Mount McKinley)	Alaska, USA	20,320 ft.
Mount Elbrus	Russia	18,481 ft.
Aconcagua	Argentina, So. America	22,835 ft.
Mount Robson	Canada	12,972 ft.
The Eiger	Switzerland	13,026 ft.
Bugaboo Spire	British Columbia, Canada	10,512 ft.
Miroir D'Argentine	Switzerland	7,626 ft.
Illiniza Sur	Ecuador	17,219 ft.
Mount Ararat	Eastern Anatolia, Turkey	16,854 ft
Jebel Toubkal	Morocco, N. Africa	13,671 ft.
Nevado Alpamayo	Peru, So. America	19,512 ft.
Pigeon Spire	British Columbia, Canada	10,354 ft.
Jungfrau	Switzerland	13,642 ft.
Chimborazo	Ecuador	20,703 ft.
Monte Rosa	Switzerland/Italy	15,204 ft.
Marmolata	British Columbia, Canada	9,905 ft.
The Matterhorn	Switzerland/Italy	14,692 ft.
Mont Blanc	France/Italy	15,780 ft.

Monch	Switzerland	13,449 ft.
Popocatepetl	Mexico	17,887 ft.
Cotopaxi	Ecuador	19,348 ft.
Mount Olympus	Greece	9,751 ft.
Pico De Orizaba	Mexico	18,701 ft.
Mount Rainier	Washington, USA	14,410 ft.
Grand Teton	Wyoming, USA	13,300 ft.
Tour d'Ai (via ferrata)	Switzerland	7,646 ft.
Crestone Needle	Colorado, USA	14,197 ft.
Mount Kilimanjaro (Kibo)	Tanzania, Africa	19,340 ft.
P. Fourche	Switzerland	11,589 ft.
Mount Assiniboine	British Columbia, Canada	11,867 ft.
Pyramid Peak	Colorado, USA	14,018 ft.
Centre Peak	British Columbia, Canada	10,033 ft.
North Maroon Bell	Colorado, USA	14,014 ft.
Mount Sinai	Sinai Desert, Egypt	7,498 ft.
Mount Magog	British Columbia, Canada	10,600 ft.
Tete Blanche	Switzerland	11,289 ft.
Mount Kosciusko	Australia	7,310 ft.
Devils Tower	Black Hills, Wyoming, USA	5,112 ft.

Many other less recognized mountains, such as Grunegghorn, Weissnollen, Pigne d'Arolla, Rosablanche in the European Alps, many of the Colorado 14,000 feet mountains, the Colorado Flatirons, in Eldorado Canyon (Colorado), in Chamonix, France, and in Zermatt, Switzerland.

Ski Mountaineering Experiences:
Chamonix-Zermatt Haute Route (Europe)
Berner Oberland Haute Route (Europe)
Wapta Icefields (Canada)
Rogers Pass (Canada)
Battle Range (Canada)
Moroccan Haute Route (North Africa)
Many other routes in North America

ABOUT THE AUTHOR

LOU KASISCHKE has lived his entire life in Michigan, but his enduring love of the mountains and alpine endurance sports have taken him to many remote parts of the world, on all seven continents.

Lou's education includes a Bachelor of Arts degree in business and a Juris Doctor degree in law from Michigan State University. Risk management was the major focus of his business degree from MSU. Already as a student, Lou was fascinated by risk, risk evaluation, and the concepts of taking and managing risk. For a career centered in finance analysis and law, he also became a certified public accountant and earned an advanced Master of Laws degree.

Lou's work career experiences were multi-dimensional. In law, this included 35 years with Dykema Gossett, a national law firm, as a specialist in corporate and tax law and in representing venture capital businesses. He authored a leading book on corporate law and was selected by his colleagues for all editions of *The Best Lawyers in America*, which represents about one percent of the nation's lawyers.

In business, Lou was a chief executive officer and a director and advisor to several major corporations on business and legal matters. His professional career, especially as a lawyer and a venture capital advisor, often focused on taking high-stakes business risks, managing risk, and making decisions with far-reaching consequences. This part of Lou's life made his several decades as a serious mountain climber a natural extension. And it also explains his perspective and the important purpose that led him to closely examine, analyze, and explain what went wrong on Everest and his experience of being there, based on the facts that matter and not on the sensational and irrelevant.

Lou is retired from law and business and lives with his wife, Sandy, on the northern shore of Lake Michigan. He remains active with alpine sports and other endurance challenges in the great outdoors.

A CONVERSATION WITH
LOU KASISCHKE

Since you say in the opening pages that most of the book was written in 1997 and 1998, why didn't you publish it then?

My reasons for writing 17 years ago were different from my reasons for publishing today. I wrote then because the aftermath reporting was like fog rolling in to obscure and distort what actually happened. Too much was written about things that were colorful for storytelling, but did not matter. This led many people to misunderstand the events and reach false conclusions about what went wrong. And so, I wrote things down to solidify and preserve my experience and insight about what happened and why.

But, at that time, I had no interest in publishing. Since the story about what went wrong is about mistakes—human failings—I did not want to be one more voice of criticism about people who were my friends. And who were dead. It just didn't feel right. I was content for 17 years to have my writing reside in a file cabinet.

So then, why did you decide to publish the book now?

My writing 17 years ago went beyond what went wrong. I also wrote a highly personal (and mostly untold) story about how and why I survived. The tragic story was one I wanted to forget. The personal story was one I wanted to remember. It's about my wife Sandy's role in my survival. A story about the voice of the heart. A love story.

Sandy and I have loved each other 48 years. We have been married 47 years. Today, Sandy is seriously ill. During her illness we have spent many hours reflecting on our lives together. Thinking back to those critical life and death decision moments at noon on 10 May 1996, it was Sandy's love and influence that gave me the inner strength I needed to make the right decision that saved my life.

After The Wind tells the details of that personal story, which can only be told in the context of the bigger historic story. And now is the right time to publish. I do so to honor and to pay tribute to Sandy while we are still together, to share our love story with others, and to thank God for the gift of her love. By publishing , I hope to give a broader and longer life to a story about the voice of the heart as a source of strength.

Climbing Everest, and facing a decision dilemma near the top, is also just the backdrop for an everyday life story — about the human struggle to make hard choices in the face of everyday life pressures. And it's also an example of the role and influence of a personal relationship as a source of inner strength to make the right choices.

What are some of the edits you made to a story written 17 years ago? For instance, what did you feel you needed to take out? And why?

In late 2013, when I decided to publish my story, I discovered I had written 166,000 words. For normal book length, I needed to cut the number of words in half. My approach was to first cut a 40,000 word "after story," which covered experiences of some others and myself in the aftermath. Then I cut stories about events on the mountain that I no longer wanted to tell, and some that were not mine to tell. Today, 19 years after the tragic events, it's clear to me that some stories may (and perhaps should) never be told.

My editing was also about storytelling structure. For instance, I originally wrote too much about other team members. I wanted to respect their privacy and leave the others to tell their own stories, if they chose to. And so, I only told so much about others as was necessary to tell my own story.

I also feared that some stories about the events, and my views, could attract overshadowing attention, and the story I most wanted to tell would be lost. I didn't want that. I wanted *After The Wind* to be read and remembered for my story—my personal survival experience and my causal analysis of what went wrong.

I also cut many details from my analysis of what went wrong. That part of my story dominated in the number of words written. I needed to cut it back to bring it in a better balance with the personal story. I also wrote too much about myself as a climber, about my life outside climbing, and about how all that shaped who I am. And so, for balance, I cut.

Jon Krakauer, who was part of the same climbing team, wrote the book, Into Thin Air. What was your reaction to it? Did you write your book as a response to it?

Jon Krakauer wrote the Everest story the way he wanted to write it. I wrote it the way I thought it should be written. *After The Wind* tells the Everest story that *Into Thin Air* doesn't tell. So, in that sense, each book compliments the other.

My book has a materially different focus, but it is not a response to *Into Thin Air*. If I had wanted to draw attention to our different viewpoints, I would have published it 17 years ago.

The two books actually highlight a fascinating issue—how can people in the same situation experience it differently? The difference can't be in what happened. That was a constant for everyone.

The climbers who lived this story brought "who they are" to the experience of, and their responsive insight about, the events. We are not all alike. I guess that's what individuality is about.

Individuality, and the resulting different experience, occurs because each of us brought something different with us to Everest—different life and career experiences, different expectations, different motivations, different agendas, different influences, different vulnerabilities, different values, different roles in life, different habits, and different personal relationships. All of these affect what we see, think, feel, and do.

Each of us sat in a different seat in the stadium of Everest. Each of us experienced the same events, but from our different view. Each of us took something different away.

So, from these differences, each of us has a different story to tell. I acknowledge the difficulty of people who were not there to understand and evaluate the story. What they are told about this tragedy depends upon who is doing the telling. And who you are tells what you tell.

Why did you choose independent (Indie) publishing over traditional publishing for your book?

I didn't need a traditional publisher. Indie is practical, easy, and fast. And because of Sandy's poor health and my reason for publishing, time was of the essence. I didn't have the 18 to 24 months it would take to go the traditional route. And frankly, I thought I would have a higher quality outcome going Indie. I feared that, by the time all the editors were finished rewriting, I might not recognize my own story. I wanted my writing to be me, with all my shortcomings as a writer. I wanted readers to hear my voice — not the voices of a team of editors. I write simply and from the heart. That's what matters the most.

Are you planning a follow-up to After The Wind?

Maybe, but probably not. That will depend upon whether readers first care about *After The Wind*. But I actually have more to say. During editing, I cut a 40,000 word "after story," which covered Everest related personal growth experiences in the aftermath. I called that time my journey to understand and to be. Someone famous once said that the true worth of your journey through life lies not in how far or how high you go, but in who you come to be along the way.

DISCUSSION QUESTIONS

1. What do you think draws people to such extreme high risk challenges as climbing Mount Everest?

2. Can you see from the story what individual qualities or attributes enable them to endure extreme suffering and hardship to achieve their goals?

3. Because of the high risks, what responsibility do they have to the other team members? How about to their families back home?

4. Why do you think Rob Hall, as team leader, continued to climb to the top after it was too late and past the safety turnaround time? Why did some of the team climbers follow? Why did some not follow?

5. Do you think embedding in the team a writer for publicity and business promotion added to the risks and influenced leadership decision making, especially on summit day?

6. What do you think the roles of both the leaders and the climbers are on these expeditions? Should both be held responsible for the outcome? How does ego, peer pressure, and ambition come into play here? How about the quest for publicity? Should the leadership be mixing together business and climbing safety decisions?

7. It came out early that the assistant leadership team was inexperienced for an Everest climb. Would a stronger leadership team have resulted in a different outcome?

8. What if, after six weeks of climbing you were close to the top (minutes away), but it's too late by all measures to continue. What would you do? Is turning back defeat or good climbing?

9. It's easy to understand what prepares you to have the physical strength needed to face the challenges of climbing a mountain of rock, snow, and ice. But what prepares you to have the inner strength needed to face conflicting pressures within yourself to make a hard choice? Where can you go for the needed inner strength?

10. Do you find it ironic that a majority of the climbers who died were the most experienced?

11. Why do you think Lou included the episode about Bruce Herrod on the evening of May 9? What does it contribute to the story?

12. Why do you think the aftermath reports clung to the false idea that a storm was the cause of the tragedy? Was it simply that a storm makes for more dramatic storytelling? Or was it for some other reason, such as distraction from human error as the cause?

13. Do you see the story as having any meaning for non-climbers in facing their everyday life challenges, especially making hard choices? What lessons from the story would parents likely pass on to their children? Would how to find the strength to say no be one of them?

14. Do you see anything from Lou's experience that's inspirational?

15. Do you think it's ironic that, at the pivotal life and death moment, thinking about others saved Lou's life?

16. Lou dedicates his book, "To Sandy, A Story I Can Tell." Can you see from the events the idea of "living a story you can tell" as having meaning and guidance in everyday life?

17. Lou writes about the sources of inner strength to make hard choices, and that for him what mattered the most was the power of a personal relationship — the influence of his wife Sandy's love and his promise to only live a story he could tell. Discuss the other sources of inner strength that Lou writes about.

18. Lou called it the still, small voice of the heart. But how would you explain the drama ("uncommon moments," according to Lou) of the beating heart and sheer silence as Lou made his decision to turn back?

19. This is a very personal story to Lou. How did you feel about Lou and his wife Sandy at the start of the book? Did your feeling change as you read? How did Lou's views of himself change through the pages? How did his relationship with Sandy change by the end of the story?

20. In the book, Lou is also asking questions. See pages 234 and 235. What do you think about these questions?

Summit 29,028'

South Summit
28,700'

Hillary Step

High Camp
26,000'

Lhotse 27,940'

Lhotse Face

Camp 3
24,000'

Western Cwm

Camp 2
21,300'

Camp 1
19,000'

Khumbu Icefall

Base Camp
17,500'

Khumbu Glacier

Six Week Route to High Camp